DINU LOGOZ

JOHN MAYALL
The Blues Crusader
His Life – His Music – His Bands

DINU LOGOZ

JOHN MAYALL
The Blues Crusader

His Life – His Music – His Bands

C

EDITION OLMS ZÜRICH

First published in Switzerland by
© 2015 Edition Olms AG, Zürich

EDITION OLMS AG
Willikonerstr. 10
CH-8618 Oetwil am See / Zürich
Switzerland

Mail: info@edition-olms.com
Web: www.edition-olms.com

ISBN 978-3-283-01228-1

Editing & proofreading: Eugene Edwards
Design & Typesetting: Weiß-Freiburg GmbH – Graphik & Buchgestaltung

A catalogue record for this book is available from the Deutsche Bibliothek
More detailed information under
http://dnb.ddb.de

Printed in Lithuania

Table of Contents

Foreword

It must have been in the summer of 1967 when a school friend first showed me "A Hard Road", the first John Mayall LP I had ever seen. Although familiar with "Moanin'" by Art Blakey's Jazz Messengers and "Can't Buy Me Love" by the Beatles, it was "Stevie's Blues" by the Spencer Davis Group and "Little Red Rooster" by the Rolling Stones that really caught my attention. I soon found out that these two songs had something in common which was called the blues. I started to become fascinated by everything about Mayall, and found out that he could play guitar, harmonica, piano and organ, called his band the Bluesbreakers and even designed the LP covers! A few weeks later I discovered that Eric Clapton had played with him, and that "Crusade", his third LP, featured another brilliant young guitar player called Mick Taylor. Mayall soon became my musical guiding light and role model, but some facts were confusing me. How could the Bluesbreakers have been the band where Jack Bruce and Eric Clapton first met when the only bass player ever mentioned on the LPs was John McVie? And how come the Bluesbreakers had had a single on the Immediate label when all their other releases were on Decca? It just didn't add up.

Problems such as these prompted me to start a life-long investigation of all things Mayall-related, all of which I have religiously collected and noted down. This has over the years expanded into a vast and highly intriguing story about Mayall's various band line-ups, a school for outstanding musicians, with many remarkable off-shoots. And also of course about Mayall himself, a charismatic personality and exceptional band leader with extraordinary staying power. Why no one else has ever thought of writing a book about the godfather of British blues is a mystery to me, but the man himself may have put his finger on it when he said: "Let's face it, I've never had a hit record. I've never even been nominated for the Rock 'n' Roll Hall Of Fame. I've only got one Grammy nomination. You've got to realize, I'm pretty much an underground figure except to blues lovers who follow me and my career." This book is for them.

It has been a labour of love collecting information, clippings and facts over such a long period of time. The early years with Clapton, Green and Taylor are well documented in several books and publications, one of the finest being Christopher Hjort's excellent "Strange Brew", which focuses on the British blues boom of 1965–1970. Much more research was needed for the decades after the 1970s up to the present. I got in touch with many of Mayall's former sidemen via e-mail, many of whom willingly supplied me with precious information, much of which I have been able to include. As often as possible I have given space for the musicians to speak for themselves, in order to give fans direct and authentic insight into the events surrounding Mayall and his career. My original intention was to give readers as much information as possible about Mayall: his life, his musicians, his records and his tours, the lot! However, popular biography must be anecdote-led, and strive to strike a balance between story telling and dry fact; only academic studies need contain all the details. To this end, I am indebted to editor Eugene Edwards for correcting my original manuscript, and transforming it into a shorter and more readable account.

– *Dinu Logoz*

I would like to dedicate this book to the following musicians who are sadly no longer with us:

Sonny Boy Williamson II	*Dec. 5, 1899–May 25, 1965*
Magic Sam Maghett	*Feb. 14, 1937–Dec. 1, 1969*
Jimi Hendrix	*Nov. 27, 1942–Sep. 18, 1970*
T-Bone Walker	*May 28, 1910–Mar. 16, 1975*
Duster Bennett	*Sep. 23, 1946–Mar. 20, 1976*
Freddie King	*Sep. 30, 1934–Dec. 28, 1976*
Blue Mitchell	*Mar. 13, 1930–May 21, 1979*
Jimmy McCulloch	*June 4, 1953–Sep. 27, 1979*
Bob the Bear Hite	*Feb. 26, 1943–Apr. 5, 1981*
Muddy Waters	*Apr. 4, 1915–Apr. 30, 1983*
Alexis Korner	*Apr. 19, 1928–Jan. 1, 1984*
Sonny Terry	*Oct. 24, 1911–Mar. 12, 1986*
Sippie Wallace	*Nov. 1, 1898–Nov. 1, 1986*
Paul Butterfield	*Dec. 17, 1942–May 3, 1987*
Roy Buchanan	*Sep. 23, 1939–Aug. 15, 1988*
Shakey Jake Harris	*Apr. 12, 1921–Mar. 2, 1990*
Rick Grech	*Nov. 1, 1946–Mar. 17, 1990*
Mike Gardner	*July 20, 1946–May 18, 1991*
Champion Jack Dupree	*July 4, 1910–Jan. 21, 1992*
Albert King	*Apr. 25, 1923–Dec. 21, 1992*
Albert Collins	*Oct. 3, 1932–Nov. 24, 1993*
Eddie Boyd	*Nov. 25, 1914–July 13, 1994*
Brownie McGhee	*Nov. 30, 1915–Feb. 16, 1996*
Ronnie Barron	*Oct. 9, 1943–Mar. 20, 1997*
Ted Gardestad	*Feb. 18, 1956–June 22, 1997*
Luther Allison	*Aug. 17, 1939–Aug. 12, 1997*
Junior Wells	*Dec. 9, 1934–Jan. 15, 1998*
Nigel Stanger	*Jan. 16, 1943–Mar. 15, 1999*
Don Sugarcane Harris	*June 18, 1938–Nov. 30, 1999*
Tommy Eyre	*July 5, 1949–May 23, 2001*
John Lee Hooker	*Aug. 22, 1917–June 21, 2001*
Soko Richardson	*Dec. 8, 1939–Jan. 29, 2004*

Clifford Solomon	*Jan. 17, 1931 – June 21, 2004*
Dick Heckstall-Smith	*Sep. 26, 1934 – Dec. 17, 2004*
Billy Preston	*Sep. 2, 1946 – June 6, 2006*
Steve Thompson	*Oct. 17, 1950 – Dec. 2007*
Jeff Healey	*Mar. 25, 1966 – Mar. 2, 2008*
Mickey Waller	*Sep. 6, 1941 – Apr. 29, 2008*
Bo Diddley	*Dec. 30, 1928 – June 2, 2008*
Roger Dean	*Mar. 16, 1943 – Aug. 3, 2008*
Davy Graham	*Nov. 22, 1940 – Dec. 15, 2008*
Freddy Robinson	*Feb. 24, 1939 – Oct. 8, 2009*
Paul Lagos	*July 9, 1940 – Oct. 19, 2009*
Johnny Almond	*July 20, 1946 – Nov. 18, 2009*
John Slaughter	*Aug. 12, 1944 – Aug. 15, 2010*
Jay Spell	*Dec. 22, 1945 – Dec. 30, 2010*
Gary Moore	*Apr. 4, 1952 – Feb. 6, 2011*
Keef Hartley	*Apr. 8, 1944 – Nov. 26, 2011*
Hubert Sumlin	*Nov. 16, 1931 – Dec. 4, 2011*
Etta James	*Jan. 25, 1938 – Jan. 20, 2012*
Red Holloway	*May 31, 1927 – Feb. 25, 2012*
Victor Gaskin	*Nov. 23, 1934 – July 14, 2012*
John Juke Logan	*Sep. 11, 1946 – Aug. 30, 2013*
Jack Bruce	*May 14, 1943 – Oct. 25, 2014*
Andy Fraser	*Aug. 7, 1952 – March 16, 2015*

CHAPTER 1

Cheshire, the tree house, art school and Korea
Early days and the pre-Bluesbreakers years, 1933–62

John Bromwell Mayall was born in the northern English market town of Macclesfield, just south of Manchester, into a working class family on November 29, 1933. Mayall comments: "The only reason I was born in Macclesfield is because my father was a drinker and that's where his favourite pub was! We lived near Cheadle Hulme and Bramhall in Cheshire, that's where I grew up". His father, Murray Mayall, not only enjoyed a pint of ale, but was also a music lover, playing guitar and banjo for fun with the Cam Collegians, a college jazz band. "My father, who had an M.A. in Classics from Cambridge, was a musician, and played a lot in dance bands in his spare time." He earned his living as a clerk and had a huge collection of jazz recordings, which exerted a considerable fascination over his son. However, Mayall felt closer to his mother Beryl, and maintained a good relationship with her until she died in 2006 at the age of 97. A warm-hearted person, and very well liked by musicians, she even went on the road with John and his bands in the 60s.

John's interest in music started very early: "When I was about three, I got addicted to the early 1930s recordings of the Mills Brothers, who imitated the jazz and blues sound with their voices," Mayall recalls. "And it all grew from there. My father had a fairly large collection of 78s; many of them black American music. Through him, I was exposed to a great many styles of music, mostly guitar-orientated: Segovia, Dick McDonough, Carl Kress. But primarily it was all early jazz, people like Louis Armstrong, Django Reinhardt, Charlie

Christian, Lonnie Johnson and Eddie Lang. From there, the dividing line between my interest in jazz and blues was very fine. The guitarists I used to listen to when I was about 6 or 7 were Django Reinhardt and Charlie Christian."

When he was ten, John went to prep school at Alderley Edge, but detested it. He ran away regularly: "I hated that feeling of regulation, of being caged in. I had fewer friends than most. I was a shy, retiring kid." When John was eleven, his parents divorced, and together with his mother, brother and sister, John went to live with his grandfather. When he was twelve, Mayall began playing the guitar and the ukulele. He never received any guitar lessons from his father. "He had a Gibson with terrible action on it and I couldn't even get the strings to reach the frets. I got myself a ukulele instead, which only had four strings and was very much easier. There was a very famous comedian called George Formby who had published a book 'The George Formby Chord Book for the Banjo', so I worked with that. Later on, when my fingers were strong enough, I got a guitar and started off with four strings, which I added one to later. On the guitar, I was playing a lot of Josh White songs, Big Bill Broonzy tunes, and things by the Spirits of Rhythm, Teddy Bunn and Leadbelly." Until he was thirteen, Mayall went to the local council school, where he was blissfully happy. Afterwards, he attended art school. "When I was thirteen I went to Junior Art School in Manchester. It was a two-year course where they taught you a minimum of English, maths, geography and history, and everything else was art. So I thought it was terrific. It got me out of doing any examinations as well as providing me with a basic art training." At roughly the same time he took up the piano. "When I was about thirteen, I started to get into blues and boogie-woogie, having heard records by people like Meade Lux Lewis, Albert Ammons, Pete Johnson, Jimmy Yancey and Pinetop Smith. They got me hooked, as did Josh White, Leadbelly, Big Bill Broonzy and Muddy Waters a bit later on." Within two years, he had taught himself to play the piano. "We never had a piano at home, but I liked the idea of playing, I never did learn to read music and I still can't today. As we didn't own a piano, I had to learn at the art school piano or rely on other people's." Mayall remembers: "In England, in the late 40's, there was a traditional jazz band boom; these bands played Dixieland or 'trad' jazz. In each town, they'd have their own bands. In Manchester, it was the Saints Jazz Band that was the big crowd puller. You'd get the London bands, guys like Humphrey Lyttleton, and a little bit later on, Chris Barber, coming up for one-nighters. And then you got Lonnie Donegan, who, within the Chris Barber jazz band had a smaller group, which was covering Leadbelly-type stuff. And they titled that skiffle; an offshoot from the trad thing. I just went for the pianists. John Fish was the pianist in the Saints Jazz Band. In '48, '49, I got close to him, I used to hang on like a groupie, sit at the end of his keyboard and watch. He let me go over to his house and listen to records. He told me about Big Maceo, Jimmy Yancey and Cripple Clarence Lofton. The first record I ever bought was Albert Ammons's 'Shout for Joy'; on the B-side was 'Bear Cat Crawl' by Meade Lux Lewis. That was at a record store in Manchester and I was about 13, so it must have been about 1947. Everything was 78s; it was before LPs even were invented."

After finishing junior art school aged 15, the young Mayall first went to work for a reputable advertising agency in Manchester. For five days, he brewed tea and took letters to the post office. He never saw a drawing board, or, for that matter, an artist. On the Friday, he collected his pay, never to return. Mayall commented on the experience thus: "If that was advertising, I didn't want to know." Several weeks later, he went to work for a large department store as a window dresser, which lasted for two years. It was around this time that he demonstrated his independence and eccentricity by moving into his backyard tree house, built with the help of his brother. The tree house was like one more room for John, away from the house but near enough so he could run electricity up there. Here, without interference, John and his friends pursued their hobbies: listening to jazz records, painting, puppetry, and dressing up to look like figures in horror films. Mayall's penchant for living in tree houses would continue on and off until his early twenties. All in all, he lived in three different ones!

At 18, Mayall first heard Big Maceo Merriweather playing 'Chicago Breakdown' which had a huge impact on him. "At that particular time, probably 1949–50, I was saving up my coins to buy 78s. Anything that had the word 'boogie' on it, I bought it! That led to a lot of stuff that I'd buy and then say, "This isn't 'boogie!' Some of the big band things said 'boogie', but it got me onto Lionel Hampton, and one thing lead to another and you start finding out how massive the variety of music there is to choose from in jazz and blues. There's no stopping!" Mayall became a keen recordcollector, writing away to America for copies of records that didn't stand a chance of finding a British release. He also listened to the blues on his short wave radio. As drummer Keef Hartley writes in his wonderful book 'Halfbreed': "I asked John how he learnt all these obscure blues tunes whilst living in the sleepy county of Cheshire. I expected him to say that he had a friend who brought records over from the States. No, the answer was that John had built a forty-foot tall radio mast in his back garden. This had been hooked up to a radio, and from there, to a reel-to-reel tape recorder. This meant he could pick up and record blues broadcasts on the 'Voice of America' radio station. From these, John learnt the music of Robert Johnson, Willie Dixon and many more."

At 18, Mayall was plunged into the army. "I stupidly signed on in the Royal Engineers for three years (March 1952–55), and became a corporal a week before I came out." He also found time to play his first solo concerts when on leave in 1952 and 53, singing songs by his heroes Josh White, Leadbelly & Big Bill Broonzy, and accompanying himself on guitar. Then they decided to send him to Korea to fight, but good fortune decided otherwise. Mayall arrived in Korea but a week later the Armistice was signed, so he worked as an army clerk, and did not take part in any fighting. When John embarked for Korea, a local newspaper noted that he was "carrying a heavy kitbag, large pack, small haversack, water bottle, steel helmet, rifle, and a guitar." On the way to Korea Mayall formed his first group. "We were on board for two months and I formed a band that consisted of myself on guitar, a second lieutenant on sax and a Scottish accordion player who hogged the entire show!" While on leave in

Tokyo 1954, John purchased his first electric guitar for $25. As he had a great deal of spare time in Korea, he used to practise a lot: "It was a pretty cheap way to idle away those long hours in the tent." Later, Mayall modified this guitar by adding three more strings, and it became his main guitar in the 60s, even featured on the cover of the 'Blues Alone' LP. The idea of the 9-string-guitar might have come from country bluesman Big Joe Williams, who used guitars he festooned with extra machine heads to accommodate nine or more strings.

Following his creative muse, John planned to continue his art education. He began a four-year course in graphic design at the Regional College of Art in Manchester, also an ideal place to put together bands. Mayall used to play with other students at lunchtime jam sessions and local dances. One of the first was with Mart Rodger, who played clarinet and sang. They called their duo the Dreamland Boys, and the Manchester Evening News reported on March 4, 1955: "Clarinettist Mart Rodger and guitarist John Mayall, two young soldiers from Cheadle Hulme, made their debut as the Dreamland Boys at the Lancashire Society of Jazz Music last weekend. John and Mart play and sing in Scat style, doing earthy race music and middle-period classics such as 'China Boy' or 'Who's Sorry Now'." Mayall and Rodger also played in a trad jazz band from 1955 on, with Cephas Howard on trumpet (who later formed the Temperance Seven), an unknown trombone player, Roger Woodburn on banjo and Peter Ward on drums, the latter joining the Bluesbreakers a few years later. Mayall played guitar and occasionally sang. Other combinations were The Featured Five in 1956, with Mayall on electric guitar, and Martin Roger's Hounds of Sound around September 1956 to January 1957, all playing trad jazz. Playing traditional jazz instead of blues and boogie-woogie must have been a compromise for Mayall, who later commented: "Trad bands were playing the blues, but not the type of blues I wanted to listen to." At that time, virtually nobody knew anything about the blues in Britain, with the exception of musicians such as Alexis Korner, Cyril Davies and Chris Barber. Mayall formed his own blues band in 1955, calling it John Mayall's

Powerhouse Four. It lasted until 1958 and its members were all students of the art college like Mayall himself. Besides blues and boogie improvisations, the band played songs like 'How Long Blues' by Leroy Carr and 'Too Close Together' by Sonny Boy Williamson, as well as Big Bill Broonzy and Spirit of Rhythm tunes, among others. "We tried to achieve a gutsy blues sound in the style of Big Maceo Merriweather, Cripple Clarence Lofton, Jimmy Yancey and Big Bill Broonzy," Mayall remembers. "Off and on I'd also play piano for a local group. It was hybrid kind of thing, most of our audience didn't really understand the blues—this was the time of Elvis Presley and rock 'n' roll, remember. But as long as there was a strong beat to what you played, they didn't mind!"

Despite the flourishing popularity of American rock 'n' roll such as Bill Haley & the Comets, Mayall's love for the blues continued undiminished. The Powerhouse Four played at local clubs and universities in Manchester, Macclesfield, Liverpool and clubs where the group worked four hours a night for a pound! Mayall started playing mouth harmonica around 1956–57. "I adopted the harp because it was essential for different blues players that I adored—the two Sonny Boy Williamsons, Sonny Terry, Little Walter and James Cotton. I quickly used it together with the piano, playing both in unison." The main influence on Mayall's harmonica style was Rice Miller, a.k.a. Sonny Boy Williamson II.

In June 1956, the Manchester Evening News reported: "Backstage at the Free Trade Hall recently, visiting American jazz star Brownie McGhee bumped into 22-year-old John Mayall, who invited the folksinger out to his flat. They played their guitars and sang the blues for hours. Later, Brownie reminisced about his life and wanderings in America and it was 4 a.m. before he went back to his hotel." This must have been one of the rare occasions when young Mayall had the chance to hear authentic live blues. "Horst Lippmann was bringing across the American Folk Blues Festivals only from 1962 on," Mayall remembers, "so I saw all those, with John Lee Hooker, T-Bone Walker, Muddy Waters and so on." But in the 50s, the British blues scene was virtually non-existent, apart from Chris Barber. "He had a traditional jazz band, but he did have blues in his set. He was the only one, really" remembers Mayall.

Mayall sometimes worked as a jobbing music teacher, which is how he met drummer Hughie Flint, who was to play a major role in Mayall's future bands. Flint remembers: "I first ran into John Mayall in Manchester around 1957 or '58. I was in a crowd of friends who dragged me up to a youth centre in Wythenshawe where John was a so-called teacher. It was one of those twice a week things where he was paid by the council to get musical events organised. It was a real hotch-potch of jazz, blues and skiffle. We used to go up there and jam, basically. John played marvellous barrelhouse piano and a bit of harmonica and guitar. We became very good friends and I would go to his house every weekend. He had shelves and shelves of tapes and hundreds of records. It was just incredible." A number of generous newspaper reviews pretended that the Powerhouse Four were a successful blues band, but in reality the public showed hardly any interest; Britain was still in the grip of the trad jazz boom. John eventually became disillusioned by the lack of response or recognition, and left to concentrate on his art career and family. "I never considered that the blues might be a direction for a career. It never even crossed my mind that I might earn a living at it and become a professional musician, because I was trained in art; that's what I got my degree in, and that was my career, so I pursued graphic design. Music was just a hobby for me. That didn't happen until I was thirty. What I always wanted was to play the blues, but there was no demand for it; it was just all for myself." All of this was well before the discovery of the great American blues artists that precipitated the British blues boom, and of course, well before the Beatles and the Stones exploded onto the scene. Authentic black American blues musicians touring the UK in the 50s and early 60s were really only playing to jazz club audiences; there was virtually no public interest. It was Alexis Korner and Cyril Davis who pioneered the British blues scene, producing the first white blues recordings around 1957, but they were noticed only by a handful of fans.

The public started to show an real interest in blues music only around 1962, with the American Folk Blues Festivals. These were showcase tours that German promoters Horst Lippmann and Fritz Rau had put together. The first featured T-Bone Walker, John Lee Hooker, Memphis Slim and Willie Dixon. Shortly afterwards, the first rumblings of rhythm 'n' blues as a commercial sound began to make its way north to Manchester. Alexis Korner and Cyril Davies were bringing amplifiers into the clubs, which was considered heresy; they were playing *electric* blues music! This was what Mayall had been playing since the mid-50s, so perhaps now people would discover what the fuss was all about.

Mayall's second band was called the Blues Syndicate, formed in 1962 together with trumpeter John Rowlands, guitarist Ray Cummings (ex-Powerhouse Four), alto saxophonist Jack Masarak and drummer Hughie Flint. There was no bass player. Pete Frames' Rock Family Trees mentions Nigel Smith as the bassist, and Bob Brunning's book claims Alain Ditchburn played guitar, but both are mistaken. The Blues Syndicate was together for just a few months, and played most of their 11 concerts in and around Manchester, often opening for jazz bands or for Alexis Korner's Blues Incorporated. On their rare excursions up north, Korner's band greatly impressed Mayall, who later remarked: "When he came to Manchester, that's where I first met him. This was just after he'd split up with Cyril. He had Johnny Parker on piano, who came from Humphrey Lyttleton's band, from the trad thing, Dick Heckstall-Smith on tenor, Graham Bond on alto, Ginger Baker on drums, Jack Bruce on string bass—it was just amazing that line-up, it just blew me away. That was a hell of a band!" Opening for Blues Incorporated at the Bodega Jazz Club in Manchester one night, Korner befriended Mayall. He was quick to see John's talent, and encouraged him to move to London where the blues boom was about to explode, telling him he would certainly make it in the capital, where the burgeoning scene would offer steady employment to the multi-instrumentalist, bandleader and singer.

CHAPTER 2

Trial and Error

London and the first Bluesbreakers, 1963–65

Mayall arrived in London in January 1963, aged 29. "I came to London to sing the blues and have a band. Every band has to have a name, so I wrote down about 50 with the word "blues" in them, and picked one out of a hat." This was "Bluesbreakers", an apt name for a band whose leader wanted to make blues music popular. Mayall moved to London on a trial basis; his family didn't want to join him unless things were going to work out. Still working as a graphic artist, he easily got a job as a studio manager for an advertising agency, which provided him with a steady income, and in the evenings played gigs. Mayall remembers: "Alexis Korner and Cyril Davies were the founders of the British blues movement. Korner helped introduce me to the right people in London; he opened doors for me and became a great friend. He paved the way for the whole phenomenon. And practically every British jazz musician had played with Alexis. He seemed to have massive experience of running bands, and the trials and tribulations of musicians, vans breaking down and all those matters." As things in the capital started to work out, Korner helped to get his family down to London. "He got John gigs, helped us find a house and got the kids into school. He was great shoulder to lean on," Pamela his wife at the time, recalls.

Korner continued to mentor Mayall by introducing him to the growing number of musicians who were seeking to play in a blues band. Right from the start, Mayall had a keen eye for talent. He went through a lot of musicians, looking for the right people. By February 1963, Mayall had established his first Bluesbreakers, even if the early line-ups were very transitory: "It was more like an informal jam session rather than a band, we never rehearsed and so the gigs became the auditions. Alexis had done all the groundwork, so there was an audience. Our problem was being good enough for them." For several months, Mayall fronted what he subsequently described as "some appalling bands", and endured derisive audiences on many occasions. "We played some oldies, plus Chicago blues covers, done very badly but earnestly, and tunes by Muddy Waters, John Lee Hooker or Robert Johnson, as well as a lot of my own stuff." Many musicians passed through the ranks of the early Bluesbreakers, some staying just for a single gig. They ranged from complete unknowns to musicians of outstanding talent. Folk guitarist Davy Graham was one of the latter, Mayall recruiting him from Korner's Blues Incorporated. He remembers: "Davy and I did a lot of gigs, we even shared a flat near Baker Street. But it didn't really work out because it was a different kind of music, Davy being a folk guitar player." Graham recorded with Mayall some 37 years later, contributing guitar to a new version of "California" for the album "Along for the Ride".

The first Bluesbreaker bass player was Ricky Brown, who had played with Cyril Davies' R&B All Stars, but he didn't last long, and was replaced by Pete Burford. By April 1963, Mayall had recruited the 17-year old John McVie to play bass, and he became a cornerstone in Mayall's band for the next four and half years, although their relationship was erratic due to McVie's drinking habits. McVie remembers: "I knew nothing at all about blues music. Mayall just gave me a stack of records, and asked me to listen to them to see if I could grasp the style and feeling." Mayall advised him to keep the bass parts as simple as possible, and this helped take McVie a long way in the music business. McVie: "The first gig I did with him was at The White Hart in Acton. He said 'OK, let's try a 12-bar in C, and I had to ask him what he meant! He just told me to follow his chords, and over the months I began to learn what the blues was all about. Mayall taught me the rudiments of the blues. It was only about a year and a half after I joined the Bluesbreakers that I began to understand what I was playing, through John playing me records and telling me what to listen to. Mayall was playing the music that I wanted to play, and he was a very good guy to work for, very honest and fair. One of his strongest talents is putting people together who can bounce off each other well."

Having found the right bass player meant that only guitarists and drummers remained a problem. Mayall wanted Flint to leave Manchester and come to London to play, but that wasn't yet possible. Flint recalls: "The plan was for John to come down to London and establish something, then I would join him, because when he left Manchester, I'd recently married, and he he'd already got a wife and three kids, so we couldn't go the whole hog straight away." While waiting for Flint to arrive, Mayall employed several other drummers: Sam Stone, Brian Myall and then Keith Robertson all had short stints with the early Bluesbreakers. Already a versatile musician, Mayall moved freely on stage between guitar, organ and harmonica, and because of his skills as a multi-instrumentalist, he was soon being billed as Britain's answer to Roland Kirk!

When Bluesbreakers' guitarist Gilbey quit in July 1963, Mayall recruited Bernie Watson as replacement. Watson stayed for nine months, and Mayall remembers how introverted he was: "Bernie was classically trained and hated rock 'n' roll, but did it so well. It's amazing; he had such a wonderful feel for it. But it was just hell to get him to play. He used to sit with his back to the audience, and only if he felt like playing a solo would he do one; half the time he wouldn't." By the summer of 1963, Mayall had a relatively stable line-up with John McVie on bass, Bernie Watson on guitar, and Peter Ward on drums. Incidentally, Mayall was one of the few who dared perform blues songs he had written himself. Alexis Korner and Cyril Davies had been mostly content to recycle the music of the American greats, and had little interest in writing their own tunes. With the creation of original material, the blues became British, whatever that means! Now the Bluesbreakers had an attractive repertoire consisting of rare Chicago blues covers, original Mayall songs and some lesser-known Chuck Berry instrumentals, perfectly imitated by the seated Bernie Watson.

Mayall's first major breakthrough came when he managed to talk Manfred Mann into giving the Bluesbreakers the interval spot at the legendary Marquee Club for £15 a night. At that time, top groups could choose their own intermission band. His first Marquee gig was on November 4, and after a few months, the Bluesbreakers were reportedly blowing the headliners off the stage. Mayall was one of the few who played the Flamingo *and* the Marquee, both situated in Wardour Street, in central London. Usually if you played one, you didn't play the other. At the time, all the London R&B groups rotated around a handful of clubs like the Fishmonger's Arms, the Black Prince in Bexley, Klooks Kleek, the Ricky Tick, the Windmill and the Manor House, but the Flamingo became the Bluesbreakers' de facto headquarters. At the end of the year, drummer Peter Ward quit, as he didn't like being on the road full-time, and Mayall temporarily replaced him with Martin Hart until Flint arrived from Manchester.

Around this time, Mayall had signed a management agency deal with Rik Gunnell. The Gunnell Agency, Rik and John Gunnell's stable of artists, had on their books Georgie Fame and the Blue Flames, Chris Farlowe and the Thunderbirds, Ronnie Jones and the Night-Timers (with John Paul Jones on bass and John McLaughlin on guitar), and the Cheynes, all of whom played the same club circuit. The Bluesbreakers were now booked into a succession of one-nighters up and down the country.

In 1963, blues music suddenly became fashionable among the London crowd, and the new generation of listeners meant the audiences grew very quickly. This was still several years before the press started reporting on it, or anybody had made any records. At the time, the press was more preoccupied with the Beatles and all the other groups emerging from Liverpool, but the London clubs and pubs were starting to teem with blues music. Mayall recalls being impressed by some of the young British bands, recalling: "The Stones were always very exciting; I liked Georgie Fame and the Blue Flames, Spencer Davis with Stevie Winwood, and the Animals were a good band." The Bluesbreakers worked semi-pro until spring 1964, which meant they all kept their day jobs. Besides working for advertising agencies, Mayall made a good living as an illustrator of science fiction books. In May 1964, the Bluesbreakers turned professional.

Mayall signed a short-term record contract with Decca, who already had the Rolling Stones under contract, and had released albums by Alexis Korner on Ace of Clubs, their sub-label.

The first studio session took place at Decca studios in West Hampstead in March and on April 20, 1964, with Ian Samwell producing. Samwell was the former guitarist and songwriter for Cliff Richard and the Drifters, having produced Richard's first hit, and went on to produce the early Georgie Fame releases, as well as the Small Faces and the Aynsley Dunbar Retaliation in later years. Two songs were recorded with the Mayall, Watson, McVie and Hart line-up, and both were original compositions: the Ray Charles-influenced "Crawling Up a Hill" and the slow blues "Mr. James". Mayall remembers: "Crawling up a Hill was our first chance at making a record. We did 42 takes; we were burnt out, and I can still hear the frenzied desperation when I listen to it!" "Crawling up a Hill" was a flop, selling a meagre 500 copies. Although Mayall dismisses it today as "a clumsy, half-witted attempt at autobiographical comment", it did provide Georgian-born singer Katie Melua with a hit in 2003, and went on to become one of Mayall's biggest selling songs!

In spite of poor sales, both songs were included on a Decca compilation released in August, called simply "Rhythm And Blues", with contributions by Alexis Korner's Blues Incorporated, the Graham Bond Organization, Zoot Money's Big Roll Band and Dave Berry.

Shortly after Flint had arrived, Watson left to study classical music, and Mayall was in trouble to find a suitable replacement. After several tries, Mayall recruited Roger Dean, who had been playing in country and western bands like Bob Xavier & the Jury (with Albert Lee), Russ Sainty & the Nu-Notes, John Layton and Bobby Vee, among others. Dean, although very capable, was an odd choice because he played in the Chet Atkins style, much more country than blues. Mayall remembers: "Roger Dean was a very pleasant fellow. He wasn't a blues player, just a fast guitarist. He impressed audiences by his speed and facility." The line-up with Mayall, Dean, McVie and Flint remained stable for about a year from May 1964. Flint recalls: "We did the whole London circuit:

Klooks Kleek, Cooks Ferry Inn, Crawdaddy, and so on. We even started to go to Manchester, Newcastle and the provinces to play a lot of college gigs. We were doing gigs with acts like the Who and the Kinks. We even did the May Ball at Oxford University with the Rolling Stones" (on June 16, 1964).

By 1964, the Bluesbreakers had become the backup band of choice for touring American blues greats. The first of them was John Lee Hooker, who arrived from Detroit to team up with the Bluesbreakers in June and July, 1964. It was Hooker's first time in England; the Bluesbreakers played their set and then backed Hooker during his. The four-week, 25-date tour was so successful that it pushed Hooker's latest release, "Dimples", up to number 23 in the British singles charts. The extensive series of concerts also brought the Bluesbreakers to the attention of a wider public, and resurrected Decca records' interest in the group, which had been flagging somewhat since "Crawling up a Hill" bombed so badly. Mayall remembers: "When we played with Hooker, there were queues right down Wardour Street. I think guys like John Lee, or T-Bone Walker, were flattered and kind of surprised that their music had an appeal to a bunch of white kids over in England. They were pleased we were playing their music, although I don't think they thought we were very good at it!" Playing with Hooker must have been a real challenge for the Bluesbreakers, as the legendary bluesman changed chords regularly and unpredictably. Mayall remembers: "I think the band in general had a little bit more trouble than I did. He was difficult to follow; it turned out it was a listening thing, really. You just keep your ears open and try to follow it. The singing part would have tipped you off where the changes would come." Mayall later commented: "Hooker was very important for us, 'cause we learnt a lot about not overplaying." On his encounter with the Bluesbreakers Hooker reportedly commented later: "Man, that John Mayall, he got the most hard-hitting blues band in the city of London. He's my boy!" Unfortunately, no recordings are known to exist from this unique Mayall-Hooker tour, and fans had to wait until 1998 before they played together again on "Padlock on the Blues".

The Bluesbreakers also played a few concerts with another blues legend, Sonny Boy Williamson II, who was an incredible harmonica player and a musical genius. Williamson came over to Europe with the American Folk Blues Festivals in 1963 and 1964, and liked it so much that he stayed for several months, recording with Roland Kirk, Dexter Gordon and Memphis Slim, as well as the Yardbirds, the Animals and Brian Auger, but unfortunately not the Bluesbreakers. Mayall recalls: "Sonny Boy Williamson was my mentor for the harmonica, he was very cantankerous, always drunk and you never knew quite where you were going with him, but I'm really glad that I got to know him and work with him. He showed me quite a few things on the harmonica." Sonny Boy reportedly said about Mayall: "Him and me played like a charm together. He's got a whole lotta soul!" However, it's true to say that Williamson viewed white blues musicians with a certain contempt. He reportedly said about one of the British groups that were backing him: "They want to play the blues so bad, and they play the blues so bad!" Future Bluesbreakers guitarist Eric Clapton remembers Williamson from his tour with the Yardbirds in the winter of 1963/64: "He had a pretty tough character and he didn't like us. He subjected us to a few racial humiliations... were his little white boys, and we'd have to get down on our knees and he'd walk around."

Rock historian Pete Frame remembers the first time he saw the Bluesbreakers in concert: "(It was) at Dunstable Civic Centre around August 64, supported by Steve Marriott & The Moments. Most impressive. Mayall had a rack of harmonicas hanging round his neck, and jumped around at this big old battered brown organ. John McVie stood at the back, serious and practically motionless throughout. Hughie Flint looked like a modern jazzer, the erudite beatnik. Roger Dean, very neat in a suit and tie, played an orange Gretsch guitar while seated!"

Decca's renewed interest led to an offer to record their first LP, a live album taped at Klooks Kleek, then a leading R&B club. It took place at the Railway Hotel in West Hampstead, conveniently close to Decca studios, the close proximity making the recording process much simpler. For Decca, it was common practice to tape live shows at nearby Klooks Kleek; they had already recorded the Graham Bond Organization here in October 1964. It took place on Monday, 7 December 1964, buoyed by an enthusiastic audience. Although the resulting LP was given the unimaginative title "John Mayall plays John Mayall", the sound was promising and distinctive, but by today's standards, poorly recorded. There were eleven Mayall originals and two R&B standards: "Night Train" and Little Richard's "Lucille".

Nigel Stanger, on loan from the Alan Price Set, contributed some superb saxophonist to several songs. The album was released on March 26, 1965, just eleven days before Mayall replaced Roger Dean with a young and promising guitarist by the name of Eric Clapton.

"John Mayall plays John Mayall" is a trailblazing album, brilliantly capturing the tremendous atmosphere, and a good example of early British R&B, equal in every way to the first live Graham Bond or Alexis Korner albums.

In spring 1965, the Bluesbreakers were hired to back Texan guitarist and singer T-Bone Walker on a three-week British tour, starting in early March. After two days' rehearsal, they appeared on the popular TV show "Ready Steady Go!" on March 5, a vital piece of promotion and Mayall's first ever TV appearance.

T-Bone Walker was famous for his flamboyant showmanship, and was one of the first black bluesmen ever to adopt the electric guitar. The original guitar hero commented in an interview with Melody Maker: "These John Mayall's Bluesbreakers I'm working with, they're dedicated to the blues. They give me the idea of Jimmy Reed, people like that. My way's a little different, but they're good for what they do." On another occasion, Walker commented: "This is the greatest group I've had working with me in years. Soon as I get back to the U.S., I'll be telling everybody!" Mayall remembers affectionately: "T-Bone Walker was wonderful and a lot of fun. He taught me a lot of showmanship, he was a real extrovert, and would do things like playing his guitar behind his back. And the audience reaction we got was amazing." The experience of playing with an authentic blues guitarist of the calibre of T-Bone Walker persuaded Mayall to look for a replacement for the more country and western-oriented Dean. When he read in Melody Maker that Eric Clapton was leaving the Yardbirds, he tried to track him down, eventually discovering that Clapton had gone to stay with his friend Ben Palmer in Oxford. Despite his tender years, Clapton was a blues purist, and deeply dissatisfied with the commercial direction the Yardbirds had taken. He hated "For Your Love", their latest single, and badly wanted to play in a blues band. For his part, having listened to Eric's chops on "Got to Hurry", the B side of the latest Yardbirds single Clapton so despised, Mayall was convinced that Eric was the guitarist he had been seeking since founding the Bluesbreakers.

CHAPTER 3

Eric is God and the Beano album
The Bluesbreakers with Eric Clapton, 1965–66

Mayall remembers: "Eric had the magic touch. On "Got to Hurry" it was all definitely right there, irresistible. It just gave me chills. There was something there that cut right through me. To have such mastery and feel at that age is pretty remarkable; it's scary, actually! So the fact that he left the Yardbirds was perfect timing." "Got to Hurry" was a bluesy guitar instrumental in the Freddy King idiom, with stunning, stinging guitar lines played through a Vox amp, cranked up full with plenty of buzz, sustain and crackle. Clapton recalls: "John Mayall called me up about two weeks after I'd left the Yardbirds. It suited me fine because it was a blues band. For me, in those days, I didn't like anything else. What I saw was a frame I could fit into. And I was very grateful that someone saw my worth." While many British groups started as blues or R&B bands, and rapidly became mainstream thanks to chart success (the Rolling Stones, the Kinks, Manfred Mann, the Animals, Spencer Davis, the Pretty Things and the Yardbirds), Mayall and the Bluesbreakers remained true to the blues. Mayall was immersed in his music, the complete anthesis of a pop star, and something of a blues purist himself. Mayall let Eric move into his house in Blackheath, London, in early April 1965, where he was given a tiny room of his own. Eric mostly stayed there, practicing and listening to Mayall's vast collection of blues records, probably the finest in England at the time. Having finally found a guitarist who really knew how to play the blues was manna from heaven for the 31-year old Mayall. He also found a soul mate in Eric's character. As Clapton remembers: "I think that until I came along, Mayall had been quite isolated in his musical tastes, and now he'd found someone just as serious about the blues as he was." Clapton had just turned twenty and was looking for sanctuary. In Mayall he had found someone he could relate to who was also a strong bandleader in the Muddy Waters tradition. And not only that, but the Bluesbreakers also had a great rhythm section. What Clapton says about Mayall speaks for itself: "He was very good in that he'd listened to me about music, one of the first people who did. We would listen to a lot of blues, and pick songs that were right for the stage. He was easy company, older than me, but keen to draw me out and find what I thought. It was most unusual, a very important band for me. I did flower a lot during my time with John Mayall. He had a hell of a lot of responsibility on his hands. I mean, he used to take care of everything: bookings, everything. He was a good father figure. And he never gave me terms like you can't leave this band: once you get good, you're staying with it. It was more like once you've got on your own two feet, make your own way."

Clapton made his first live appearance with Mayall's band on Tuesday, 6 April 1965. "There were no rehearsals," drummer Hughie Flint recalls. "I first met Eric on the street outside my house. We got in the van and went off to his first gig, wherever it was, and Eric played just like Eric can play." McVie remembers: "Eric came in like a powerhouse, very strong and intense. He was almost unreal." Clapton was still using his trusted red Fender Telecaster from his Yardbirds days. Clapton's impact on the band was immediate. Not only did he win over existing fans, but brought his own substantial following with him. His stunning technique and style, coupled with his anti-hero stance, ensured that within weeks people were flooding in to see him play. Clapton's chops were influenced by Freddie King and Buddy Guy; he was louder and more aggressive than anything that had been heard in England before. He would often play with his back to the audience, as like this he could achieve better feedback-fuelled sustain. On stage, his physical presence was striking. He stood stock still, often with his eyes closed in a world of his own, refusing to put on any sort of show. His devastating technique and deep soul seemed somehow ill at ease with his quiet but friendly, unassuming character. Thanks to the new guitar player, Mayall's career blossomed as well. Clapton enabled his boss to reach a much wider audience, as crowds filled the clubs to catch a glimpse of the new guitar hero. Flint commented: "It was the Eric Clapton show, it wasn't John Mayall's Bluesbreakers: there were more people coming along to see Eric!" Producer Mike Vernon remembers: "Eric's joining the band changed it totally. With Clapton, the band had two focal points, and the power of the band was so much greater with him in front, playing in this really strong Freddie King, or B.B. King, kind of style. I think it was a real shock to people who'd only seen him play with the Yardbirds. He'd stepped into different shoes altogether; it was like he came from another planet. I was very impressed, particularly by the aggression of his playing and the toughness. When Eric joined the Bluesbreakers the audiences grew at an alarming pace."

New publicity photos of the Bluesbreakers taken around this time show a smart looking Eric Clapton sporting a tiny moustache, while John Mayall holds his newly acquired, first solid-body guitar, a Burns with three pickups, that he had cut around, decorated and hand painted, an instrument that he often used as a five-string guitar with open tunings in E or C for slide playing. Mayall had also built himself a harmonica harness with a built-in microphone to free up his hands, so he could simultaneously play organ and harp. He had also upgraded his Farfisa Compact with the more powerful Hammond M100 organ, already popularized in Britain by Georgie Fame, Zoot Money, Graham Bond and Brian Auger. Around the end of May, Clapton found a second-hand sunburst Gibson Les Paul Standard in Lew Davis's guitar shop in Charing Cross Road. The sound was heavier and creamier than anything British beat-boom guitarists had produced thus far, with a rich, gritty, warm, singing tone. Suddenly, Clapton had much more sustain, and his unique, violin-like sound with rich, distorted overtones was to influence generations of guitar players. Eric remembers how he found his signature sound: "It really came about accidentally, when I was trying to emulate the sharp, thin sound that Freddy King got out of his Les Paul, and I ended up with something quite different, a sound that was a lot fatter than Freddy's."

30

Now Mayall had almost everything he needed, a well-equipped band and the best blues guitarist in all the land. What he didn't have was a record deal, for it was around spring 1965 that Mayall's contract with Decca expired, and after the poor sales of the first three releases, they didn't renew it. Instead, Mayall accepted an offer by Andrew Loog Oldham (who managed the Rolling Stones) to record a single for his newly established Immediate label. As a result, two Mayall originals, "I'm Your Witchdoctor" and "Telephone Blues" were recorded at Pye studios in early June, produced by the highly respected 21-year old session guitarist Jimmy Page. The A-side featured inventive single note feedback solos from Eric, with notes being progressively sustained a little longer at each chorus. The B-side was a slow blues, inspired by a track with the same title by Chicago harp ace George "Harmonica" Smith. Jimmy Page remembers the sessions: "The engineer, who was used to doing big bands and orchestras, suddenly turned off the machine and said: 'This guitarist is unrecordable!' I told him just to record it, and I'd take full responsibility. The guy couldn't believe that someone was getting that kind of sound out of a guitar on purpose." The single was eventually released in October 1965 and was easily the best electric blues single of the year. Melody Maker wrote: "A superb disc which deserves to be a hit." Although never chart material, "I'm Your Witchdoctor" was one of Immediate's biggest-selling early releases, and the closest Mayall got to a UK hit. It was re-released in 1967 when Clapton was successful with Cream, and both tracks found their way onto many compilations and reissue albums. This track eventually became one of Mayall's most covered songs, with versions by Them and even Motörhead!

Always recognizing a good guitarist, at one point Mayall asked Page if he would be interested in joining, but the latter didn't want to join a touring band as he had too much session work. Even Jeff Beck was asked when Clapton left for the first or second time. Clearly, Mayall always had an eye open for replacements, fully aware that new and talented musicians alter the chemistry, and bring new life to any band. Confusingly, Page remembers further Mayall-Clapton songs being taped at this or later sessions, not only "On Top Of the World" and "Double Crossing Time", but also songs such as Mayall's "So Sorry" and Freddie King's "Someday After Awhile", both mentioned on album liner notes. However, many remain unissued, and due to a cock-up of monumental proportions, virtually all Immediate's master tapes were wiped in error. As a result, several studio-recorded Mayall-Clapton outtakes will never see the light of day.

On May 25, the Bluesbreakers played Klooks Kleek, one of Mayall's mainstays from 1964 to 1970. American blues pianist and singer Champion Jack Dupree, now resident in Europe, was on the same bill, and that meant long jam sessions with Mayall's band! A talented young guitarist from Putney, London by the name of Peter Green witnessed these concerts, and raved: "Wonderful, absolutely out of this world. Nothing I had ever seen up to that point was better than Clapton." At this time, the set list included "Chicago Line", "Heartache" and "I Need Your Love", as well as Freddy King's instrumental "Hideaway", Little Walter's "My Baby is Sweeter", "Red Beans & Rice" by Booker T & The MGs, "I Ain't Got You" by Billy Boy Arnold, "Bad Boy" by Eddie Taylor, "My Last Meal" by Jimmy Rogers and of course Ray Charles' "What'd I Say". With Eric, the Bluesbreakers played mostly Chicago Blues, while more jazz-tinged songs, disliked by Clapton, vanished from their repertoire. During one of Mayall's weekly visits to the Pontiac club in Putney, southwest London at summer, Jeff Beck and Jimmy Page turned up to see Clapton play. At one point, Beck and Page were invited up on stage, forming an impressive three-guitar line-up. Several fans clearly later remember that night, although oddly enough Mayall himself has no memory of it.

Around this time, the relationship between Mayall and Clapton was becoming tense. Eric could be moody, and had the tendency to pick holes in a situation. Clapton recalls: "I have always found something that isn't right, things that you're slightly ashamed of being in a band for—I mean, just quirks. In this band, it became John Mayall himself. Together with a couple of the other members of the group, we started to gang up on John behind his back. Since Mayall was that much older than the rest of us, and was to our minds a respectable middle-class man living with a wife and kids in suburbia, the dynamics of the band were very much 'him and us.' We saw him in the role of schoolmaster, with us as the naughty boys. He was tolerant up to a point, but we knew there was a limit and we did our best to push him to it. We would take the mickey out of him behind his back, muttering about him not being a good enough singer, and being too flamboyant and eccentric in his presentation. We were giggling when he went on stage bare to the waist. He was a well-built man, and more than a little vain, and we liked to see just how far we could go before he lost his temper. John had many quirks, and we used to really take the piss out of him behind his back on stage. He was amazing; no one was allowed to drink! John McVie got slung out of the bandwagon halfway between Birmingham and London one night because he was drunk, and had to make his own way home. And if we did a gig in Manchester, where Mayall's parents lived, he'd go and stay the night at his mum's and we'd have to sleep in the van. He didn't get us a hotel or anything. So there were disadvantages!"

Mayall was undoubtedly a gifted bandleader but was often accused of running a tight ship. He responded thus: "Not a tight ship but a professional ship. If you work seven to nine gigs a week, you have to." In contrast to most blues musicians, Mayall had his life organized down to the last detail. He confirmed that Eric could be moody, and added "By that I mean he'd conjure up these incredible moods and intensity. The things he did with a slow blues: when he felt like playing a slow blues, he could send shivers down your spine. But it was always awkward dealing with Eric because you could never read what mood would take with him. There were nights when Eric would be on stage and wouldn't feel like playing for one reason or another, and he would stand there and more or less just strum. Mick Taylor had that disease, too. But that was all part of the person. Eric and Mick made up for that with total brilliance on nights when they did feel like playing."

Eric also had quirks, and was not one hundred percent reliable. From time to time he didn't turn up, or was late, to the consternation of his boss. He sometimes preferred to jam with other bands, and it was not unknown for him to be seen playing at the Marquee with Stevie Winwood in the Spencer Davis Group when the Bluesbreakers were booked to appear down the road at the Flamingo. When this happened, the Bluesbreakers appeared as a three piece!

There was still something of the wandering minstrel to Eric. After about four months with Mayall, it had become a job, and Clapton longed to have some fun. In the summer of 1965, he moved out of Mayall's house. He had become restless and bored with the seemingly endless succession of one-nighters, and was also probably a little overwhelmed by all the attention he was getting as a guitar superstar. He just wanted to abandon the treadmill and follow his wanderlust with some friends. So, together with Ben Palmer and four others, he put together a group called The Glands, and set off on a "trip round the world", which actually only got as far as Greece! Mayall remembers: "Well, Eric going off to Greece was a bit of a surprise, because I thought things were going so well." Although Mayall had no choice but to let Eric go, he was full of praise for his apostate young guitar god. He even wrote an appreciation of him for R&B Monthly, the magazine edited by Mike Vernon and Neil Slaven, which is worth reproducing here in full:

AN APPRECIATION OF ERIC CLAPTON by John Mayall

On the 29ᵗʰ August, Eric Clapton made his last appearance in a British club with my band before setting out on a globe trotting project to enable him to temporarily 'get away from it all'. The pressures of playing blues in this country under the bastardised banner of R'n'B can at times become a little discouraging, and Eric felt that isolation from the British scene for a while would help to clear up some of his emotional problems.

In my opinion, Eric (now only 20 years old) is fast developing into one of the finest blues guitarists in the world, and I say this being quite aware of the stature of his mentor B.B. King and the younger generation players employing this style such as Freddie King, Otis Rush and Buddy Guy. I know damn well that many so-called purists would say that because Eric wasn't born an American Negro he couldn't seriously be compared with these giants. I feel this is a very narrow attitude when we consider the growth of appreciation and interest in blues music in all countries during the last decade. I believe that if a person is attracted at an early age to this music and seriously feels that this is the only natural outlet for his self-expression, he should be judged impartially on the strength of his playing, without regard to where he comes from or the colour of his skin. Eric has been playing the blues since he was old enough to hold a guitar, and is constantly driven towards mastery of his instrument by the ever-present frustration that he is not good enough, and that there will always be so much to learn. This frustration is one of the major ingredients in a person's ability to play the real blues, and communicate his moods. With the American Negro these frustrations can be sparked off by the social inequalities of life in White America, producing the feeling of being an outcast.

Speaking for myself and for Eric, I know we both feel we've been outcasts from the beginning. I have been playing the blues for the last twenty years and know full well what it means to feel the loneliness of playing for myself and perhaps a handful of record-collecting friends who understand and appreciate the blues. In Eric's case, he was soon made to feel an outcast playing within the commercial limitations of the Yardbirds music and their 'success' accelerated his feeling of isolation. The Yardbirds, although well intentioned and pleasant characters offstage, have an almost negligible conception of the true meaning of the blues which is apparent in the way that they have since settled down to pop material that is more natural to them. When Eric left them and joined the Bluesbreakers he was able to play professionally for the first time the kind of music he loves.

During the last five months with us he has quickly developed himself to the extent that he is an instantly recognizable stylist, and has established an individuality all his own. As evidence of this, listen to the things he creates on our new single track 'I'm Your Witchdoctor' and 'Telephone Blues' available on the Immediate label.

On leaving my band he says that he hopes to rejoin soon when he feels that his break has been beneficial to him and so, on behalf of all of us in the John Mayall Bluesbreakers and Eric's many followers throughout the country, we hope he won't be away too long. His great talent will be sorely missed."

After Eric left on August 30, 1965, there was an almost tangible air of disappointment in the clubs when audiences realised that he wouldn't be playing. Many of Clapton's followers stopped coming when they found out he'd left. It was of course a drastic situation for Mayall, who commented at the time: "we'd come to rely on him so much and he left this large gap. That dropped me into a real problem situation because there were so few people to choose from as a replacement, certainly nobody who could easily follow in Eric's footsteps. We got countless replies from a Melody Maker advert, and in the week after the ad was printed, I probably got through a guitarist a night, none of whom were it. So a lot of different guitar players were tried out on different gigs. We weren't doing any rehearsals because I had a full calendar, all the gigs were there, and by then I had a certain reputation to fulfil. So any changes in the line-up, I couldn't stop to cancel gigs and get in new musicians. So the auditions were gigs, I was struggling around and there was a massive turnover of guitarists."

The first substitute from September 1 to 6 (before the Melody Maker ad) was 18 year-old John Weider, who had played with Steve Marriott in the Moments, the Tony Meehan Combo and Johnny Kidd & the Pirates. Then John Slaughter, on loan from Chris Barber's band, replaced Weider for a couple of nights. Even John McLaughlin deputised for Clapton, appearing with the Bluesbreakers in September. To complicate matters further, Mayall became fed up with McVie's excessive drinking and fired him on October 3. When news reached Mayall about Jack Bruce's departure from The Graham Bond Organization in September, the fiery virtuoso Scot, whose roots were more in jazz and R'n'B, immediately replaced McVie. Bruce was a veteran of Alexis Korner's Blues Incorporated, and had recently been forced out of the Graham Bond Organization by drummer Ginger Baker, mainly as a result of friction between the two. Although a very busy player, perhaps too much so for the Bluesbreakers in 1965, John Mayall had no qualms about asking him to join: "Yes, he did overplay a bit, but he was a blues player, so there was no problem". Already considered one of the best bass players in the country, Bruce was also a great harp player and a fabulous vocalist. Playing both upright bass and a Fender VI six-string bass, he brought tremendous power and dynamism to the band. "He invited me down to his place," Bruce recalls, "and so my wife and I went there by train and had this sort of interview over stew and potatoes. He asked me to join, so I did." Bruce demanded a proper rehearsal when he joined, although this was at odds with Mayall's laidback style of introducing brand new songs on stage, and rarely using a fixed set list. However, rehearsals were duly arranged. They included Mayall and Bruce working on two-part harmony vocals for some songs, while Bruce introduced a Duke Ellington number called "Dooji Wooji" which he brought with him from Blues Incorporated. The other was a harmonica number by Forrest City Joe called "Train Time", later also covered by Cream. Sometimes Bruce would also sing a fantastic version of Clifton Chenier's "Why Did You Go Last Night", with Mayall on backing vocals. Before Bruce, John's way of introducing new songs was to sing them in the van on the way to gigs. Now with Bruce in the Bluesbreakers, improvisation started to get the upper hand. Now the Bluesbreakers line-up was Geoff Krivit (guitar), Jack Bruce (bass guitar, double bass, harp), Hughie Flint (drums), plus Mayall. They recorded five selections for BBC radio on

October 25. Three of the songs (all Mayall compositions) have survived, thanks to overseas broadcasting, and were released more than forty years later by Decca. They were "I'm Your Witchdoctor", probably to promote the new single with Eric Clapton (rearranged to allow the organ carry the middle eight), "Cheatin' Woman" (with a guitar riff blatantly copied from James Brown's "Papa's Got A Brand New Bag") and, best of the lot, a jazzy thing called "Nowhere To Turn" which featured Bruce on a superbly swinging upright bass, Flint on brushes, and Mayall singing and playing harp and organ. Krivit plays rhythm guitar only. The other songs they recorded have sadly been lost forever.

During Krivit's stint with the band, a cockney boy with mutton chop sideburns kept coming to the gigs and hassling Mayall, saying: "I'm much better than he is. Why don't you let me play guitar for you?" It was the 19 year-old Peter Green, who was trying to bully his way in. Mayall remembers: "He got really nasty about it, so I said 'Have you got a guitar?' No, he said, I'm a bass player—but I'll get a guitar! He kept following me around all the gigs within reach of London and pestering me—a pain in the arse! So I finally let him sit in and said: OK, then prove it! And he did; he just plugged in and played. No nerves. He played brilliantly; he had the feel, that touch! The cocky bugger was right. He was the better guitarist, so I hired him straightaway." Krivit was sacked on October 27, and later joined Dr. K's Blues Band and recorded with Fairport Convention.

All this took place just a week before Eric Clapton returned from Greece, which was very bad luck for Peter Green. As his money had run out, Eric was forced to return to England. Remembering his old boss had said the job was his whenever he felt like coming back, as soon as he got off the train at Victoria Station he called Mayall, who immediately welcomed him back, no questions asked. Eric was immediately reinstated, leaving Peter Green, who had just turned 19 and played only three concerts, bitterly disappointed. Mayall: "It really pissed Peter off because he'd fought so hard to get in the band, and now he was going straight out again." Of course, Green could not have known that just eight months later he would return to the

Bluesbreakers as lead guitarist. The announcement of Eric's return caused a huge stir on the English club scene, with Mayall even giving Eric equal billing on concert advertisements.

In early November, shortly after his return, Clapton and Mayall were invited to participate in recording sessions with black blues singer and piano player Champion Jack Dupree for his album "From New Orleans to Chicago". Dupree was probably the first US blues-man to move to Europe. Blues fan and Decca producer Mike Vernon wanted to produce the sessions, which led to his working with Mayall later. Vernon, an enthusiastic follower of the Bluesbreakers, had been to virtually all of their live shows. Vernon would later play a significant role as the leading producer of the British blues boom, working on recordings by Savoy Brown and Ten Years After for Decca and Deram, as well as producing for Fleetwood Mac, Chicken Shack and Duster Bennett for his own highly influential Blue Horizon label.

When Clapton rejoined the Bluesbreakers on November 6, he was surprised to find that Bruce had replaced McVie on bass. Bruce had a jazzier style and tended to improvise much more than his prede-cessor. Clapton was astonished by the bass player's versatility and said later: "Musically he was the most forceful bass player I had ever played with. He approached the gig almost as if the bass were a lead instrument, but not to the point where it got in your way, and his understanding of time was phenomenal. We hit it off really well. There was something creative there. Most of what we were doing with Mayall was imitating the records we got, but Jack had some-thing else; he had no reverence for what we were doing, and so he was composing new parts as we went along. So playing with Jack was more exciting then with John McVie." And Jack Bruce remem-bers: "When Eric started to play... phew! I'd never heard anything like that before. When we played together we had an instant rap-port. There was a great thing between me and Eric even then. He'd seen me with Graham Bond a couple of times and he dug my play-ing." The combination of Clapton and Bruce was musical dynamite, a sort of controlled anarchy. Mayall gave Clapton the freedom to stretch out, but he had a hard job holding both of them together. The pair loved taking extended solos, and it was an experience neither would forget. Clapton knew right away that Bruce would be the first choice in any future group he might dream of forming, not just as a bass player but also as a singer and composer. Although the Bluesbreakers with Clapton and Bruce lasted only six weeks, some live recordings survive that bear witness to their amazing interplay. The tapes were made at the Flamingo Club on Sunday, November 7, and the band did T-Bone Walker's "Stormy Monday", John Lee Hooker's "Maudie", the two Freddie King tunes "It Hurts to Be in Love" and "Have You Ever Loved A Woman", Mayall's harp feature "Bye Bye Bird", and the Muddy Waters standard "Hoochie Coochie Man". Despite the rough quality, the playing is inspiring and creative, anticipating early Cream. The songs are taut, solos are kept in check, and the ensemble playing is first rate. Eric's guitar playing is incendiary throughout, but especially on "Stormy Monday", where his timing, phrasing and attack are jaw-dropping. The pure emotion here has probably never been equalled, and the solo is perhaps the most brilliant by Clapton you will ever find anywhere on record. Thanks to modern technology, Decca was able to re-release these historic recordings in incomparably better quality on their Mayall-Clapton deluxe edition in 2006. For a long time, there was a lot of confusion about the recording dates of these six live tracks. Christopher Hjort supplies the solution in his excellent book Strange Brew. As Mayall was still signed to Andrew Loog Oldham's label in November 1965, the recordings belonged to Immediate. When they were released on Decca, the recording date was conveniently changed to spring 1966 to avoid legal complications.

Although Jack Bruce's stay in the band was brief, he managed to play at least 26 concerts, twelve with guitarist Krivit, three with Green and the last eleven with Clapton. Manfred Mann came to a gig and lured Bruce away with the promise of better money; his band had already had two hits and promised far greater earning potential. Having just got married, the temptation was too great, so Jack took up the far more lucrative offer with Manfred Mann and quit the

Bluesbreakers, much to Mayall's disgust. When Bruce left, Mayall tried out three other bass players without much success, so, near the end of the year, he allowed McVie to return on the solemn promise to moderate his drinking, which he did, at least for a while.

The beginning of 1966 saw the Bluesbreakers return to their classic combination of Mayall, Clapton, McVie and Flint, which was to last until the summer. It was around this time that the notorious "Clapton is God" graffiti started to appear. Various explanations for this mysterious phenomenon exist, Clapton himself commenting in his autobiography that "someone had written the slogan on the wall of Islington underground station. Then it started to spring up all over London. I didn't really want that kind of notoriety; I knew it would bring some kind of trouble." Adverts in the music press now read John Mayall's Bluesbreakers featuring Eric Clapton. Flint remembers: "When Eric came back, things went from strength to strength. It was like the Eric Clapton show, it wasn't John Mayall's Bluesbreakers: there were more people coming along to see Eric. He was an incredible draw in the band. He just got better and better." Mayall muses: "Eric was always doing different things to himself: long hair, short hair, moustache, sideburns, and he was one of the pioneers of clothes like military uniforms. One night in Newcastle, a pretty tough town to play in, at the Club-A-Go-Go, the stronghold of the Animals, a really working-class atmosphere with bottles flying, he turned up in a priest's habit, the white collar and everything. People just stared in disbelief." On stage, Clapton usually stood quite still, deep in concentration, sporting mutton-chop sideburns, cropped hair, jeans and T-shirt, and let the blues flow from his fingertips. Although not the object of hysterical adulation by crowds of screaming teenage girls like the Beatles, he had nevertheless became a cult figure for intellectuals, hippies, art-students and beatniks.

Now free of his recording contracts with both Decca and Immediate, Mayall was free to record with whatever label he pleased. Blues aficionado and producer Mike Vernon used the opportunity to ask Mayall and Clapton to record a single for his tiny Purdah label. This was just a back-room operation with records available only through mail order, made by blues purists for like-minded fans. Mike Vernon remembers: " I just said to John 'Look, do you fancy doing an out and out blues thing, just for collectors? It could be a lot of fun, and we could probably sell a thousand copies'. I promised to give them 50 % of the profits after the costs. They went away, discussed it and finally agreed." So, sometime in February 1966, Mayall and Clapton went into Wessex Studios in the Old Compton Road, Soho. Vernon wanted to make a real down-home blues record, without a rhythm section. They taped two duets: "Lonely Years" with guitar and harmonica/vocals, and "Bernard Jenkins", a jaunty guitar-piano instrumental recreating the Forties duo work of Tampa Red and Big Maceo Merriweather. Vernon recorded the session using simple but effective techniques: "We did it straight mono: one microphone in the middle of the studio, just piano, voice and a guitar, and to this day it's the only record I've ever done that sounds as if it was made in Chicago. Within three hours of our arrival the job was completed. We spent much of the time repositioning the one microphone, searching for that sonic picture that would create the illusion of Chicago recordings from the early Fifties". Vernon had successfully captured the authentic raw Chicago blues sound. The music was rough-hewn and unpolished, but the feel was good. The limited edition of five hundred copies sold out rapidly when the single was released in early August 1966.

Vernon later sold the tapes with both titles to Decca, who released them in early 1967 on their bargain sampler Raw Blues, while the original Purdah single became a collector's item. "Bernard Jenkins", the unusual title of the B-side boogie-woogie, came from the band's fondness for "The Caretaker", a bleak Harold Pinter play. The Jenkins in question was the main character in the 1963 movie of the play.

Two radio sessions for the BBC were recorded in early 1966. The first took place on February 9, for the BBC Light Programme Jazz Beat, (broadcast February 12), with "Little Girl", "Hideaway", "Tears In My Eyes", and "Parchman Farm". The second was on March 14 for BBC's Saturday Club.

Mike Vernon worked hard to persuade Decca that they were wrong to drop Mayall from their label, especially as Clapton had now re-joined, and the band had become one of London's hottest draws. Mayall had become a little disillusioned with Decca, but Vernon was able to persuade him to re-sign by explaining that Decca was one of the only record companies with people who knew anything about the blues. Mayall insisted on having Mike Vernon as producer, which is how the legendary Bluesbreakers album with Eric Clapton, their first ever studio album, came about. In March 1966, Mayall, Clapton and the others entered Decca Studios, intending to capture the intensity of their live set as quickly and as simply as possible. "We had no trouble selecting what songs would go on it," recalls Mayall, "it was just what we were doing every night in our set." The budget was small; they were allocated the No. 2 studio, which was undersized and sparsely equipped. Assisting producer Mike Vernon was Gus Dudgeon, a freelance engineer who had little or no experience with electric blues (Dudgeon was later to find fame as producer to Elton John). Mayall remembers: "We just went in there. I think it was either one or two days, it didn't take much more than that. Basically, we were just playing the stuff that we were doing in the clubs, so the material was totally familiar to us. It felt pretty natural. The only difference was that we had to play a little quieter than we might have done in the clubs. Dubbing was difficult in those days, because Decca only had a four-track machine. It was pretty primitive. As I remember, the bass and drums had to be mixed onto one track before we recorded, so they had to be balanced up. Then you had one for the keyboards and one for the guitar, and left one for the vocals. Things like overdubs had only just started to come into the picture, so if Eric had a rhythm guitar part, we had to work out a way of doing it. I recall there was some doubling had to be done in order to get what we wanted. I think all Eric's solos were overdubbed, as were my vocals. That was what everybody did; that makes the most sense, because you don't want to keep going through something where the rhythm section was perfect on the first take but the vocalist or the soloist had made a mistake. That way you capture the freshness of those first takes. The art of making records is knowing what elements to keep, but I've always believed in going for that first, spontaneous take." Flint recalls: "On the two slow blues "Have You Heard" and "Double Crossing Time", Eric soloed on the original tracks and maybe overdubbed some rhythm guitar later to beef it up." Nobody was expecting a hit record. Mayall recalls: "All we were thinking was to do the best job possible on it". As a major blues enthusiast himself, Vernon seems to have allowed the band to be pretty much as they were, without the sort of input that might even have been expected from more pop-conscious producers on the big labels. "John didn't know what the hell was going on as far as technical terms were concerned," recalls Vernon, "he was just interested in making the music. And Eric would play loud, which we hadn't had to contend with before, and Hughie was loud, but his snare wasn't as loud as anything else, and John McVie would usually end up having a few too many drinks. So in one way or another there were lots of little hangups." Clapton resolutely refused to turn down his amplifier. Playing at club-volume levels would be the key to getting the tremendously dynamic, aggressive sound of his guitar onto the record. His Gibson Les Paul, inserted into a Dallas Rangemaster treble booster, played through his Marshall 60-watt combo amp, was recorded at stage volume. This was the only way to obtain the feedback, sustain, fuzz and distortion required for his searing solos. As can be expected, back in 1966, this approach created a fair amount of technical difficulties for the sound engineer. The usual practice in the studio in the 60s was to play very quietly in order to ensure maximum separation between instruments. For Clapton, this would have meant 'direct injection' i.e. plugging his guitar lead directly into the recording desk, thus eliminating the need for amplification. Clapton, in his typically uncompromising way, insisted that he wasn't going to play with a clean sound at all. To achieve what he wanted, he had to drive his amp to the limit. "He had a terrible time with the engineer," says Hughie Flint, "because he wanted his amp up, which meant that it was distorting. Gus Dudgeon was tearing his hair out and said: "Turn it down!" Eric, ever the individual, said, "No; I can't play unless I play like I play on stage." Gus put the mike in front of Eric's amp. Eric picked up his amp and took it across the studio, as far away as possible from the mike. Much of Eric's guitar on the album was actually picked up by Hughie Flint's drum mike. Dudgeon later explained: "Eric absolutely insisted that he wasn't going to play with a tame sound. So I simply waited for Mike Vernon, told him what was up, and he went to have a word with Eric." And Vernon remembers: "I went to talk to Eric. Is this absolutely essential? Because Gus is having kittens, he doesn't know how to record it. He's never had to deal with anything like this volume in his life. Can't you turn it down? And Eric said very politely: 'No, I can't, because if I turn it down, the sound changes. And I can't get the sustain I want. He's the engineer, you're the producer: tell him to engineer it, and you produce it. But I'm not turning it down.'" Finally, Mayall, having realised how important Eric's sound was to the way he played, made sure Clapton prevailed by telling the engineer and producer to "give God what he wants!" For this, all future electric guitarists should be eternally grateful to Mayall, because from that moment on, they were permitted to play in the studio at volume levels similar to their live set. The result was a fabulously thick, high-sustain tone, and some of the most powerful blues guitar ever recorded by Clapton (or anybody else, for that matter). At the end of the sessions, Vernon said: "I was very impressed, particularly by the aggression of his playing, the toughness." And Eric later summed up his performance as "a combination of real anger, frustration and arrogance. I was convinced I was the only person who knew what was going on."

This seminal album was released on July 22, 1966, and contained the following tracks:
- "All Your Love (I Miss Loving)". In 1966 a modern Chicago blues with minor key elements. The signature guitar riff (sliding up the whole neck on the top string), and the rhythm changes make this Otis Rush tune interesting for guitar players and very distinctive. Mayall had the rare single on Cobra from 1958 in his vast collection and played it to Clapton, which is how it came to

be part of their repertoire. Peter Green recorded it later, as did Gary Moore. It became the inspiration for "Black Magic Woman", the Peter Green/Fleetwood Mac original that became a massive hit for Carlos Santana.

- "Hideaway". Freddie King's biggest instrumental hit made #3 in 1961, but evidence shows that this tune was used as the opening number for Hound Dog Taylor for several years before it was recorded by King. Clapton's version injects the original with pure adrenalin. He even felt free to add the riff from the then famous Mancini tune "Peter Gunn". It's really his tour de force and a definite highlight on the album, with Mayall playing some cool Hammond organ (the stereo version is better for this). Mayall and Clapton made Hideaway famous, and it has become a standard for practically every contemporary blues band since.
- "Little Girl". A fairly typical Mayall composition of the time which lifts its basic form and signature riff from Howlin' Wolf's "Forty Four", which featured guitarists Humbert Sumlin and Jody Williams. Clapton's solo builds to a sensual climax.
- "Another Man (Done Gone)" is a traditional Alabama chain-gang song, closely linked to the folk movement, sung and recorded by Odetta, Harry Belafonte and even Johnny Cash. Mayall: "This was taken from field recordings of prison work songs [taped by Alan Lomax on one of his field trips in the 1930s], which I converted into a harmonica solo."
- "Double Crossing Time". Mayall: "We did this song before the Bluesbreakers album. It was intended as a B-side for "On Top Of the World" on Immediate, which never came out. So we put it on the album instead. It was originally called "Double Crossing Man" after Jack Bruce, who walked out on us to join Manfred Mann." Recorded in December 1965, with John Bradley on bass and probably Martin Hart on drums. Here, another Clapton guitar track was put on top of the original recording.
- "What'd I Say". The well-known Ray Charles hit from 1959 was the group's usual set-closer because it had such a good beat. Ray Charles was very popular in places like the Flamingo, and every

British R&B band at the time played it. "What'd I Say" is often cited as the beginning of soul music. The song is brightened by Clapton quoting from the Beatles' hit "Day Tripper", clearly showing that he was far from being the narrow-minded blues purist he sometimes appeared to be.

- "Key to Love". A slight but jolly tune with Clapton's distinctive ascending solo. The horn section was overdubbed later with Alan Skidmore (tenor sax), Johnny Almond (baritone sax) and Dennis Healey (trumpet).
- "Parchman Farm". When originally recorded by country blues singer and guitarist Bukka White in 1940, this was an autobiographical piece about Parchman Penitentiary, the state prison of Mississippi. White jazz-blues singer and pianist Mose Allison changed it to a piano song in 1957. Mayall: "I was a big Mose Allison fan. Georgie Fame was very close because we played the Flamingo together. He put that in the repertoire but I turned it into a harmonica feature with a faster pace. Eric didn't play on this one. He found the same riff too boring, so I took it over as just bass, drums, harmonica and vocals."
- "Have You Heard". According to Mayall, he wrote this 12-bar blues with a pretty standard arrangement in the studio, more or less making up the words as he went along. With a running time of almost six minutes, this is by far the longest track on the album, one of the songs on which Eric was allowed to stretch out. Surprisingly, the song kicks off with Alan Skidmore's excellent tenor saxophone solo for one chorus. "I knew Alan Skidmore and his father Jimmy through their work at jazz clubs," remembers Mayall. Skidmore contributes almost as much to the take as Clapton, blowing up a veritable storm! Eric's solo comes in at 3.25, and is delivered as though his very life depended on it. It is still regarded as one of his best solos ever, absolutely devastating!
- "Ramblin' on My Mind". This was Eric's vocal debut, and he made sure the others had gone home before he recorded several takes. His inhibitions had prevented him from ever singing on stage with the Bluesbreakers. Mayall recalls: "Eric hadn't done any singing

before, so I encouraged him to have a go. We recorded it with just Eric and me on piano. He was a bit shy about singing for the first time on record, but it worked out after a couple of takes." Clapton had chosen a number by his hero Robert Johnson (1911–1938), the legendary and influential Delta blues genius with almost supernatural guitar skills, who died tragically at age of 26, poisoned by the jealous husband of a woman he had been flirting with.

- "Steppin' Out". Another obvious guitar feature for Eric that crackles with energy. They took this blistering instrumental from the 1959 album "Memphis Slim at the Gate of Horn" with Matt Murphy on guitar. Eric easily adapted the original piano part on his guitar.
- "It Ain't Right". A harmonica showcase for Mayall taken from a 1955 Little Walter single for Chess /Checker and featuring Clapton on rhythm guitar and no solo. "Little Walter was one of our favourites, especially for his song writing, and this song suited my voice, its range and whatever else," is what Mayall remembers about the closing track.

The precise recording dates of the 1966 Mayall-Clapton album seem to be one of the best-kept secrets of music history. During the 60s, the dates were always listed as March, although decades later, they were changed to April or May. One of many Clapton biographies mentions it was a Saturday afternoon in March. The only Saturday possible (with no daytime gigs) would have been March 12, but Mayall says it was recorded in two days plus a third day for overdubs. Mayall: "We just went into the studio in the daytime and did the gig that night. On all my albums, we start early, about 11:00, and are out at about 6:00 pm." If we believe the mixing was done on April 2, the obvious answer must be sometime during March 1966. "Probably no-one will ever know for sure" as Mayall once wrote.

Mayall took the unprecedented step of giving his guitarist equal billing on the album sleeve, but this is the only time he ever did. The Bluesbreakers album cover quickly became something of a classic in itself, showing Eric calmly reading The Beano, a well known

British children's comic, while the rest of the band gaze mournfully into the camera, pondering the meaning of life, or their unpaid bills! This light-hearted gesture, together with Eric's barely suppressed grin, clearly show that his attitude to the photo session was less than 100 % serious. The shot, showing the four musicians against graffiti-daubed inner city decay, started a fashion in British blues LP sleeve designs. Bands such as Fleetwood Mac often used the "urban-decay-back-alley-street-scene" image to present their music. The garbage bins and empty bottles created a kind of south side of Chicago or Maxwell Street vibe, with the musicians shown quite self-consciously down at heel. By the time the album was released in Britain on July 22 (initially in mono only), the line-up with Eric was already history. He had left five days earlier to form the supergroup Cream, with Jack Bruce and Ginger Baker.

Fans soon baptised it the "Beano album", as it didn't have any short or catchy title. Looking back, it is impossible to overstate the seismic impact and influence of it on the music scene on both sides of the Atlantic, and on electric guitarists in particular. It effectively launched blues rock in the UK, and was influential in America too, where one of its many purchasers was a certain James Marshall Hendrix Jr. Shortly after arriving in England that autumn, Jimi bought his own Marshall kit, inspired by Eric's example. In Britain, the album had a massive effect on many other guitarists, spawning a host of Clapton imitators. It also introduced the idea of the guitar hero, setting a benchmark for all British blues bands to come. A whole new generation of guitar players began to emerge, fronted initially by Clapton and his Yardbirds' successors Jeff Beck and Jimmy Page, but joined shortly after by Peter Green, Mick Taylor, Kim Simmons, Stan Webb, John Moorshead, Miller Anderson, Dave Clempson, Martin Stone, Pete Haycock, Tony McPhee, Alvin Lee and Rory Gallagher, to name but a few. For many, Clapton's playing on that record has never been equalled from the point of view of aggression and attack. It achieved wide acclaim and made Clapton a star. His guitar playing is a revelation throughout, all underpinned by John McVie's solid bass and Hughie Flint's swinging touch. Almost overnight, slick, popular guitar-based bands like The Shadows seemed hopelessly outdated. The blues in the hands of Clapton and Mayall appeared so much more accomplished. Although heavily rooted in electric Chicago post-war blues, it is Mayall's introduction of the Hammond organ that gives the album a uniquely British slant. This instrument was foreign to just about all Chicago blues recordings. Interestingly, B.B. King replaced the piano with a Hammond organ in his band at around the same time. And because the album was recorded so quickly, it has a raw, live, edgy quality that made it special. The album quickly achieved cult status, surprisingly achieving no. 6 in the UK album charts. Nobody could believe it, least of all Mayall. It stayed there for two months, probably one of the earliest examples of success without the release of a single to boost sales. "No British musicians have ever sounded like this before on record. It is a giant step. It is a credit to John and his musicians" wrote Melody Maker. The album laid the foundation for the renaissance in British blues that followed. Alexis Korner, originator of the earlier R&B boom, acknowledged: "That's where the blues renaissance built from, basically through John Mayall and Eric Clapton." The album clearly demonstrated that young white British musicians could aspire to play the blues with a sincerity and intensity previously credited only to black Americans. According to Mike Vernon, the album really opened up people's ears: "The album was tremendously important. It was the first time a blues album had hit the top of the charts. I know John and Eric would say: 'Well, B.B. King, Freddie King and Buddy Guy were doing all this stuff years before,' but by the same token, those guys didn't even have record deals. The album also helped B.B. King and Freddie King to tour Britain and Europe and get record deals. There's no doubt that the Bluesbreakers album (and possibly the first Fleetwood Mac album also) were the most important releases of their time."

Beat Instrumental gave the LP high marks: "John Mayall's voice may not be the greatest example of blues singing there is, but he is sincere, and... it's Eric who steals the limelight." Mayall says: "Unfortunately, the version found everywhere now is the stereo one.

It was made as a mono record so that's the best way it should sound." Luckily, some of today's CDs contain both versions, so fans can compare for themselves. Thanks to the good sales, Decca was very pleased, and allowed Vernon and Mayall to do follow-up albums.

By this time, however, Eric had become very erratic, often not turning up for gigs at all, forcing the others to play as a trio. Drummer Hughie Flint recalls: "It was pretty dire, but John insisted on carrying it off and getting paid, but two solid hours of John Mayall, John McVie and myself must have been pretty heavy when most of the people wanted God. Can you imagine the audience shouting 'Where's God?' with John saying 'F... that', and playing relentless, endless piano and harp solos?" Mayall recalls: "I wouldn't criticise Eric for when he started not turning up at gigs—he was just Eric. If there was something he didn't feel like doing, he wouldn't do it. I don't think he thought he was more important than the rest of the band, it's just that he didn't take the whole thing that seriously". Eric remembered in 2004: "I behaved very badly, didn't even show up to gigs sometimes. But John always forgave me. Perhaps he fined me once or twice. But I got away with it." One such occasion was April 18, 1966, when the Bluesbreakers were scheduled to play in Welwyn Garden City, a new town north of London. Eric decided to go and see The Loving Spoonful at the Marquee Club, together Spencer Davis, Stevie Winwood, John Lennon and George Harrison.

Mick Taylor was a blond, shy, 17-year-old guitar player living locally who went to see the band. "Some friends and I had gone along to see the Bluesbreakers, but Eric never showed up—his guitar was there but he wasn't. They played the first set without him, just the three of them and then, after much persuading from my friends, I went to see John in the interval to see if I could play the second set. I'd seen Eric with John at the Flamingo and knew all the songs, what key they were in and everything. John was a bit sceptical at first, but he let me do it. I was very nervous. I played Eric's guitar. I was still kind of learning how to play blues guitar—I was really not that good. I'd learnt all the licks but I couldn't play the blues—I could copy the blues. But I knew the songs and it obviously sounded better with me playing then it did with no guitar at all!" is how Mick Tayor remembers that night. By the end of the evening, Taylor had impressed Mayall with his technique and maturity but, typically, disappeared without leaving even a telephone number! 14 months later, however, when Taylor answered Mayall's advert in the Melody Maker after Peter Green had left, John immediately knew who he was and gave him the job right away. It is interesting to note that both Green and Taylor "auditioned" for Mayall by standing in for Clapton during his unscheduled absences, and both would join the Bluesbreakers a short time later.

With Clapton unreliable and John McVie temporarily fired for drinking again, it looked like Hughie Flint was the only easy-going guy in the band. Flint, however, had a few problems of his own. Mayall commented: "Hughie was going through some personal problems at the time and was feeling rather depressed. This was towards the end of Eric's time with the Bluesbreakers and Hughie resigned shortly afterwards." Hughie thus had no objections when drummer Peter "Ginger" Baker sat in with the Bluesbreakers when they played in Oxford on May 13, 1966. Since Hughie was quite a Ginger Baker fan, he was glad to sit out for a few numbers and just listen. The rapport between Eric and Ginger was immediate, and it was after this concert that Baker clandestinely approached Clapton to ask if he would like to join the new trio he was intent on forming. Clapton showed great interest, but stated that he would only do so if Jack Bruce could be persuaded to join them as the bass player. Although Baker and Bruce had enjoyed a turbulent relationship in the Graham Bond Organisation, Ginger was forced to relent, and thus Cream was born. Unknown to Mayall, Clapton, Bruce and Baker then began rehearsing for several weeks on the sly, although still continuing to work with their respective bands. Trying to keep it hushed up proved impossible, however, and on Saturday, June 11, 1966, Melody Maker announced: "Eric, Jack and Ginger team up. Sensational new group starring Eric Clapton, Jack Bruce and Ginger Baker! Top groups will be losing star instrumentalists as a result. Manfred Mann will lose bassist, harmonica player, pianist and singer Jack Bruce; John Mayall will lose brilliant guitarist Eric Clapton; and The Graham Bond Organisation will lose incredible drummer Ginger Baker. The group say they hope to start playing at clubs, ballrooms and theatres in a month's time. It is expected they will remain as a trio, with Jack as featured vocalist."

John Mayall was not amused. Flint remembers: "John and I were sat in his back garden and when John read this, he was very displeased, he even went ballistic and erupted with violent fury, quoting from the paper that 'Clapton, Bruce and Baker are rehearsing the new group in an anonymous church hall'. I was very sad because it meant that Eric was going to leave, and I didn't know what was going to happen at all." For Mayall, it was "Double Crossing Time" again. Clapton was summoned and said, "I'd like to give a month's notice," and Mayall agreed. In fact, Mayall got angry enough to fire him before Clapton had played out his notice in full, eventually telling Clapton: "You can leave tomorrow because we've got another guitarist".

Eric Clapton remembers his last days as a Blues Breaker in his autobiography thus: "Ginger let the cat out of the bag by giving an interview to Chris Welch of Melody Maker, and all the hell broke loose. Jack was furious about it and almost came to blows with Ginger, and I had the unenviable task of explaining myself to John Mayall, who had been like a father to me. It was not a happy experience. I told him I was leaving because I had come to a fork in the road and I wanted to form my own band. I was quite surprised by how upset he was, and though he wished me well, I was left in no doubt that he was pretty angry. I think he was sad too, because I had helped take the Bluesbreakers to another level." Eric played his last concert with Mayall on July 17, 1966 at the Black Prince Hotel in Bexley, southeast London, never having played outside Britain with the band. The year or so with Mayall saw Eric's playing mature from that of boy wonder to fully-fledged electric guitar superhero. When he became a Bluesbreaker his playing was considered merely brilliant, but by the time he left, he was rated among the best in the world. Rarely has there been such a meteoric rise to fame. Only thirty songs featuring Clapton and Mayall exist from the 60s, but Mayall still maintains to this day: "In my opinion, Eric Clapton is the greatest blues guitar player who ever walked on earth."

CHAPTER 4

The Bluesbreakers with Peter Green

Peter Green and the birth of Fleetwood Mac, 1966–67

When Clapton quit the Bluesbreakers to form Cream with Jack Bruce and Ginger Baker, it would have been a devastating blow to most bandleaders, but not Mayall, who said about it: "When Eric left for good, I went straight away to Peter Green. We'd sort of been friends before he joined. We used to hang out. He was hesitant to join because it had fallen through before, but he eventually did." Green recalls: "When Eric went for good and John asked me back I was very happy, because I was getting an outlet for the type of stuff I really wanted to play."

According to Mayall, it wasn't all that easy to lure Green back, because he was still angry at having been dismissed when Clapton had returned from Greece. "He really made me wait around for a decision on it. It was like, 'Now aren't you sorry you had Eric back?' He definitely wanted to keep me on the hook and make me have a hard time getting him back, so there was a bit of revenge there. I had to try and find a way of talking Peter back into the band after treating him so shabbily. He made me sweat for about a week before he accepted the offer!" At the same time, Green had had an offer from Eric Burdon to join the New Animals and go on tour in America. While he was eager to see the States and go to Chicago to meet blues people, Green loved playing pure blues more than the Animals' chart-friendly music. Finally agreeing to join when his relationship with Shotgun Express singer Beryl Marsden broke up, Green officially became a Bluesbreaker again on July 18, 1966.

Peter Green had learned to play the guitar when he was about eleven years old after his brother Michael had taught him a few chords. He swiftly became, as he put it, "an experienced three-chord merchant." His main influences were Hank Marvin and B.B. King. He was first drawn to the blues after hearing Muddy Waters' "Honey Bee" aged 14. The first amateur band he played with was the Strangers, a skiffle group that played school dance halls and youth clubs for fun. On leaving school, Green played part-time for rock 'n' roll group Bobby Denim and the Dominoes, then the Muskrats, an R&B band with Dave Bidwell on drums. After a spell in the Tridents playing bass, he had his first brush with Mayall in autumn 1965. This whetted his appetite return to lead guitar, inspired by Clapton. After the first short stint with Mayall, Green found a regular spot in Peter B's Looners, a Stax-styled instrumental quartet led by keyboard player Peter Bardens, which is where he met Mick Fleetwood. The Looners soon took on two singers, Beryl Marsden and Rod Stewart, and became Shotgun Express. Liverpool girl Marsden proved a special attraction to Green, but when she turned down his offer of marriage, the chance to join the Bluesbreakers proved irresistible. Green walked away from gnawing heartache and threw himself into an all-consuming love affair with the blues. Mayall recalls: "Peter's character was very pushy, and he was determined to prove himself. He was just a staggering player, such an uncomplicated, straightforward blues player, completely different from Eric personality-wise, but just as good a musician. He had an aggressive attack in a good way. He was gung-ho, a real battler. He wanted to get over to the audience that he was the best, and that always came over in his playing. So Peter was a lot easier and more reliable to play with than Eric had been. I guess from a musical point of view, I was a kind of father figure. We spent just a lot of our free time talking and listening to blues. Peter wanted to hear more or less everything from my vast record collection." For a year or so, Mayall and Green lived in the same building in Porchester Road, Paddington, south-west London, a strange huddle of rooms on the top floor of a seedy block of flats. Daily the blues percolated down one storey from John's flat to Peter's:

old 78s from John's wall-to-wall collection, sparking impromptu jam sessions and caffeine-fuelled conversations at all hours. At just 19, Green wasn't just a fluent guitarist with a fascinating combination of blazing intensity and remarkable restraint, but also a great blues singer (Clapton didn't contribute much singing while with the Bluesbreakers). Bluesbreakers' later bassist Keith Tillman recalls that Green was also a very able harp player long before he joined Mayall's band, good enough to have worked out note-for-note "Juke", Little Walter's signature song. As soon as Green teamed up with Mayall, he also began to write his own songs. Preparing himself, Green was given an advanced copy of the Beano album to learn from. He recalls: "I didn't learn Eric's parts, I just enjoyed them. And when I joined John, I played things my own way." Peter had been in the band for only four days when the Beano album was released on July 22.

Taking Clapton's place was a tall order for Green, as the new guitar player not only had to match his predecessor's ability, but also live up to the expectations of the public and the press, most of whom would make immediate comparisons. But Green kept his nerve, and far from being withdrawn or unassuming, he was bright and self-confident, being quite aware of his exceptional abilities. There are varying opinions from this time as to the audience reaction to Mayall's young new lead guitarist with his mutton-chop sideboards, blue jeans, Canadian lumber jacket and sneakers. While history has it that in his first few weeks as a Bluesbreaker, Peter was frequently heckled at gigs, with shouts from Clapton fans like 'Where's Eric?', band members do not remember this being the case. Hughie Flint remembers: "I didn't remember anyone heckling or booing then, or anything like that. Peter came in and did the job very well." Despite this, Green complained to Beat Instrumental: "I just wish people would stop comparing me with Eric. I'd just like them to accept me as Peter Green, not 'Clapton's Replacement.' I've felt terribly conscious of this on stage. I can feel them listening for special phrases. They want to see how I compare with Eric. It makes my job tougher, because, just lately, I've been really trying hard all the time. Sometimes I try too hard and overplay. If I make a mistake when

I'm doing this, I'm spoiled for the rest of the evening." A year later, Green told Record Mirror: "The verbal taunts weren't the kind of things which made me play better; they would just bring me down. For a long time with John I wasn't playing at my best. Only in the last few months with him could I really feel uninhibited." To promote the new album, Green had to play a lot of songs Clapton had made his own, although Mayall did change the repertoire slightly, so that direct comparison between the two guitarists became more difficult. To continue the Freddie King instrumental theme, they played "The Stumble", and it became Peter's showcase. Soon, some of Green's own compositions were added to the set list. For a long time, however, Peter had to play the songs from the Beano LP, but there was another, more subtle difference: Green played at a much lower volume than Clapton, making for less impact. Soon, Peter learned to do what audiences were expecting of him: "The applause I get when playing fast, this is nothing; I like to play slowly and feel every note; it comes from every part of my body." Back in 1966, this kind of restraint went against the grain: guitarists had learnt that flash, if nothing else, meant cash. Not for Peter Green, who became famous for his impassioned, economical playing, which conveyed a broad range of emotion with a minimum of gimmickry. Within a short time, the band had gelled, and fans began accepting Green. Mayall told Beat Instrumental, "In Peter Green we have a young genius. He's better known than Eric was when he joined, and for my money, he'll be better than Eric. Peter is more interested in playing blues than being a star." It didn't take long before Peter received adulation for his unique, minimalist, bent-note style, and soon new graffiti appeared: "Green is better than God"! His self-assured performances at gigs elevated his stature, and made him one of the most prominent guitarists in the country. More than anyone else, it was Mayall who helped to form Green's character as a blues musician, teaching him discipline, taste and song writing skills.

Only seven weeks after Green had joined, drummer Hughie Flint quit, playing his last night on Sunday, September 4 at the Marquee. He had been the Bluesbreakers' drummer for over two years, but no records were cut by this line-up. Bassist McVie also got his marching orders at the same time, once again for drinking, just as he had eleven months before. In on drums came Micky Waller, a man with an impressive pedigree, having played with the Flee-Rekkers, Joe Brown & Bruvvers, the Cyril Davies R&B All Stars, Long John Baldry & the Hoochie Coochie Men, Marty Wilde & the Wild Cats, and Brian Auger & Steampacket. After considering Bugs Waddell from Chris Farlowe & the Thunderbirds as his new bassist, Mayall settled instead for the young Steve Usher, an unknown quantity. This also allowed him to toy briefly with the idea of expanding the line-up with horns. Mayall would return to the idea the following summer, as promised on the cover notes of the "Hard Road" album.

The line-up with Usher and Waller lasted a fortnight only; Usher rejoined the Blue Monks and McVie returned on bass. Mayall had been loath to let him go because, as he told Beat Instrumental "he has a good tone and can really swing, which is what blues bass-playing is all about!" Waller joined Georgie Fame, and was replaced by the excellent Aynsley Dunbar, who had played in a host of bands. Dunbar had been inspired by the great American jazz and big band drummers like Buddy Rich, Joe Morello, Art Blakey, Elvin Jones and Max Roach, and had worked his way through the ranks of Liverpool beat bands before ending up in London, just as the British blues scene was beginning to take hold. Dunbar remembers how became a Bluesbreaker: "Mayall called me up and said, 'I was wondering if you'd come down and sit in with my band.' I didn't know who the hell John Mayall was, so I asked my wife, and she said she thought he was a country & western singer. Oh no! But he was nice enough to call me, so I thought I'd go down and listen to him. I was completely overawed by Peter Green's playing, but I didn't think the band was backing him properly. He was doing great solos, but the band was always playing the same level of intensity behind him. I wanted to play. So John Mayall said, 'Well, we've got a gig tomorrow night. Be at the house at so-and-so, and have your drums there and we'll go up to the gig.' No rehearsal—just get on stage and play. He'd just call out a song and tell me whether it was a shuffle or whatever, and give me a nod if there was a break. I just kept my eyes on him all evening." Mayall commented: "We got Aynsley Dunbar when Peter was really beginning to find his feet, and because he was such an aggressive guitarist, we needed a more aggressive approach on the drums. So we got Aynsley in. I'd never heard the other bands he was in, but he was recommended by someone as being very good, and he was." Dunbar recalls: "John Mayall put me into the blues thing; it built me up, because I was playing with good musicians, and hearing all types of blues. When I heard about Mayall, I was told he was playing just country blues. But it wasn't like that. It was good, solid and full." The new Bluesbreakers line-up was exciting, and in spite of Mayall's desire to become more dominant, it featured Peter Green's rapidly developing guitar style, which was bringing him the kind of following which Clapton had enjoyed. This quartet version of the Bluesbreakers with Green, McVie and Dunbar remained intact for half a year until April 1967.

The schedule was gruelling, as Mayall recounts: "A lot of time, we were doing eight, nine, even ten gigs a week, afternoons and evenings at weekends. The Flamingo was still our mainstay, because we were being booked by Rik Gunnell, and so on Friday night we'd play a ballroom somewhere, then come back to the Flamingo and do an all-nighter; same routine on Saturdays too!" As a travelling bandleader, Mayall would make the most of what little sun Britain's summers offered by sunbathing on the roof of the group's van, even as it motored along to the next gig. As riding on the roof is illegal, Mayall built small barriers at the sides and on the top to remain undiscovered by the cops!

Green's recording debut with Mayall came on September 30, 1966, when the Bluesbreakers recorded a single at Decca, pairing distinctive covers of Johnny 'Guitar' Watson's catchy R&B workout "Looking Back", with Otis Rush's "So Many Roads", released three weeks later.

Mayall's original plan was to record an EP, the idea being to let Green stretch out. Mayall added a horn section consisting of Johnny Almond (baritone saxophone), Nick Newell (tenor sax), and Henry Lowther (trumpet). On this first recording, Green sounds enormously like a Clapton copyist; Green himself felt that he had overplayed, especially on "Looking Back".

Immediately after the recording, Mayall came close to losing Dunbar to a young, unknown American guitarist named Jimi Hendrix. Just arrived from the States on September 24, Hendrix was accompanied by his manager, ex-Animals bass player Chas Chandler, and they were looking for a drummer. They were unable to decide between him and a certain Mitch Mitchell, who was playing with Georgie Fame. As Dunbar wanted £30 a week and the gig paid just £20, the position went to Mitchell, and Dunbar remained a Bluesbreaker.

Only eleven days after recording the single, Mayall, Green, McVie and Dunbar were back at the Decca again, this time to record an entire album. The sessions for "A Hard Road" produced twenty-two tracks, fourteen of which appeared on the LP. Mayall was prolific, and wrote eight songs, some of which are still considered his best ever.

- The title track is a meaningful slow blues with a strong piano-guitar riff. Green makes his presence felt within seconds, complementing Mayall's pleading vocal with tightly-coiled restraint that exemplifies the tension and subtlety that typifies his work with the Bluesbreakers. Mayall recorded this track again for his album A Padlock on the Blues 31 years later.
- "It's Over" is a swinging organ and harmonica shuffle with sublime interplay between Green's guitar and Mayall's harmonica. Alan Skidmore plays tenor sax.
- "Another Kinda Love" is a passionate but gloomy tune with an ominous groove and burbling organ, later covered by Joe Bonamassa.
- "Hit the Highway" is the boogie piano feature, a duet between Mayall, on piano and double-tracked vocal, and Green on guitar.
- "Leaping Christine" is a wonderful jazzy, driving track with organ and harp. Both Green and McVie disliked it, both professing to loathe jazz. This ideological battle between blues men who hated

jazz and jazz men who disliked blues was difficult to understand, especially as the blues has always been the backbone of jazz.

- "There's Always Work" was a bizarre, gloomy kind of chain-gang holler, with Mayall on dual harmonicas and ethereal vocal chant.
- "Top of the Hill", which was originally recorded as "Mama, Talk to Your Daughter" by J.B. Lenoir, Mayall shrewdly replacing the original vocal track.
- "Living Alone" features Mayall playing slide on his 9-string guitar, with harmonica, piano and vocals.

The album also contains four blues covers, including two by Freddie King. "The Stumble" is an up-tempo guitar instrumental, "Someday After A While (You'll Be Sorry)", a great gospel-tinged slow blues, with more complicated chord changes than most slow blues played at the time. The other two are "Dust My Blues" by Elmore James, and "You Don't Love Me" by Willie Cobbs, sung by Green with an arrangement lifted from Chicago harp ace Junior Wells.

Mayall also allowed Green to contribute two of his own compositions: "The Same Way" is a stop-start number with an explosive guitar solo. As a result of Mayall's enthusiasm and support, Green began to write his own songs. One of these was "The Same Way", another was "Black Magic Woman", later to become a massive hit for Santana. Peter remembered: "I wrote it when I was living in the same house with John Mayall. He started me writing blues things. If he hadn't done it first I wouldn't have done it myself. For "Black Magic Woman", I took something out of Otis Rush's "All Your Love". Everything in the blues is a borrowed thing". "The Supernatural" was a majestic, exotic instrumental with Green's unmistakable stamp: a slow samba beat underneath beautiful legato guitar, stinging with feedback and sustain. This also provided the template for Carlos Santana's trebly style. This sinister, evocative tune, with its use of elongated notes, played on a vintage Les Paul with the top pickup removed and the amp set on reverb, launched a whole new style of guitar playing. The extremely controlled feedback combined with the intense, spooky mood, presages the mystical vibe that would infuse Green's later work with Fleetwood Mac. Mayall contributed some tasteful organ licks.

Outtakes from the "Hard Road" sessions were "Sitting In the Rain", a sweet but lightweight country dance blues that gently swings, the four musicians playing at their tightest. An acoustic number by design, Dunbar was instructed to rap his sticks on the back of Mayall's guitar. "Out of Reach" was the other one, a stark, slow blues by Green, who sings with almost suicidal intensity. This is an exceptionally slow, dark, minor key blues with no keyboards, Mayall contributing just slide guitar. It has the definitive Peter Green sound, bluer than the bluest! Beautiful, heart-felt and sends shivers down the spine. Other outtakes were released on the "Raw Blues" compilation, a Mike Vernon-produced, low-price LP on Decca's 'Ace Of Clubs' budget label, and on the rarities sampler "Thru the Years". Please see the discography for more details.

Mayall decided to write the sleeve notes himself, in which he praised Green thus: "Speaking of the modern young blues guitarists that I've heard 'live', I would certainly cram Jimi Hendrix, Buddy Guy, Otis Rush, Eric Clapton and Peter Green on the same pedestal. In my opinion, they all sound completely individual but all share the same emotional greatness." Mentioning lesser-known bluesmen such as Buddy Guy and Otis Rush enabled many European fans to discover them for the first time. When the LP was released on February 17, 1967, there were hardly any new, guitar-dominated, blues-influenced British albums, just the Beano album and "Fresh Cream". Later that year came Hendrix's "Are You Experienced" (in May), Savoy Brown's "Shake Down" (in September, like Mayall's "Crusade" LP) and the first Ten Years After album (in October).

By this time, Mayall was already established as one of the U.K. blues boom's leading lights, combining a deep affinity for tradition with a restless experimental streak. While most of his peers were concentrating on covering material by American blues greats, Mayall's repertoire was comprised largely of his own compositions, which merged a knowledgeable mastery of traditional blues idioms with a more personal, contemporary sensibility. "A Hard Road" quickly stopped all talk of the band being lost without Clapton. It convinced people that the Bluesbreakers didn't need a fixed line up. Critical praise for the album was unanimous. Rolling Stone said it was "by far the best album ever put out by a white blues band, and should continue to be the same for quite some time." It climbed to number 10 on the U.K. album charts.

Only a few days after finishing the "Hard Road" sessions, the Bluesbreakers were back at Decca again, this time to record an EP with white American blues-harp player and singer Paul Butterfield. Mike Vernon was aware that the pairing of Mayall with Butterfield was quite a sensation, practically a transatlantic white blues summit. While Butterfield was touring Britain with his band (as part of a Georgie Fame/Chris Farlowe package), Vernon worked feverishly to pair the two artists. He cut a one-off deal with Butterfield's record company Elektra to enable Mayall and Butterfield to record together with the Bluesbreakers. Four songs were taped in one afternoon session, crossing Butterfield's amplified Chicago harp with the Bluesbreakers' British blues sound. The songs were: "All My Life", a slow blues by Jimmy Lee Robinson, with Mayall on vocals and piano; both Butterfield and Green contribute solos. "Ridin' on the L&N" features Mayall on vocals and bottleneck guitar, with Butterfield supplying harp and vocal harmonies. Butterfield sings a version of Junior Wells' Chicago Blues "Little By Little", supported by Mayall's backing vocals and piano, while the final track, "Eagle Eye", is a new Mayall composition. All tracks feature McVie and Dunbar, but none of the Butterfield men play on the session. The fact that the record appeared only in Britain makes it one of the most sought-after for collectors. Although the line-up of musicians was top drawer, the results were rather lacklustre.

On January 23, the Bluesbreakers were back at the BBC to record six songs, a mix of recent recordings, stage favourites and new songs; unfortunately, little from this and the follow-up session a few days later has survived. Shortly afterwards, without informing Mayall, producer Mike Vernon had Green, McVie and Dunbar record four new tracks on February 16. They were briefly toying with the idea of going out as a threesome, which was probably sound reasoning, given the recent success of power trios such as Cream and The Jimi Hendrix Experience. However, after they had let off steam on this session, the idea was dropped. The circumstances around these recordings will never be satisfactorily explained, but it was certainly done on the sly. When Mayall got wind of it he was so enraged that his relationship with Vernon soured temporarily. The churning, Hendrix-influenced, proto-metal "Curly" was probably inspired by Green's recent studio encounter with Hendrix. On January 11, Green and Mayall had been fence-riders at a Hendrix recording session at De Lane Lea studios in central London, where Jimi was working on his second single, the groundbreaking "Purple Haze". Green's hard rocking instrumental was boosted by putting the guitar through a homemade fuzz box, while "Rubber Duck" was Dunbar's vehicle for a wild drum solo, with Green overdubbing fine harmonica; "Curly" was released on Decca on March 24, 1967 as a single, credited to The Bluesbreakers. Another fantastic Peter Green instrumental was recorded entitled "A Million Knobs" (or "Four Million Knobs"), but the guitarist didn't want it released, considering it just a "sound check". However, it came out in June 1969 on the Decca compilation "The World of Blues Power" where it was entitled "Greeny". The fourth number was the short rocker "Missing You", based on Junior Wells' "Messin' with the Kid", with Green on vocals and harp, which can be found on "Thru the Years" in October 1971.

Back home after their short tour of Sweden, the Bluesbreakers returned to Decca on March 8 to record the Mayall composition "Please Don't Tell" which was intended as their next single, but the release was shelved, despite Green's wonderful, ferocious guitar. Mayall revived the song for his solo album a couple of months later.

Between March 12 and 22, the Bluesbreakers backed American blues pianist and singer Eddie Boyd on his short British tour. On March 17, Boyd and the Bluesbreakers were back at Decca, this time to record an entire album. The 16 tracks were released in late July 1967 entitled "Eddie Boyd and his Bluesband, featuring Peter Green", which was probably Mike Vernon's idea. Boyd and Mayall duet on

❶ *Mayall strumming his trusty Baldwin/Burns electric guitar around 1970.*

❷ *The famous "Beano" band, featuring Eric Clapton, John McVie, Hughie Flint and Mayall. This was the line-up that made Clapton a superstar, created the guitar hero, and contained one-quarter of the future Fleetwood Mac.*

❸ *A selection of album and single covers.*

❹ *In concert in 1972 with the superlative jazz-blues fusion line-up: Clifford Solomon, Blue Mitchell and Mayall.*

❺ *The fantastic blues-and-country fusion band in 1975 with Ronnie Barron, Don "Sugarcane" Harris, Soko Richardson, Rick Vito, Larry Taylor, Dee McKinnie and Mayall.*

two numbers: Big Bill Broonzy's "Key to the Highway" and Pinetop Smith's "Pinetop Boogie Woogie". The Boyd-penned "Vacation from the Blues" features the full line-up, and Mayall and Green deliver backing vocals on "Night Time is the Right Time".

In March 1967, Mayall met Marsha Hunt, a beautiful, twenty-year-old black American lady. In her autobiography "Real Life", Hunt writes a great deal about Mayall, and some of it is worth quoting from at length: "High on the list of English blues fanatics was a musician named John Mayall, who trailed me home one night after he'd come down to check out one of Alexis Korner's rehearsals. He had a Chicago blues singer named Eddie Boyd with him, who was doing some recordings with John's band, the Bluesbreakers. I'd never heard of either of them, but John seemed pleasant enough and I was relieved he'd come to my door, because I needed to replace a light bulb and wasn't quite tall enough. John Mayall was a bear of an Englishman, a modern, eccentric Thoreau. He wore buckskin clothes that he designed and stitched up on his sewing machine. They made him look like Davy Crockett without the coonskin cap. His shoulder-length hair and beard were in the same colour as his buckskin and his moccasins, which he'd also made by hand. The tan tone of it all gave you the impression he was tan too, although he had that English whiteness, which continued to look strange to me even after a year away from California. John did everything, made everything, and was everybody to himself. He required far more space than he had after he'd convinced me to move in with him. The fourth-floor walk-up that I shared with him, not far away from Alexis's flat on Queensway, was small, but the built-in furniture he made gave the impression that it was larger than it was. He not only made the benches and the cushions that fitted them, but also everything else in the three rooms. The bathroom was converted to a fully equipped darkroom, and he took all his own publicity pictures, including the ones of himself. I don't know how we managed to stay together for the few months we did. He was stubborn and I was wilful and I don't expect either of us was in love or had delusions about our affair lasting. He was an extraordinary collector of things and thought I was right for his collection. I was caught up in my blues-singer guise when he first met me and no doubt he was taken off guard when I showed myself in different lights.

Both of us were on the road doing our separate gigs while I was living with John. His band was popular at colleges and clubs and got booked for one-nighters throughout the week. At that time Aynsley Dunbar was the drummer with the Bluesbreakers, with John McVie on bass and Peter Green on guitar. John handled all the vocals but coaxed Pete into singing a slow blues. This was no mean feat because Peter, a brilliant, sensitive guitarist, was shy about singing solo though he had a sweet voice, more melodic than John's, but was timid when he sang. He didn't push. Eventually this became the essence of Peter Green's vocal style and made it special.

I learned more about performing at John's gigs than I did going to my own. I tried to see as many of his as I could when we didn't work on the same night. John had trouble with his band during the period I was with him, in 1967. Aynsley Dunbar had to be replaced. His successor was Mick Fleetwood. Mick and I struck up to a hearty friendship right away. He had a school boyish sense of humour and was a prankster. I tried to be supportive without getting involved. It was a very intense period for the entire band and with Pete living in the flat downstairs from us with his girlfriend Sandra; I avoided conversations about the boss and the band.

John came to bed every night with a pencil and pad and would take a phrase, turn it into a song title and add it to the list he was compiling for a new album he was planning, "The Blues Alone". He was extremely economical and didn't waste pen, paper or ideas. I know he wrote a few of the songs for me or about me, 'Brown Sugar', 'Brand New Start' and 'Marsha's Mood'. It was impossible not to respect John for his single-mindedness even though he was hard to live with. To have the opportunity of seeing how he wrote songs, managed his band and kept his eye on every aspect of the business was like taking a course, and I only ever met one better teacher. He had a few quirks. Sometimes he would come back from a week on the road with a hunger to see movies. He'd get out the newspaper and plot a movie marathon that would mean we'd see three movies in one day, four if I was unlucky. I'd be bonkers by the time I came out of the last cinema. Movie marathons were one of his favourite entertainments, and if I was working and couldn't go with him, he'd go alone, heading off his bicycle with his long hair pulled back in a low ponytail. He had the most redeeming laugh. It burst right from deep in his stomach and showed his teeth, which were like I imagine a real cowboy's, long and a bit crooked with a few missing along the side. He was a very rough-cut diamond but a diamond all the same. And I was hardly a pearl."

In 1968, Marsha Hunt landed a major role in the musical "Hair", and was featured on the cover of Vogue fashion magazine, gaining world-wide fame as a singer and model.

The "Hard Road" line-up got on reasonably well, the only problem areas being McVie's devotion to Scotch, and Aynsley Dunbar's love of the spotlight. Dunbar saw himself as a featured drummer in the jazz tradition, and so would forever be hankering after solos, often to Green's and McVie's annoyance. Mayall explains: "Aynsley was a very wild drummer with a jazz and rock 'n' roll background, and he started taking too many solos. That was a case where giving a musician his freedom backfired. He got too busy and was more dominant than the lead instruments! Peter Green and John McVie were not from a jazz background and really didn't like just standing there on stage, arms folded across instruments doing nothing! 'Don't like that, too jazzy!' Peter would say disdainfully."

Towards the end of March, tensions increased, with Green lobbying to get the extrovert Dunbar out. In early April, Mayall decided to replace him, and politely asked him to leave. The parting was amicable, as Dunbar recalled: "I was grateful to John. He introduced me to the musicians I wanted to play with, although I eventually got the sack for playing too advanced. He wanted me to sit in the background and just play straightforward blues, which I didn't want to do. I didn't think I would progress until I left." Micky Waller became the stand-in for a couple of gigs. Green suggested his friend, the lanky Mick Fleetwood, should replace Dunbar, to bring in a simpler, less technical style. "It was a strange situation", Fleetwood reflects quizzically, "because I basically had no idea why I was being invited to John Mayall's Bluesbreakers. I didn't audition, I drove down to this Mayall gig, somewhere near London, the night Aynsley was fired. The thought of taking over from him, who to this day is an incredibly capable drummer technically, was awesome. He was a great performing drummer and I was horrified to see that he had his own vocal following among the fans at gigs. I never even remotely thought of myself like that. I thought of myself as a guy that has a lot of fun banging the drums: mine was a naïve, animal approach really. I think that's why Peter and John wanted me in because Aynsley was getting too clever, playing a format of music which didn't warrant paradiddles every three seconds or drum rudiments during a blues shuffle. Even so, at the time I didn't understand and said 'Why do you want to get rid of him—he's great!' I wasn't under any illusion that I was a better drummer than Aynsley, a super-powerful drummer who liked to solo for twenty-five minutes and had a lot of technique, which I've never had at all. In fact, I've never played a drum solo in my life. I was trying to create with rhythms; but there's not a lot in what I do. I try to keep it to the simplest manner possible. For me, the point of the craft is to complement your fellow players and not to get frustrated—the drummer's malady—wanting to show off, wanting to get noticed. Since Mayall already had one of the best in England, why did he want to hire me? I joined the Bluesbreakers in April 1967. I took the gig, still muddled as to Mayall's reasoning, and said to him 'John, if this doesn't work out, don't feel bad about asking me to go.' But I was really thrilled to have somehow broken into one of the top bands in the country, even if I wasn't a blues drummer."

Fleetwood had previously played with the Senders and such London R&B bands as the Cheynes, Bo Street Runners, Peter B's Looners and Shotgun Express. In his biography, Fleetwood recounts his first night with the group in early April as a true baptism of fire: "Mayall was very professional—he managed the band, arranged travel and got many of the gigs—and very meticulous, and was in general a pleasure to work for. Plus the band made me feel very welcome. My first Bluesbreakers gig was at some out-of-town club. We walked in and I could hear the fans literally howling for Peter and John. I took a gulp. This was the big time, the Bluesbreakers! As I sat down at the drum kit, there were shouts from the audience. 'Where's Aynsley?' My heart sank, and we started to play. Then another punter screamed out at me. 'You're not as good as Aynsley!' I wanted to die, but suddenly John McVie stopped playing bass, walked up to the mike, and yelled, 'Why don't you fuck off and listen!' I loved John McVie from that moment on. His comment gave me back my confidence and put the whole thing right. And off we went. Our friendship has been cemented ever since the day he stuck up for me."

Fleetwood wasn't a particularly heavy drinker when he joined the band, but a few evenings in McVie's company changed that! He writes in his autobiography: "John [McVie] and I got on great together instantly. From the moment I joined we did a lot of heavy drinking; in fact we were drunk most of the time, the two of us, and this had a lot to do with me receiving my marching orders from Mayall shortly thereafter. I didn't have a drinking problem when I joined John Mayall, but I may have had one by the time I was fired. My departure was of course, not unexpected. Indeed, it could have been predicted. I even had a graph chart of how I was doing, taped to the wall of the Bluesbreakers' van, a date sheet, like a calendar, and I remember one time ticking off the gigs; I showed it to John and everybody had a laugh, but practically that same day I was given my marching orders. My actual downfall came in Ireland. McVie and I had a few drinks before we played, and I was fired before we travelled back to England by ferry the following day." This was the 10 May, 1967.

On a historical note, this was the first band with Green, McVie and Fleetwood playing together. For a very short time, then, an embryonic Fleetwood Mac existed within the Bluesbreakers, Fleetwood and McVie going on to become one of the world's greatest rhythm sections. At the time, however, Fleetwood regretted being sacked: "I was very sad to leave the Bluesbreakers, mostly because Peter Green was incredible. And I also loved playing with McVie, whose style perfectly completed my own. I play slightly behind the beat, while John plays slightly ahead of it. We meet somewhere in the middle and to us it sounded just right. It was a real blow to leave Peter Green and John McVie." During his short spell as a Bluesbreaker, however, Fleetwood did manage to add his sparse drumming to their next single. On 19 April, 1967, they recorded two blues standards they sometimes performed live: Otis Rush's ultra-slow, down-to-earth, minor-key blues "Double Trouble" and Elmore James's wonderful, eight-bar blues "It Hurts Me Too". The reviews were perhaps the strongest Mayall had received for any of his singles so far, with Fleetwood contributing some characteristically simple but effective drumming, along with Green's exemplary guitar and a great vocal performance by Mayall.

Mayall had already set his eyes on Fleetwood's successor, the twenty-three year old Keef Hartley, who joined on May 13, 1967. Mayall had first met Hartley in November 1965, when the two had played together on sessions with Champion Jack Dupree and Clapton. Hartley had started drumming with the Thunderbeats aged sixteen, before moving to Liverpool in 1962 to replace Ringo Starr in Rory Storm & the Hurricanes, when Ringo left to join the Beatles. Hartley moved to London 1964 to play with the Artwoods for three years, an R'n'B band run by Ron Wood's older brother Art, and featuring future Deep Purple organist Jon Lord. In April 1967, the Artwoods replaced Hartley with drummer Colin Martin. In his highly recommended autobiography Halfbreed, Hartley writes how he became a Bluesbreaker: "On the way home from what was my last gig with the Artwoods, we pulled into the Blue Boar services as usual. This motorway café was one of the few places open all night, and a regular stopping off point for musicians returning to London from shows in the north. Climbing out of the van I heard a voice shout, 'Keef'. I turned to see the grinning face of John Mayall who asked, 'What are you up to?' I explained that I was returning from my final gig as an Artwood and was now looking for a new job. 'That's lucky; I've just sacked my drummer. Want to join?' What a stupid question! John's reputation as a blues player was second to none, and just about anyone would have leapt at the chance to join the Bluesbreakers. I only had one question, 'Can I wear a T shirt on stage?' 'Yeah' he replied,

'You can wear whatever you want.' I took his address and agreed to call round the next day." Hartley debuted as a Bluesbreaker on May 13, in Southport, with Green and McVie. Hartley stands out as one of Mayall's best ever drummers, together with Jon Hiseman and Aynsley Dunbar. He has an immediately recognizable, economical style, faultless timing, and his solos are always exciting.

On 1 May 1967, Mayall started recording a 100 % solo album entitled "The Blues Alone", a project dear to his heart, as he wrote all the songs, played practically all the instruments, designed the album sleeve, and even took the cover photographs. He felt he needed to offer the public a package on which he did almost everything himself, showcasing his ability as a multi-instrumentalist. The only Bluesbreaker Mayall recruited was Keef Hartley, who overdubbed his atmospheric drumming around May 22. Later, Hartley remembers how it happened: "John Mayall asked me to be at the Decca studios on the following Monday morning. It turned out he was making a solo album to be called "The Blues Alone", but desperately needed a drummer. He had an ambition to make a solo album in the true sense of the word. This was to be a side step away from the Bluesbreakers, with John playing every instrument himself. We finished it in two long sessions. I used John's drumming as a guide, but worked my own stuff over the top. At the time some critics claimed it to be the one of the purest British blues albums ever made. The aim from the outset was to record a stark and dark album, stripped down to the bare bones. This is exactly what came out and it still is one of my favourite albums from this period. Sadly Decca had little faith in it, issuing it on their subsidiary label, Ace of Clubs. To me it really stands the test of time. Some albums seem to quickly sound out of date, but "Blues Alone" is timeless to my ears." Mike Vernon and Mayall produced it, and DJ John Peel wrote the sleeve notes. Not released until November 3, "The Blues Alone" got to number 24 in the U.K., and number 59 in the U.S. album charts. Critics praised the album, commenting: "This is interesting because it shows that Mayall alone is slightly different to when he is with the Bluesbreakers: sadder, more melancholy... the album's as good an example of pure blues as is ever likely to come out of Britain." Please see the discography for more details on individual tracks.

Hartley recalled the mood in the Bluesbreakers at the time: "Following "The Blues Alone", my friendship with John grew much stronger and I soon realized there was a certain amount of disharmony in the band. We were roughly split into two camps with John Mayall and me on one side, and Peter Green and John McVie on the other. Peter liked playing with the Bluesbreakers, but clashed with John over the direction the band should take. It was apparent from an early stage that two such forceful personalities could not co-exist without a shared vision, and no one was really surprised when Green quit the band in mid-June to work with Mick Fleetwood." Mayall himself commented later: "Keef wasn't the right drummer for Peter, so Peter left. There were all these overlaps, all due to musical or personality clashes." Like Clapton before him, Green was getting restless, and was keen to visit Chicago, home of so many blues greats. His plans were not yet 100 % clear, but he handed in his resignation at the end of May. Green later explained: "The most important thing was that I didn't agree with the kind of material being played. It was becoming, for me, less and less the blues. And we'd do the same thing night after night. John would say something to the audience and count us in, and I'd groan inwardly." Peter Green played his last gig with the Bluesbreakers on June 11, not long after Fleetwood had been given the boot. Unfortunately, work permit and visa hassles scotched the idea of moving to Chicago, so Green took a short holiday in Spain with his girlfriend to contemplate his future.

Mayall wasn't a man of remorse and dealt with Green's departure very well. On the contrary, the bond between mentor and protégé remained strong as ever: "The rapport that brought me into contact with him in the first place, and that made us so close" John proudly points out, "once you get that kind of friendship, you never lose it. It's always there, right to this day."

Returning from Spain, Green wanted form an undiluted blues band, a pure blues trio in the style of Buddy Guy, with that sparse Chicago sound. This was in stark contrast to Mayall's band, which had been reaching out to soul and jazz. The first person he recruited was drummer Mick Fleetwood, and Mike Vernon was an early supporter. Green then approached McVie, but the latter was initially reluctant to leave the financial security of the Bluesbreakers. However, he did agree to do some demo recordings, supervised by Vernon. These were taped at night and unofficially in the second half of June, in a single session at Decca's London studios in West Hampstead, which explains why no documentation exists for these sessions. They recorded "First Train Home", "Looking for Somebody", Howlin' Wolf's "No Place to Go" plus an instrumental entitled "Fleetwood Mac". Although none of the musicians knew it at the time, blues-rock history was made that day. The title stuck as the group's moniker, and Fleetwood Mac went on to become one of the biggest bands of all time. Green became *the* British blues guitar hero! This Mayall-trained Jewish cockney went on to write many hits, all of which have proved timeless: "Albatross", "Oh Well", "Green Manalishi", "Man Of The World", and "Black Magic Woman", the latter covered by Santana in 1970 to become a huge hit. In Europe, Fleetwood Mac even outsold the Beatles.

Yet in May 1970, Green gave it all up, leaving Fleetwood Mac only three years after he had helped create it. After a concert in Munich on Sunday 22 March, he was invited to a commune outside the city. Green was given wine spiked with LSD, and all hell broke loose inside his head. The next day Fleetwood found him lying in a sunken den, obviously out of his mind, and barely coherent. Only after long persuasion were the band members able to get him to return, but the person they brought back would never again be the man they'd known. Fleetwood would later say: "Peter should never have taken acid. He was charming, amusing, just a wonderful person, but off he went and never came back." Intake of LSD induced irreversible personality breakdown with Peter, who often appeared confused and disoriented. Tragically, Green slipped into a decades-long abyss of psychiatric illness. He was later institutionalized, given electroshock treatment and psychotropic medication for paranoid schizophrenia. This heartbreaking descent into mental illness would lead him to withdraw from music industry. Mayall remembers: "He just got weirder and weirder. It's a sad loss because he's the completely opposite of what he used to be, an entirely different character. When he was in my band he was aggressive and pushy in a good way. Great sense of humour, always up for a laugh. Now he's just turned into a ghost, it's really a dreadful shame."

With a return to better health, the mid-1990s found him touring and recording again with the Peter Green Splinter Group, a band he had formed with Nigel Watson and drummer Cozy Powell in 1996. The band released several fine albums, although the fire in Green's guitar playing was only rarely glimpsed. In 2000 and 2002, the Splinter Group undertook three package tours, together with Mayall's Bluesbreakers, two in Britain and one in the US. In 2004, Green opted to leave the music business again, but in 2009, he started a third comeback as Peter Green and Friends, fresher and more lucid than for many years. By August 2010, however, he was so exhausted that he had to cancel all live commitments on health grounds.

CHAPTER 5

From Crusade to Laurel Canyon
The bands with Mick Taylor, 1967–69

With Peter Green leaving to form Fleetwood Mac, Mayall was faced with the task of replacing a guitarist who had built up a considerable personal following. As Mayall explained to Melody Maker on June 3, 1967: "I could form a new band from people I know, but I want to find out if there are other aspiring bluesers I don't know about. While I'm about it I shall be adding horns." He placed a "musician wanted" ad in Melody Maker on June 10: "John Mayall requires lead guitarist to match the brilliant standards set by Eric Clapton and Peter Green (B.B. King, Otis Rush style). Candidates must have an unswerving dedication to the blues." McVie decided to stay with the Bluesbreakers after all, so Mayall didn't need to find a bass player, at least not for the moment.

Mayall did not only rely on musicians replying to the ad but also searched for other guitarists he knew. His first choice was 16 year-old Davey O'List from the Attack, a group that already had some singles out and opened for the Bluesbreakers on April 8, 1967. O'List briefly gained notoriety because John Peel liked to use his guitar solos as catchy sound bites on his shows on Radio London. O'List turned Mayall's offer down and joined Keith Emerson's new group the Nice, a decision he was to regret. Another contender was the 18 year-old Mick Taylor, who had made quite an impression on Mayall when he stood in for one night in April 1966 when Clapton failed to show up. Taylor had been fully familiar with the band's repertoire, knowing everything virtually note-by-note, and performed admirably. After the show, the shy teenager had disappeared before Mayall could get his phone number. All Mayall knew was his name. Luckily, now Taylor had seen the ad, and picked up the courage to phone. Mayall remembers: "He answered the ad and auditions for a new guitarist stopped. He had so much talent. He was the obvious replacement for Peter."

Taylor became interested in joining a band after his parents took him to see Bill Haley & the Comets. His uncle John played the guitar and exposed him to all the great rock'n'roll heroes of the 1950s: Bill Haley, Elvis Presley, Fats Domino, Jerry Lee Lewis and Little Richard. By the age of 11, he had started to play guitar in earnest, teaching himself, and by 1962 he had joined his first band, the Strangers. His next group was the Juniors, with whom he recorded his first single in 1964, but it was with Hatfield-based outfit called the Gods that Taylor began to be recognized. The Gods also featured keyboardist Ken Hensley (later of Uriah Heep), and bass player John Glascock (later of Jethro Tull and Chicken Shack). During his teens, Taylor discovered the blues after listening to B.B. King's classic "Live at the Regal". He also enjoyed Memphis Stax R&B material. Mick had learned guitar licks by playing along to records, and when he joined the Bluesbreakers on a permanent basis, he was only 18, very nearly the same age as Clapton and Green had been at the same point in their careers. In order to be closer to the action, Taylor decided to leave his parent's home and move to west London, where he shared a flat with Bluesbreakers' drummer Keef Hartley.

Mayall enjoyed a solid fan base, ensuring full houses everywhere, and could now afford to expand his line-up. Although he had thought about horn players before, and even featured them on occasional recording sessions, this change of direction may have been to shift the focus away from lead guitarists. After swearing not to augment the Bluesbreakers with horns (on the "Hard Road" LP sleeve, he assured his fans that the use of horns on certain tracks was purely for studio purposes), he'd obviously changed his mind. Mayall comments today with a laugh: "By 1967, the players I had found were just too good not to be added to the band." The Bluesbreakers' first horn section brought a touch of soul, and consisted of tenor sax player Chris Mercer and baritone man Rip Kant. In record time, Mayall had gathered together a new group.

Taylor didn't seem particularly worried about replacing Peter Green. Taylor: "I was very conscious I was following in the footsteps of Clapton and Green. They were the two English guys who, for me, exemplified that white English guitarists really could play the blues. I knew that I was potentially a good blues guitar player, but my sound and my style were very influenced by B.B. King and Clapton." Keef Hartley remembers: "The replacement for Peter Green was a slightly built, fair and retiring young 18 year-old by the name of Mick Taylor. In those first days, Mick hardly spoke, and this seemed very strange after the outgoing and opinionated Greeny." Taylor wasn't a singer, unlike his famous predecessors, but he did use the same guitar, a late '50s Gibson Les Paul Standard, plugged into a 50 watt Marshall half stack.

The new six-piece line-up had been together for only three weeks when it entered Decca studios on July 12 to record "Crusade", the next album. In typical Mayall style the album was cut in a single day. "Having performed most of the songs on the road, they had already got a handle on them," Mayall explained. "Most good music comes in the first take, and certainly the third take at the most. After that, things tend to go downhill, because you lose that creative spark. The band weren't sure they were ready but I kept pushing them. We just went for a nice, gritty live feel that's not over-produced." Like "Hard Road" or the Beano album, the songs on "Crusade" are a mix of Mayall compositions and covers of blues songs. This time, Mayall had carefully chosen among his heroes, including lesser-known musicians, in order to give them more recognition. The album also included a Freddie King number, "Driving Sideways", plus "Snowy Wood", an instrumental to show off the chops of the Bluesbreakers' new guitarist. "The Death of J.B. Lenoir", the album's standout track, is Mayall's haunting and emotive tribute to the Mississippi-born, Chicago-based musician and songwriter. His death on April 29 from a heart attack affected Mayall deeply, as he was in the process of persuading Lenoir to collaborate on a future recording project. "I Can't Quit You Baby" is another wonderful, slow Chicago blues featuring a brilliant feedback and sustain-drenched Mick Taylor solo. Once again, Mike Vernon and Gus Dudgeon produced and engineered the sessions. As for the title, Mayall was on a self-appointed crusade to awaken interest in the blues, and get blues artists onto the radio and TV more. As he described it in the liner notes: "It's about time that the blues fraternity made an outcry against a system locked in the belief that blues fans are only a small minority in the world of popular music." Mayall's campaign must have been successful, as some 60,000 fans signed his petition for more blues to be played on the BBC. Taylor's debut was impressive, demonstrating a fluid style right from the start. He provided clean-cut and confident guitar with a sure-fingered vibrato far beyond his tender years. Despite his obvious talent, he owed a lot to Clapton as well as Albert King and B.B. King, but there's also a very linear, lyrically melodic approach that gives his playing a personality and a distinct identity. With his economical single-line playing, melodic invention and gifted bottleneck style (the latter not yet fully developed), he brought a new dimension to the band's style. Not only Taylor, but the horn section is also impressive, and Mayall's voice is at its best. The "Crusade" album received mixed reviews in the British music press when it was released on September 8, 1967, although many positive comments were made about Taylor's studio debut. The album climbed to number 8 in the English charts, staying in the Top 50 for 14 weeks. It also marked Mayall's first appearance in the American charts, the album peaking at 136. In Sweden it reached number 3 and in Finland number 1!

During the summer of 1967, Mayall appeared at Kingsway Studios, London, to make unspecified contributions to a new album by Roger McGough & Mike McGear. Both were members of a band called The Scaffold; Roger McGough was a witty and inventive poet who belonged to a group of writers who had emerged from Liverpool at about the same time as the Beatles. Mike McGear was Paul McCartney's elder brother, and both McGough & McGear were taking time out from their regular band to collaborate on a new album. The result is a wry collection of poetry, music and black humour. The LP features John Mayall (piano), Jimi Hendrix (guitar), Paul McCartney (mellotron), Graham Nash (guitar), Dave Mason (guitar), Spencer Davis (guitar), Zoot Money (keyboards), Mitch Mitchell (drums), Noel Redding (bass) and Paul Samwell Smith (guitar). It was released in April 1968 and is more interesting for fans of blues and poetry than pure blues.

Mayall and Paul McCartney briefly socialized in the mid 1960s, as McCartney recalled to biographer Barry Miles: "John Mayall was another hangout, not very often, but a few times after a club he'd still be around, and we'd go back to his house. He was a blues DJ too, fantastic collection. He first played me B.B. King; Buddy Guy he'd play a lot. Then he'd play me some early Eric Clapton stuff, which was: 'God, it's amazing!' You could really see where Eric was getting some of his stuff from, but Eric was making his guitar sound like a violin. It was a great education."

On August 13, the Bluesbreakers played at the 7th National Jazz and Blues festival in Windsor. They were on the same bill as Peter Green's Fleetwood Mac (their first gig, with Bob Brunning on bass), The Aynsley Dunbar Retaliation (also their first gig), Cream, Chicken Shack, Jeff Beck and others. The festival marked the start of the British blues boom, with attendance totalling 50,000. The blues was fast becoming the most important music for the youth in Britain. The Bluesbreakers were one of the best-received acts, and Mayall's band was the only one called back for an encore. Following the festival, Mayall and the Bluesbreakers took a summer break until August 24.

The Windsor festival was Rip Kant's last gig. When Mayall heard that Dick Heckstall-Smith was out of the Graham Bond Organisation, he wasted no time. Heckstall-Smith was easily the most experienced British R&B saxophonist of the time. He happily signed with Mayall, and was a great asset to the band. By putting the saxophone further up front, Mayall brought another dimension to the Bluesbreakers' sound. When he joined on August 25, Dick Heckstall-Smith was almost 33 and cut a striking figure. He was quite bald and always wore black; for him, all that counted was the music. He had learnt the continuous breathing technique after studying jazz giant Roland Kirk and would, like his idol, play two saxes simultaneously! And he produced a fabulous elastic "rubbery" sound on his horn. The day after Dick joined, the group made a lightning visit to Copenhagen to appear on the Danish TV show "Top Pop", which was broadcast one month later. This was Mayall's first television appearance since the Clapton days. Performing live, the group plugged Mayall's latest single "Double Trouble", Albert King's "Oh, Pretty Woman" plus the new instrumental "Snowy Wood". Afterwards, the group took the ferry across to Sweden to play a concert in Malmö.

Recruiting Heckstall-Smith was too much for McVie, who still considered himself to be an out-and-out blues musician, and whose aversion to sobriety was matched only by his dislike of brass sections in blues bands. "To me, back then, brass equalled jazz", the bassist remembers. "Peter Green was very persistent. I kept saying, 'I've got a nice steady gig here, everything's fine.' I was making forty pounds a week and doing well. But I left John because I thought things were getting too jazzy. I was a blues fanatic—if it wasn't straight Chicago Blues, then forget it. We were doing a gig in Norwich, and we did a sound check, working some arrangements out, and one of the horn players asked: 'What sort of solo do you want here?' John said: 'Oh, just play free-form.' I thought: 'OK, that's it!' We played one set and I marched to the phone box across the street with all the indignation a blues purist could muster. I called up Pete and said, 'Do you still want me in the band?' He said he did, so I gave in my notice to Mayall and that was it." McVie played his last gig with Mayall September 3, 1967, at Union Rowing Club in Nottingham. He had been Mayall's longest serving sideman, but the parting was amicable. Years later, McVie played on Mayall's 1976 album "A Banquet in Blues", as well as on "Along for the Ride" in 2000. He even returned to play with the Bluesbreakers in 1982 for five months, together with Mick Taylor and Colin Allen.

The day after McVie's departure, the Bluesbreakers were back on stage with new bassist and singer Paul Williams, who joined September 4, after having been in the Wes Minster Five, Alexis Korner Band and Zoot Money's Big Roll Band. In the September issue of his fan club newsletter, Mayall broached the subject of his reputation as an unreasonable taskmaster who hires and fires at will. "I am always being plagued with questions like 'Why did so-and-so leave?' or 'What happened to so-and-so?' Bluesbreakers tend to fall into two categories, those who are asked to leave because their playing styles alter to the extent that they are no longer able to work in the same musical direction of the rest of the band—for example Roger Dean, Hughie Flint, Aynsley Dunbar, Mick Fleetwood, Rip Kant—and those musicians, usually guitarists, who have developed their own confidence and playing ability to the point where they want to set out on their own in a different branch of blues like Eric Clapton, Jack Bruce and Peter Green." Mayall was probably the first British musician who appealed to rock fans, but abandoned the idea of a stable group in favour of continuous change. He would surround himself with musicians of choice in much the same way as jazz musicians had been doing for years. Though the personnel might change or evolve from album to album, with Mayall being the only constant, the sound was always the Bluesbreakers' own, thanks to John's bandleading ability. Parallels to this ever-shifting line-up can not only be found in jazz, but also in the blues. The legendary Muddy Waters Blues Band from Chicago had many different line-ups, all of which were firmly anchored by Muddy's larger-than-life presence. During the fifties, many great blues musicians like Little Walter, Otis Spann, Jimmy Rogers, James Cotton and Buddy Guy all emerged from the Muddy Waters band. "The Bluesbreakers have been like a continuing college of the blues" John Mayall has said. It is true that his ever-changing line-ups became a training ground for some of Britain's finest musicians. Bands of cult status such as Cream, Fleetwood Mac or Colosseum may never have formed if Mayall had not brought some of the founder members together and developed their musical direction. Rolling Stone has referred to him as "one of the most famous talent scouts in rock music". When Mayall was asked about stories depicting him as a callous firer of musicians, he answered: "Well, that sometimes happened. There seems to be a nasty stigma attached to the phrase 'being fired' in this country. It implies a loss of grace or something, that the person being fired is inadequate or even incompetent. But in music, it's different; there's usually a reason for it, and I don't think it's because the guys couldn't handle their instruments, which is the only area they should feel disgrace about, really. It's always been a question of my having played with a particular set of musicians for so long that I need a change. I usually know what I want to do next. I find that by continually changing my bands I don't get stagnant as a performer, nor does my music as a composer. When I feel that the music with the musicians concerned has gone as far as it can possibly go, I start to think about organizing a new set of musicians and some new music." In other words, Mayall has always created bands that reflected his changing tastes and interests.

The Bluesbreakers (Taylor, Hartley, Mercer and Heckstall-Smith) together with Paul Williams, their new bass player, did some radio recordings for the BBC in September 1967, including some songs from the "Crusade" LP. They also did the Mayall oldie "Another Man", plus some blues standards never recorded before or since, such as B.B. King's "Sweet Little Angel" and Booker T's "The Hunter". Mayall compositions were "I Can't Sleep", "Not at Home" (both composed on the spot!) and "Supermarket Day". The BBC has never released songs from any of these sessions. Please see the discography for more details.

The Bluesbreakers entered Decca studios on September 14 to 15 to record the next single, this time a Mayall original entitled "Suspicions", an earthy horn-driven rhythm and blues number with a strong but simple riff, played by Mayall on guitar, and providing plenty of space for Taylor and Heckstall-Smith to stretch out. The song comes in two parts to accommodate the single format: "Suspicions Part One" with Taylor's guitar solo upfront is much shorter (3:18) than "Part Two" (5:27) which features Heckstall-Smith on multiple saxes. Mayall brought in extra horns, hiring an additional seven players. You can hear a baritone and an alto saxophone, two trombones and three trumpets. Commenting afterwards, Mayall said "it was just written so we could have a bash with a big band!" The focus on integrating a full horn section caused anguish among some diehard purists, but Mayall's first priority was to be true to himself, so it couldn't be helped.

In September Taylor's Gibson Les Paul was stolen. His search for a replacement led him to Keith Richards of the Rolling Stones, who had one for sale. It had a beautiful sunburst finish and was fitted with the rare Bigsby vibrato; Richards had bought it during the Stones' first US tour in June 1964 and to get it, Taylor had to part with £200, a lot of money in those days. Taylor and the Stones were to meet again before long, but under entirely different circumstances.

In October 1967 Alexis Korner, the highly respected blues aficionado, talent spotter and bandleader, targeted Mayall in a stinging article published in the Melody Maker. While not naming names, it was clear that Korner was criticizing Mayall for taking the blues in an aggressive, electric, "urban" direction, and thus away from its "roots". Korner even accused Mayall of cashing in on the blues-boom by making records that were deliberately commercial, a grievous sin in the eyes of certain "serious" or "purist" musicians! Although Korner and Mayall had got on well enough before, Alexis was not one to allow friendship get in the way of his strong views on music, especially when it came to the blues. The following week, Melody Maker published Mayall's reply, and it's clear he was totally nonplussed by Alexis' comments, especially as Korner had written the sleeve notes for the Bluesbreakers' first album. Today, it seems incomprehensible that Korner could have seen the success and development of the Bluesbreakers as a betrayal. It is quite possible that he envied their success, or thought that, as another blues pioneer, he deserved more of it himself. If a record sold well, it was commercial and therefore not real blues. Bluesmen had to suffer, and if they earned good money, they didn't suffer any more and were thus no longer able to play real blues! Real blues musicians were supposed to live and die in poverty, or else they were not the genuine article. Fortunately, the discord between Mayall and Korner blew over relatively quickly, and six months later, Alexis invited Mayall to his fortieth birthday party, where the guests included Mick Jagger, Marianne Faithful, Ginger Baker and Ornette Coleman.

On Tuesday, 17 October 1967, the Bluesbreakers were playing at Klooks Kleek in West Hampstead; when the band came back after the break John announced, "We have a special guest who's going to play the next set with us" and out walked Jimi Hendrix, to gasps and cheers from the audience. Taylor handed his Les Paul to Hendrix, who, being left-handed, turned it over and began to play. To the total amazement of the crowd, including Taylor, who stood at the side of the stage the whole time, watching and shaking his head in admiration, Jimi proceeded to play a whole set of incredible blues, with the fat E-string closest to the floor! Obviously, Hendrix could even play with the strings upside down!

Around this time, Mayall had the idea of producing a special kind of live recording. His last three LPs had been in the studio, and his only live album to date had been recorded at Klooks Kleek three years previously. Mayall planned to release a kind of audio diary, so decided to tape the next sixty shows they were booked to play in the two months between October and December 1967. The edited highlights would be issued the following year as two separate albums entitled "The Diary of a Band". As Mayall commented at the time: "I've always steered clear of making a live LP because of the hit and miss element of a good or a bad night, not to mention the strain of playing to an audience and everybody being aware of the engineers, etc." With no additional budget from Decca available, John relied instead on his trusty Truvox Stereophonic P99 reel-to-reel, placed on top of his Hammond organ. The recordings were made very simply using a pair of stereo microphones, and little trouble was taken to achieve perfect sound quality. What mattered was to capture forever those magic moments when his musicians felt inspired and the music flowed freely. Interestingly, John was also keen on recording snippets of conversation, press interviews and comments from the audience, and the result was a stack of live recordings bristling with spontaneous humour and brilliant improvisation.

When Paul Williams quit the Bluesbreakers to join The Alan Price Set as their lead singer, he had only been with them for eight weeks. Mayall was quick to recruit Keith Tillman from Aynsley

Dunbar's Retaliation. Tillman had previously played with Ralph Denyer's Rockhouse, Stone's Masonry (who disbanded when guitarist Martin Stone left to join Savoy Brown), Tony Knight's Chessmen and Alexis Korner's Free At Last. He had only been with Aynsley Dunbar for a few months, but, having seen them live several times, had a good grasp of the Bluesbreakers' repertoire. Tillman was also a wholehearted blues fan and an enthusiastic record collector. As a Bluesbreaker, Tillman's first job was to contribute to another BBC radio recording on 30 October. Exceptionally, the sessions avoided blues covers and kept strictly to Mayall originals. The next day saw Tillman's live debut in front of a full house at the Marquee club, with John McVie in the audience. However, McVie was more interested in seeing the Bluesbreakers' support band Chicken Shack, whose singer Christine Perfect made quite an impression. Later, the two were to marry, and Perfect was invited to join Fleetwood Mac. On November 2, the Bluesbreakers played the Speakeasy Club again. They closed the evening with a slow instrumental, which Mayall later edited as "Blues in Bb" for release on the "Diary" album. Hendrix was in town and sat in with the Bluesbreakers again. Mayall told a journalist thirty years later: "To hear Hendrix live was always exciting. He sat in with us two or three times. And it was so unlike what you'd expect of Hendrix, so quiet and subtle... the most low-key thing he could have possibly played." Hendrix's contributions were, in fact, never officially released, although some poor-quality bootlegs from the evening have survived.

On November 13 and 14, the Bluesbreakers returned to Northern Ireland for a couple of gigs. In Port Stewart, at the farcical insistence of the venue manager, the band had to close their performance with "God Save The Queen", resulting in what must be the only modern jazz version. Mayall remembers: "It was just hilarious. The promoter said 'I'm terribly sorry, but it's the rule of the ballroom that you play the national anthem,' so we had to do it. Musical chaos!" In the middle of the tour, Mayall found time to record another solo single, but not with his current band. He recruited ex-Bluesbreaker Peter Green (now with Fleetwood Mac) on guitar, and on December 4, they recorded "Blues for Jenny", a heroic ballad with Mayall on piano, guitar and overdubbed three-part vocal. Mayall handled production himself. The next day, Mayall and Green recorded "Picture on the Wall" with Green playing Jeremy Spencer's National resonator steel guitar, and Hartley on brushes. Mayall: "Every time I hear it, it tells me everything about Peter's music that I love. The thing with Peter's playing, and people like Eric and B.B. King, is that they have that touch: they can pick up a guitar and play just two notes and you know who it is. Now that's a very rare thing." The single was released on February 9, 1968 and was the last solo single Mayall ever recorded like this. Future Decca singles were simply album tracks released to promote forthcoming LPs.

After having selected what he considered to be the best performances, Mayall gave the tapes to producer Mike Vernon and engineer Gus Dudgeon to edit. As Decca were unsure of the viability of releasing a double album of live recordings made on a domestic tape recorder, the decision was made to release two separate LPs on the same day (February 23, 1968) in virtually identical Mayall-designed sleeves. They were named simply "Volume One" and "Volume Two". Giving fans maximum value for money, Mayall ensured that each record clocked in at nearly 48 minutes, the maximum running time of an LP. As the Bluesbreakers had begun to make extended improvisation the cornerstone of their live performances, a lot of good material had to be cut. However, thanks to modern technology, Decca were able to re-release the complete recordings on a re-mastered double CD set in 2007. The albums are true musical treasures and probably the most innovative British blues ever released by Decca up to that point.

1968 started with four gigs in Britain in early January, the first at Klooks Kleek on January 2, with Jimi Hendrix sitting in again. Then the Bluesbreakers left for their first tour of the United States from January 9 to February 12, which proved to be quite an eye-opener for all concerned. On January 8, the band had to endure a nail-biting wait, as their visas did not arrive until very late. The next day, the group's flight out of London was delayed because of snow. They finally took off at 5:30 am, the same day that Mayall's residency at New York's Café Au Go Go was due to commence. For their first journey across the Atlantic, Mayall had got over the high cost of air fares for the band by doing a deal with London Records and West Coast impresario Bill Graham, who booked Mayall for several appearances in San Francisco for the beginning of February. During their successful 13-day stint at the Café Au Go Go, Blood, Sweat & Tears and The Steve Miller Band were support. A Billboard reviewer wrote of the Bluesbreakers' performances: "Musically, the group evokes an exciting sound without the loudness usually associated with blues-rock," while Hartley remembers: "We played our first American gig to a sell out crowd." The Bluesbreakers then moved on to the Grande Ballroom in Detroit for a single performance on January 23. Tillman recalls: "The gig was great. Interestingly enough, it was largely a black audience." From Detroit, the band flew to Los Angeles for an extended weekend with four gigs at the Whiskey A Go Go from January 25–28. Mayall remembers: "We sold those out and then the club added an additional four days." However, Mayall's abiding memory of California was that he instantly fell in love with the place: "When I touched down in Los Angeles, all of a sudden I knew that this is where I wanted to live. It was in January, and in New York the weather was pretty much like in Britain until we got to California. I was from Manchester, but never really liked the English weather and I'd had 30 years of it. And everything I'd always loved was American—jazz, blues, movies, books." In a later interview, Mayall stated: "I just felt an instant identity with the place. It was the environment, the climate, the American way of life."

From February 1 to 4 in San Francisco, promoter Bill Graham had booked The Jimi Hendrix Experience, John Mayall's Bluesbreakers and Albert King to play on the same bill. Albert King was one of Mayall's blues heroes, and a guitar idol for Taylor and Hendrix. Hartley wrote later: "We were booked to play at the Fillmore West, second on the bill to the Jimi Hendrix Experience, and above the great blues guitarist Albert King. We went on stage having something to prove. We were following a master player and a musician we all looked up to. We had to be good to better Albert King's act, but under John's leadership we had little trouble. Mick Taylor excelled himself, and being sandwiched between two of the world's best guitarists only seemed to bring out his best playing. In California, he was free of the shadows of his predecessors Clapton and Green. He proved himself to be their equal, and many said he was even better. From behind my kit, I watched him rise to the challenge, and every night he left the audience reeling with his ability. Over the years John has employed numerous superb players stretching from Eric and Peter through to Walter Trout and Buddy Whittington. I've seen or played with just about every line up, but few guitarists have matched Mick Taylor in 1968."

All of the Bluesbreakers were great fans of Jimi Hendrix, and Mick Taylor recounts: "After our show at Winterland, we went and played somewhere until about five in the morning with Jimi. I've learned a lot from him. He was extraordinary. His feeling for the rhythm, this energy and his fantastic finger-vibrato, it was all just gigantic. I think that Jimi was the one who has influenced me more than anybody else" while Mayall himself reminisced: "I'm not sure how I felt sharing the bill with Jimi Hendrix. Even in those early stages, a blind man could have seen he was a true star. We played together many times and I think I even asked him to play in the band around '66 or '67, but Jimi and I were both too independently minded to be together for any length of time. He is possibly the only guitarist I ever knew who was totally "as one" with his guitar. It didn't matter if it was a Fender or a Gibson, strung for a left-hander or a right-hander, he could just play it. And man, could he play it! He once picked up my 9 string and got sounds out of it that I never believed existed. Amazing."

Back home in Britain, Mayall was voted top in the section 'Blues Artist—British' by Melody Maker readers, ahead of Georgie Fame, Alexis Korner, Long John Baldry and Eric Clapton. Mayall told the paper: "It's rather amazing, really. But it's a very nice homecoming. Winning this poll must be the culmination of all our work." On February 23, Mayall expanded his horn section by adding trumpeter (and occasional violinist) Henry Lowther, known to Bluesbreakers fans from the single "Looking Back/So Many Roads". Tillman was not fond of horn players, so decided to leave to pursue Python Records, his own label, which catered for blues purists. Bassist Tillman was replaced by the tender 15-year-old, Jack Bruce-influenced Andy Fraser. He was the Bluesbreakers' youngest member to date, but had already been playing for three years. Fraser had left school early, and was dating Korner's daughter, Sappho, at the time. He had played with a group named Lawless Breed, and then gone on to join Alexis' band. It was Korner who recommended Fraser to Mayall, although he was actually a guitarist. Andy went straight to Mayall's home to jam, and had his first gig with the Bluesbreakers the same night in Guildford, on February 25. Outgoing bassist Tillman played the first set and Fraser the second, plucking an Italian Eko bass through a 100-watt Sound City amp. Frazer may have been physically diminutive, but his bass playing was incredible. The seven-piece line-up with Andy Fraser lasted only eight weeks, too short for any recordings, but long enough for radio sessions at the BBC on March 4 and 26, providing versions of "Picture On The Wall", the instrumental "Knockers Step Forward", "The Last Time" and "Rock Me Baby", plus other unknown numbers. Only the first two titles survive on bootleg editions.

In April 1968, more line-up changes occurred as Mayall wanted to bring in a jazzier rhythm section. Jon Hiseman replaced drummer Keef Hartley, and Tony Reeves bassist Andy Fraser. The peculiarity was that Hiseman and Reeves were already booked for the recording sessions for the new Bluesbreakers album on April 3, while Hartley and Fraser remained available for concerts until April 21. Mayall had seen Hiseman in action at a gig given by The Graham Bond Organisation on March 6. Bond's regular drummer had failed to show up, so in the interval Graham asked Jon to sit in. As one number blended seamlessly into the next, Mayall saw that this phenomenally versatile and unflappable drummer was the man for the next incarnation of the Bluesbreakers. A couple of weeks later, Hiseman found Mayall waiting in his car as he arrived home from a gig at 5.30 am; Mayall had been waiting for three hours. Hiseman: "I asked him inside and he invited me to join the Bluesbreakers. I'd always considered his band rubbish, but as it turned out it was very good—much better than I'd ever dreamed." And Mayall remembers: "Jon was really very taken aback when I asked him to join. He told me he knew next to nothing about blues and that he couldn't care less about my music—but I told him I wasn't too worried about that, I just admired his playing. And that was the basis on which we worked. It fitted very well."

Hiseman had left the New Jazz Orchestra in April 1966 to replace Ginger Baker in the Graham Bond Organisation. Baker had left to form Cream with Eric Clapton and Jack Bruce, but Hiseman proved more than capable of replacing the mercurial Baker; indeed, he had acquired a considerable reputation as a drum virtuoso in his own right. When the Graham Bond Organisation dissolved in chaos in late spring 1967, Hiseman joined Georgie Fame's Band. Already known for using double bass drums like Baker, Hiseman also had a smaller maple Gretsch kit which he preferred when playing with Mayall.

Fraser played his last gig with the band on April 21, 1968. He had been a Bluesbreaker for eight short weeks, but would soon come to prominence again after teaming up with singer Paul Rogers, guitarist Paul Kossoff and drummer Simon Kirke to form the blues-based rock band Free. Replacement Tony Reeves had played double bass in jazz and dance bands since his grammar-school days, together with Dave Greenslade and Jon Hiseman. He had played on recordings by folk legend Davy Graham, one of the Bluesbreakers' earliest guitarists. His friend Hiseman told him Mayall was looking for a bass player, and suddenly he found himself recruited! The new Bluesbreakers now consisted of John Mayall, Mick Taylor (guitar), Tony Reeves (bass), Jon Hiseman (drums), Dick Heckstall-Smith (soprano and tenor saxophones), Chris Mercer (tenor and baritone saxophones), and Henry Lowther (cornet and violin); they made their live debut on April 23, 1968. The same line-up played on the next Bluesbreakers album, which was one of Mayall's most ambitious; it was a concept LP entitled "Bare Wires". Completed in just four days, it was musically more complex and experimental than any of his previous efforts, and showed Mayall was fully capable of using a wide range of innovative studio techniques and effects. Side one is taken up with the "Bare Wires Suite", a sequence of seven songs linked together to form a continuous piece, something more "progressive" bands such as the Moody Blues had also started to do around this time. Of course, the Beatles had also done it on "Sgt. Pepper", which also featured a gatefold sleeve and printed lyrics, both ideas taken up by Mayall for the "Bare Wires" LP cover. There were six more conventionally presented songs making up side two. Among the many highlights are the feedback-drenched "1 Started Walking", which features one of Mick Taylor's best ever solos; "Look in the Mirror", an uplifting piece of jazz-rock, with outstanding contributions by Jon Hiseman on his double bass drum kit, Tony Reeves on bass and Dick Heckstall-Smith playing tenor and soprano saxophones all at once! "I'm A Stranger" is a long, slow blues with powerful horn-based riffs and a great saxophone solo by the underrated Chris Mercer. "No Reply" was co-written by Taylor and became the A-side of a single released two weeks prior to the album to promote it. Obviously inspired by Hendrix, Taylor uses wah-wah and his new, white Fender Stratocaster extensively. "Hartley Quits" is a brilliant, Freddie King-inspired shuffle, written by Taylor. Two other tracks were omitted from the final album and remained in the Decca vaults until the release of Mayall rarities "Thru the Years" in October 1971. The "Bare Wires" album anticipates progressive rock by exploring the gap between blues, jazz and psychedelia; it featured uncommon instruments, sound effects and time signatures more complex than the usual blues-based 4/4. Released on June 21, 1968, ot became Mayall's highest charting album ever, reaching number 3 in Britain and number 59 in the US Billboard charts. Advance orders in the USA were an impressive 50,000 copies, double the usual amount.

With the album completed, Mayall took his new band on the road, undertaking a busy European tour until mid-July. One venue of note was Zurich's Hallenstadion, which hosted the so-called Monster Konzert from May 30 to 31. Headlining were The Jimi Hendrix Experience, supported by Eric Burdon and the Animals,

John Mayall's Bluesbreakers, Traffic, The Move, and two local bands. Chris Mercer remembers: "On the second night, we played more or less to ourselves, as the crowd was engrossed in watching the police beat off members of the audience determined to scale the stage." When it was Hendrix's turn, it was amazing to see the number of other musicians standing watching from the wings, totally gob-smacked. Only Taylor was sitting down cross-legged, contemplating his guitar guru and master. The crowd broke up many of the wooden seats, and the concert ended in fights between hot-headed fans and a Swiss police force that was obviously completely out of its depth. With truncheons drawn and dogs snarling, there were some ugly scenes.

By July 1968, John Mayall was fed up from the vigorous schedule of maintaining a seven-piece band on the road, finding the extended Bluesbreakers too cumbersome. He wanted to change the dynamics of the band radically, go back to being a quartet and carry a smaller PA, so he kept Hiseman and Taylor, but sacked all the others. Mayall's decision to break up what many considered one of his best ever groups generated headlines in the British music press. Mayall later explained to his fan-club: "You've got seven people queuing up for a blow, most of them standing around doing nothing. I was just one of the seven joining in... It produced some exciting things, but was nearer to jazz than blues... Whole evenings would be instrumental, with just a couple of choruses at the beginning and end."

After having dissolved the big band, Mayall decided to take a holiday by himself in California for about three weeks. However, he first needed to fill the vacancy for a bass player. His choice fell upon the promising but inexperienced 17 year-old Steve Thompson, with whom Mayall immediately went shopping, purchasing a Gibson EB-2 bass complete with Fender Bassman amp. Mayall told the young Thompson to teach himself while he was away in California, rightly trusting that the new man would come good if he invested in more practise.

Arriving in the States, Mayall first stayed at Frank Zappa's Laurel Canyon log cabin before moving to Canned Heat's place in nearby

Topanga Canyon. Canned Heat played a blend of electric country and psychedelic blues, and were well on their way to becoming America's most successful blues band. They had just scored US chart success with "On the Road Again", and while on holiday, Mayall contributed piano to a couple of tracks destined for the Heat's third album, "Livin' the Blues". Mayall was becoming increasingly interested in the USA as a place to live and work, especially California and the West Coast; he became so impressed by Laurel Canyon that he took up permanent residence there only nine months later. Mayall: "Having played blues music and been brought up on American culture in every area, from movies to literature, I felt bonded to America immediately." Mayall also decided to work exclusively under his own name and drop the Bluesbreakers tag after 5½ years, correctly reasoning that this would give him greater freedom.

While Mayall was relaxing in California, Hiseman decided to quit the Bluesbreakers to form his own band. He wanted to call it Colosseum, taking his inspiration from the famous ancient Roman amphitheatre. Hiseman recalls: "I phoned Dick (Heckstall-Smith), Tony (Reeves) and Dave (Greenslade), who all wanted in. Then the grapevine started, and about a week later I got a phone call from Mayall. 'I hear you're leaving us', he said with a laugh." After a week mulling over Hiseman's defection, Mayall announced that Colin Allen would take over the drum seat; Allen had played in Zoot Money's bands and with Georgie Fame before accepting Mayall's invitation.

Four months after "Bare Wires", Mayall was back at Decca to record a new self-produced album with his stripped down line-up. "Blues from Laurel Canyon" was Mayall's last recording for Decca, and it set out to convey his impressions of the US West Coast in the form of a musical diary. The twelve songs were all Mayall originals; there were no instrumentals. Among the highlights are "Vacation", a rousing, rock-oriented opener, starting with jet engine noises; here Taylor's stellar guitar work displays heavy vibrato and a storm of feedback. "2401" is a guitar and organ-led rocking blues, the title of which refers to Frank Zappa's address on Laurel Canyon Boulevard. "Medicine Man" introduces native American (Apache) rhythms to produce a highly evocative piece; "Miss James" is a jazzy shuffle with one of the best organ solos Mayall ever recorded; "Long Gone Midnight" features another superb Mick Taylor solo. The closing track "Fly Tomorrow" starts with a hypnotic Colin Allen tabla pattern, the ambient introduction gradually giving way to a fabulous Taylor solo. Taylor excels on the entire album, especially with his slide guitar work. The release coincided with Mayall's 35 birthday and, like "Bare Wires", Decca issued a single to promote the album. "Blues from Laurel Canyon" received varied but mostly positive reviews, many of them praising Taylor's talent. This did not, however, translate into strong sales; the LP was not as successful as its predecessor, reaching only Number 33 in Britain and Number 68 in the US.

From September 3 to November 7, Mayall and his new, compact "backing" band returned to North America for their second tour. They flew out to California on September 3, Mayall just managing to rendezvous with Canned Heat, who were arriving in Europe for the first time to promote their latest hit "On the Road Again". The bands exchanged road crews, with Mayall's roadie borrowing Canned Heat's van for the California gigs, and Bootsie Boyle, Mayall's other roadie, assisting Canned Heat on their British tour.

By November 1968 the British blues boom had blossomed so much that bands like Mayall's were able to attract ever-increasing crowds to larger venues. For the first time in his career, Mayall was playing without support, starting November 9 at Sheffield City Hall. On November 16, Mayall headlined the Blues Scene '68 concert with a triumphant show at London's Royal Festival Hall. The line-up also featured Muddy Waters, Champion Jack Dupree and the Aynsley Dunbar Retaliation.

From November 29 to December 8, the four travelled to Scandinavia again, often performing two shows in different towns on the same night. Some venues were full, and hundreds of fans had to be turned away. This was followed by a three-day trip to Scotland starting December 13. 1968 ended with a giant New Year's Eve Gala Pop & Blues party at Alexandra Palace in north London, together with Joe Cocker, Amen Corner, Free and the Small Faces.

On January 8, Mayall's group was again at the BBC to record four selections for Alexis Korner's Rhythm & Blues radio show. It turned out to be Mayall's last live appearance at the BBC. Bass player Thompson didn't feel well and was admitted to hospital, diagnosed with pneumonia. Tony Reeves substituted for four London gigs, and when Reeves had to return to duties with Colosseum, Mayall asked ex-Bluesbreaker Keith Tillman to step in for the up-coming tour of Switzerland. Friday 17 January saw Mayall back in Zurich, this time playing two shows at the Albisriederhaus. Mayall appeared rather withdrawn, and the band played a selection from the "Laurel Canyon" LP as well as some covers, but many were off-the-cuff and organ-based, with soul and funk influences.

Back in England, Thompson was still unwell, so Mayall called on the services of bass player Jerome Arnold for the first set of gigs at Klooks Kleek on 21 January, rotating duties with Tony Reeves, who played the second set, and the following day in Croydon. Arnold was brother of singer and harmonica player Billy Boy Arnold, and had recently settled in London in order to front his own blues band.

In the late 60s, Mayall was particularly image-conscious, and used to enjoy cultivating the impression of a wild and independent outdoor type, a sort of Davy Crockett of the blues, with Bowie knife and bearskin. After ensuring all his gear was in place (suede shirt or leather jacket with tassels, broad leather bullet belt with chunky buckle, sometimes with a Stetson on top!) he would stride into the auditorium and strike statuesque poses, staring into the eyes of anyone who met his gaze. To questions from adoring fans he would bark laconic and enigmatic replies. Clearly, here was a man with more than a streak of narcissism. His outfits were often homemade, and his hairstyles always striking. He sometimes wore his hair in twin ponytails topped off with a broad headband! On stage, he was often seen in heavy boots, leather clothes, holster and woodsman's knife, swinging his shoulder-length hair from side to side as he played. This was all part of a carefully cultivated image. When giving interviews, Mayall's replies could become monosyllabic if a reporter got on his nerves. It certainly seemed to work for a time, but Mayall soon dropped such affectation when he settled down to live in the States.

The stress of so much touring was wearing Mayall out, and on January 23, he contracted 'flu brought on by physical and nervous exhaustion. On doctor's orders, he cancelled all dates and commitments until mid-February. With Mayall bedridden, Taylor did some recording sessions with Champion Jack Dupree for "Scoobydoobydoo", his new Blue Horizon album. Producer Mike Vernon had put together a stellar line-up that included two of Mayall's ex-drummers, Keef Hartley and Aynsley Dunbar, in addition to bass players Gary Thain and Alex Dmochowski. This is a wonderful and highly recommended album, not least thanks to Mick Taylor's excellent contributions.

Touring resumed on February 11 at Fishmonger Arms in Wood Green, and on February 14, the Mayall concert at the Brighton Dome was booked out, proof of Mayall's pulling power at this time. February 18 saw the band leave on yet another American tour, their third. Scheduled to last until May 3, they played about 45 concerts in 74 days. The social events organiser for Winnipeg University, Grant Boden, had booked the group for a concert there. The four musicians arrived on a flight from Toronto, where they had played at the Rockpile three nights earlier. Taylor had used the break to visit a girlfriend in St. Louis, and was rejoining the others for the Winnipeg gig before they headed off to Chicago. A short discussion ensued about the venue, equipment, stage set-up and dressing rooms before Taylor brought up the subject of his additional flight expenses in rejoining the others. He asked Mayall to reimburse him. "Mayall exploded," Boden recalls, "and refused to pay the extra cost. They were yelling and screaming at each other. "I'm not paying for your bloody excursion!" I heard Mayall shout. Then Taylor told him, 'I quit.' I couldn't believe what I was hearing. Here we were on our way to the hotel with the gig a few hours away and one of the guys isn't going to play. It was an intense experience to say the least! I've never sweated nor pleaded so much in my life." As Boden pulled up to the venue, the four disembarked and headed to the dressing room in total silence. Not long after, they went onstage to a rousing welcome and proceeded to mesmerize the adoring crowd. Taylor was the star of the show. Playing a red Gibson SG guitar through a simple Fender Super Reverb amp with no pedals, gizmos or gadgets, he was dazzling, bringing the Clapton school of pure blues to the city. Throughout the 75-minute concert he never once looked at Mayall or spoke to the audience, standing motionless to the right of the stage, his emotion expressed in his playing and the occasional arching of his back during solos. "Mick Taylor was brilliant that night," recalls guitarist Danny Casavant. "His phrasing was fluid with vibrato from heaven, and he was a great slide player, too. It was an important show for me as a young guitar player. Afterwards, a buddy of mine got me backstage, and I actually met them all! I was only 17!" Following the Cincinnati gig, Taylor, Thompson and Allen travelled to Chicago, while Mayall took the plane to Champaign, Illinois to spend a few days with J.B. Lenoir's widow and family.

From March 27–29, Mayall and his band shared the stage with Muddy Waters, Otis Spann, Bo Diddley and Magic Sam on an all-blues bill at Winterland in San Francisco, unquestionably a programme dear to Mayall's heart. April started with the Easter Pop Festival at Palm Springs, California, where Mayall played on the same bill as Ike & Tina Turner, Canned Heat, Procol Harum, and the Paul Butterfield Blues Band. The concert attracted 25,000 people. The next two concerts saw Mayall's group billed together with Deep Purple, who were more popular in the States than at home. From April 8 to 13, the Flying Burrito Brothers opened for Mayall on his highly successful week-long stay at the Whisky a Go Go in Los Angeles. Here, Mayall often jammed into the wee hours with Aynsely Dunbar and Buddy Miles.

With a week off from touring in late April, Mayall purchased his dream home, a three-storey house at 8353 Grandview Drive, Laurel Canyon. Here, Mayall would often go into the wilderness for long stretches to be alone and write.

The group flew home on May 4 after three nights in Boston. As the American tour drew to a close, Mick Taylor formally handed in his notice, one of the few who quit before being asked to go. He also had the distinction of being Mayall's longest-serving guitarist. In a similar manner and for similar reasons, drummer Colin Allen also decided to leave; both men wanted a change. Back home, the time seemed ripe for Mayall to form a group without a drummer or lead guitarist, so instead of holding auditions, Mayall visited Decca's West Hampstead studios in early May to work on the compilation "Looking Back" to fulfil his final obligations to Decca, and also found time to produce the third and final album by the Aynsley Dunbar Retaliation, "To Mum From Aynsley And The Boys". Mayall made two important decisions at this time; first, he resolved to move to California permanently, and second, to switch to Polydor, as his contract with Decca expired on May 22. Polydor offered greater artistic freedom and better money.

The quartet with Mayall, Taylor, Thompson and Allen fulfilled their agreement to play a further eight concerts in Britain from May 9 to 17 to make up for cancellations in January and February, and these were followed by a debut tour of northern Germany. A live recording taken from the Glocke in Bremen on May 22 was widely bootlegged, and the six songs it contains bear witness to the level of musicianship. Although the sound quality is far from good, the band plays with excellence and power. The highlight is Mick Taylor's incredible guitar solo on the fourteen minute-long "Parchman Farm", the song ending with an astonishing coda. On May 23 in Hamburg, Mick Taylor played his last concert with Mayall, parting after nearly two years and more than 400 shows. Typically, Taylor wanted to have a rest before making another career move, but as we know, he was invited to join the Rolling Stones to replace the departing Brian Jones. Taylor's move was made official on June 13, although his first session with the Stones took place on May 31. Everybody seems to have their own version about how Taylor joined them. Bill Wyman remembers that it was pianist and "auxiliary" Stone Ian Stewart who suggested they check out Taylor, while Marsha Hunt, once Mayall's girlfriend and now Jagger's, later wrote: "I told Jagger about Mick Taylor and I sheepishly went to Mayall's Fulham house to find out how to get hold of him." Mayall recalls: "Jagger called me on the phone and asked me if I knew a guitar player. I had that sort of reputation: 'If you want a guitar player, call Mayall, he might know one'. Mick Taylor moved up and wasn't complaining!" Colin Allen left to play with Brian Auger and then joined Stone the Crows. About his time with Mayall, Taylor later said: "Playing the sort of music, it gives you a lot of opportunity to develop your own ideas; it gives you a lot of freedom within the blues framework. So it did do me a lot of good being with John. He was only difficult to work with when I started to veer off towards other things. He's not a difficult person to get on with really, though a lot of people seem to think so. You'd have complete freedom to do whatever you wanted. On another occasion, Taylor has said: "It was very enjoyable most of the time, until the last six months when I began to get fed up."

Decca never really seemed to appreciate what they had in Mayall, while the man himself viewed his Decca days with stoic acceptance and modest resignation. With the end of the Decca years, a chapter had closed. "Looking Back" turned out to be a British hit for Mayall, reaching number 10, and making it to 79 in the States. The album earned some of Mayall's best reviews and good sales. Two years later, Mike Vernon released a follow-up by trawling through the Decca vaults for other singles tracks, mostly from the Peter Green period. These were released on another compilation named "Thru the Years". Another retrospective set entitled "Primal Solos" was released in 1977 in the US, finally appearing in Britain in 1983. It contained five tracks featuring Eric Clapton and Jack Bruce recorded live on November 7, 1965 at the Flamingo, plus three more with Mick Taylor from 1968. Please see the discography for more details.

CHAPTER 6
Turning Points
The first US bands and the early Polydor years, 1969–71

On the sleeve notes to 'The Turning Point' LP, Mayall wrote: "Having decided to dispense with heavy lead guitar and drums, usually a 'must' for blues groups today, I set about forming a new band which would be able to explore seldom-used areas within the framework of low volume music." Mayall could no longer see the point of employing a new lead guitarist or even a drummer; his sleeve notes continue: "Eric Clapton more or less founded a whole cult of blues guitar stylists; too many people are into that bag for it to mean much anymore." In addition, after discovering Clapton, Green and Taylor in quick succession, three of the era's most acclaimed guitarists, Mayall rightly felt that it would be virtually impossible to find anyone who could equal them. His career had reached a crossroads; if he wanted to outlive the blues boom and develop, he was fully aware that he couldn't continue simply by replicating the successful formula he had established over the previous five years. He had to change the band radically. While many of the other British blues musicians moved on to psychedelia or chart-bound pop, Mayall remained true to the blues, but tried to innovate by playing it in an entirely different way using a range of different instruments. The departure of Taylor and Allen gave Mayall the opportunity to try the outfit he had long been considering; a band where all of the musicians featured equally and, most significantly of all, there was no drummer. This meant going against musical convention, which, of course, was no problem for Mayall. He'd already discussed the idea with Larry Taylor and Alan Wilson of Canned Heat back in the summer of 1968. Mayall commented at the time: "I'd used the standard quartet formula with lead guitar and drums for long enough, and I felt like doing something different. I felt that I had explored all the avenues that were possible in the blues, and I wanted to try new things. Even though I had added horns, it really was only an embellishment of the same music. I really felt that I had to reevaluate the whole thing. 'The Turning Point' was the first time I thought I should do something different. I decided to drop the electric feel and go acoustic, without the drums. I don't want to get my ears blasted. I want to hear my musicians; I want to hear what they play. I've always tried to keep my volume down and that always seems to end up getting the most impact. The idea first formed when I saw the vast number of electric guitar groups in the States. If ever there was a time to start something new, it's now. Every band you hear in the blues field is on the same kick. It's not a new idea. My main inspiration had been the music of Jimmy Giuffre and the soundtrack of the film Jazz on a Summer's Day." Mayall had been studying Giuffre, Brookmeyer and Hall playing 'Train and the River' in Bert Stern's movie 'Jazz on a Summer's Day', filmed at the Newport Rhode Island Festival back in July 1958. There was no drummer. Giuffre's courageous compositions, experiments with unusual instruments, and development of a unique clarinet-playing technique, had won him admiration from followers of jazz's avant-garde. What made Giuffre's sound so strikingly different was his steadfast insistence on eliminating the one instrument most critics and fans considered a principal component of the jazz sound: the drum kit. Intrigued by Giuffre's work, Mayall set out to pare down his blues compositions to their melodic essentials. Unlike his previous recordings, which were steeped in standard blues structures, Mayall now resolved that each of his instruments should have an equal voice. Mayall pointed out that Muddy Waters, among others, had successfully used a line-up that had no drummer. Django Reinhardt's classic Hot Club de France quintets from 1934 to 1939 performed without drums as well. His new venture would freely blend blues, jazz, and even elements of folk. It was not in-your-face blues of the decibel kind, but a new sound and approach, considered almost revolutionary at the time. It was an acoustic-based, light and subtle kind of 'chamber blues', softer and more delicate, sometimes featuring horns, flute and acoustic guitar, and with a lot of cross-feel between the musicians. (The approach would be revived in the early nineties with the launch of MTV's 'Unplugged' series.) The next twelve years would see many changes and experiments in Mayall's music. Around this time, he also switched record labels. As his contract with Decca had expired, he signed with Polydor, the German-based company. Cream, The Who and Taste also recorded for Polydor at the time. Mayall later explained: "Polydor came up with the offer we thought most useful. I think that it turned out to be a very wise choice."

Mayall switched line-ups in May 1969, right in the middle of a three-week European tour, but the new format went down a storm, and Mayall was rewarded with excellent reviews and strong sales in the following months. Mayall's new line-up included a fine tenor saxophone player by the name of Johnny Almond; only bass player Steve Thompson was retained from the last band. Almond had already spent two years with Zoot Money's Big Roll Band, together with Colin Allen, and had had the opportunity to display his mulifarious talents at freelance recording work. He had spent a year and a half with the Alan Price Set, which became the Paul Williams Set, and then left to join Mayall's new band in May 1969 at the tender age of 22. Mayall had previously employed Almond as a session player on the 'Beano' and 'Hard Road' albums, so he knew the man's abilities well. Shortly before joining Mayall, Almond had already recorded his first solo album entitled 'Patent Pending' with his own jazz septet, produced by Mike Vernon. Almond can be heard displaying his 'chops' on nine different instruments! Mayall explained his choice: "I wanted a flute player who could play tenor sax and that narrowed it down to Johnny Almond!" Now back from Germany, Mayall had decided to add acoustic finger-style guitarist Jon Mark as well. Mark was a folk club guitarist, gigging with classmate and virtuoso Alun Davies (later with Cat Stevens) before forming the band Sweet Thursday, which included Nicky Hopkins on keyboards. They released one album in the US before Mark got a job accompanying Marianne Faithfull, staying for three years. Mayall: "The only acoustic guitar player I knew was Jon Mark. I phoned him and asked about finger-style guitar players who were free, and he said he would like to come to the next session." He was soon recruited, and from May 27 to 29, the new band with Mayall, Mark, Almond and Thompson rehearsed at Mayall's lodgings in Fulham. Rather than rework Bluesbreakers staples or blues standards, Mayall elected to compose a host of new songs, specifically designed for his new ensemble. The new sound was characterized by the delicate interplay between the musicians, and the combined influences of folk, jazz and blues, while still retaining Mayall's inimitable authority and style. Here, Jon Mark's gut-stringed guitar played a predominantly rhythmic role, Steve Thompson was now heard to much greater extent, while Mayall, having dropped organ and piano, concentrated on vocals, harmonica and electric guitar. Rising to his task as principal soloist, Almond's virtuoso inventions on flute, alto and tenor sax were a revelation. Besides his skills as a multi-instrumentalist, Almond had a particularly good sense of humour and rapidly became the clown of the band, telling jokes and doing daft impressions.

The semi-acoustic quartet made its debut at the Paris Olympia on Monday, June 2, 1969; it was Mayall's first visit to France, but everything turned out well, as Jon Mark reported in Mayall's monthly newsletter: "The next thing I remember is the first number finishing, and applause like I'd never heard before. From then on the music just took over. We played for one and a half hours, and it seemed like just five minutes." The tour over, Mayall brought the same show back to tour Britain, playing at least 12 dates between June 10 and July 1, including the Bath Festival of Blues on June 28, where Mayall headlined with Fleetwood Mac, Led Zeppelin, Ten Years After, The Nice, Chicken Shack, Colosseum, Blodwyn Pig, The Keef Hartley Band, Taste, Savoy Brown and Champion Jack Dupree; the crowd was estimated at over 20,000.

Audiences took to the new band immediately, and they received ovations and rave reviews from the press. Melody Maker's Chris Welch reviewed the group's first English date at the May Ball in

Cambridge on June 10, commenting: "They're sensational! The new Mayall band has suddenly developed into the most original, refreshing and exciting group in Britain. They are creating some of the most subtle and rewarding music I have had the pleasure of hearing. The range of sounds and moods they obtain is staggering. But the most remarkable feature of the new band is their interplay and empathy." Mayall was moved to quote some of Welch's review on the cover of his next album. Mayall's vision and need for change had brought him the most commercially successful phase in his career so far, and the formula of dispensing with the drummer soon found its imitators. From 1969–70, Alexis Korner put together a quartet without a drummer called New Church, which was very similar to Mayall's band. While still on tour in England, Mayall's new band recorded their latest single on June 20; entitled 'Don't Waste My Time', it was enthusiastically reviewed by Melody Maker.

Around this time, Peter Gibson and Alex Hooper, both music fans and graduates of the Slade School of Fine Art in London, filmed parts of the British tour. Their documentary covered May 9 to June 30, including concerts with Mick Taylor, and showed a band in transition. The finished documentary, like the LP also entitled 'Turning Point', was premiered on August 28, 1970, at the Electric Cinema on London's Portobello Road, and was also shown at the Edinburgh Arts Festival before being distributed Europe-wide. After that, it sadly disappeared without trace. More recently, thanks to renewed interest sparked by the BBC's 'Dancing in the Street' series on popular music, the film was made available on VHS by Eagle records, and then re-released on DVD in the summer of 2004, in tandem with the BBC documentary on Mayall entitled 'The Godfather of British Blues'. The film also provided two valuable live recordings: 'The Masters', and 'Live at the Marquee 1969', both released by Eagle in 1999 on CD.

On July 5, the band made its US debut at the prestigious Newport Jazz Festival, alongside jazz greats Art Blakey, Gary Burton and Miles Davis. Leonard Feather, the well-known US jazz critic, reported in Downbeat that at the end of their set, 'a roar went up that could hardly have been exceeded if Mayall had announced that the Vietnam War was over!' Forever the perfectionist, Mayall told Melody Maker that for him the gig was disappointing as there were sound problems from the festival PA. On July 11 and 12, Mayall headlined at the Fillmore East, supported by the Preservation Hall Jazz Band and Spooky Tooth. The New York Times declared that Mayall led 'an unusually deft quartet' and that he could 'play with pungent charm'. Heartened by the enthusiastic reception in both the US and Europe, Mayall decided to release some live performances for his debut Polydor release. Mayall secured engineer Eddie Kramer to record both Fillmore shows, which featured all new Mayall compositions. Among the highlights were 'The Laws Must Change', a great opening number with a fine flute solo by Almond. The powerful social criticism in the lyrics was something Mayall took from his idol J.B. Lenoir, who had recorded protest songs like 'Korea Blues', 'Tax Paying Blues', 'Vietnam Blues' and others. 'I'm Gonna Fight for You J.B.' is a straightforward country blues. 'California', co-written with Thompson, uses a bass line borrowed from a Dizzy Gillespie tune. The longest track on the album, it provides dramatic interplay between Mayall and his skilled sidemen, especially Almond, who plays the highest register possible on his alto sax. The song was recorded again in 2000 on 'Along for the Ride' and in 2003 for the 70th Birthday Concert. 'Room to Move' is perhaps Mayall's best-known tour-de-force on the harp, with infectious, furious playing and featuring some remarkable vocal acrobatics. The riff was inspired by Sonny Boy Williamson's 'One Way Out' and received widespread radio airplay on the newly emerging FM radio stations all over America. One of Mayall's best-known and most requested works, there are in fact 16 different live versions! Overall, the album veered much closer to jazz than any of his earlier efforts. The music was expansive, open, and fresh, but basically still the blues. Mayall played harmonica, guitar and sang, having ditched keyboards. 'The Turning Point' was released in September 1969 in the States and on October 31 in Britain. It became Mayall's highest selling release, and was lauded by critics and fans alike. It landed Mayall his only US RIAA Gold album, although it took about ten years to do so! It peaked at number 11 in the UK and sold very well in the US, remaining in the top 200 Billboard album charts for 55 weeks.

The US-tour wound down on October 24–25 with a weekend at the Grande Ballroom in Detroit, after which Mayall and his band flew into London on October 30 to start a full-scale British tour in Croydon the very next day. Such was Mayall's drawing power, he even played the Albert Hall for one night on November 20.

From June onwards, Mayall had been regularly visiting various US and London-based studios to record for his next, strictly solo album, though Mark, Almond and Thompson accompany him on several tracks. The result was 'Empty Rooms', a more refined but less exciting release than 'Turning Point'; it got to 33 in the US and 9 in the UK album charts. After the Christmas break, the band embarked on a 30-day tour of Europe starting January 2, 1970. As bassist Steve Thompson couldn't play because of illness, Alex Dmochowski took over halfway through the tour. A superb bass player, Dmochowski had played with the Aynsley Dunbar Retaliation before joining forces with Mayall. On January 31, Mayall was invited to perform two songs live on German TV for Beat Club; both can be seen on a DVD called 'The Lost Broadcasts' which was released in early 2012.

To inject that certain something to the band, Mayall decided to add Duster Bennett for the coming US-tour. Bennett was well known in Britain as a one-man band and blues performer; he sang, played guitar, bass drum, high-hat and harmonica all at the same time, and had already recorded two albums for Blue Horizon. Rather than being a full-fledged member, Bennett became a featured performer, doing some solo numbers and sitting in on selected songs. Adding Bennett emphasised the blues elements in the band. Duster's show was something to behold, a high-energy, powerhouse of sound, but done with great subtlety. Bennett was charming and charismatic and an outstanding harmonica player. Despite a special agreement between Blue Horizon and Polydor, no album featuring Mayall and Duster together has ever been released. On May 1, Mayall and his band 'featuring Duster Bennett' returned to the UK for a 17-day

British tour, performing 13 concerts. This was followed by another short European tour, including a live TV show in Lyon for French television, three songs of which were released in 2012 on a DVD entitled 'Sweet Little Angel'.

The current ensemble had been together for a year, so it was time for Mayall to move on again. He commented later "It went on longer than it should have done." What had happened was that the acoustic-based chamber blues experiment became a victim of its own success, and the subtle melodic interplay was lost in the noise of the increasingly large venues. Duster Bennett went back to being a solo performer, and then an interesting plan was hatched to play with Georgie Fame, and appear at a Japanese music festival in August, both of which sadly came to nothing, although Mayall did sign up again for the Bath Festival of Blues & Progressive Music. For this one-off show, held over the weekend of 27 and 28 June 1970, Mayall put together an all-star band, managing to recruit Peter Green on lead guitar, Larry Taylor on bass (who had recently quit Canned Heat) and half-brother Rod Mayall on organ. Although the one-off band was meant to be drummerless, the excellent Aynsley Dunbar stepped in at the last minute. Bass-player Taylor was also unable to appear, so Mayall had Ric Grech, the ex-Family and Blind Faith virtuoso, step in. Despite the showery weather, festival organisers were rewarded with a crowd of 150,000, over double the expected 60,000! Mayall and band were to appear on Saturday, but the programme fell well behind schedule, and they ended up having to follow Pink Floyd's late night show at 5:00 am on Sunday, June 28. It was still raining and many fans were asleep in their tents, but the surviving bleary-eyed audience loved it. They delivered a completely unrehearsed jam, blasting their way through an inspired set of six numbers, and putting down a good groove. Mayall was later to comment rather critically: "That band was tremendous, but the situation was so drawn out that I feel it was wasted."

Coming home to Los Angeles, there was panic at Polydor to come up with a new LP, so Mayall got on the phone right away to round up a new band, his first with all American musicians. Mayall was looking to shift gears, wanting to trade Jon Mark's acoustic guitar for an electric sound, but again without a drummer. First hired was bassist Larry Taylor, a seasoned pro already known to Mayall from Canned Heat. Luckily for Mayall, Larry had just quit the band in anger and was therefore 100 % available. One of the best blues bassists in the world, his fluid, swinging lines were an outstanding feature of the Heat's music. Earlier on, Taylor had backed Chuck Berry and also been a member of the Moondogs alongside P.J. Proby in the late 50s. Taylor had played on the sessions that produced the first two Monkees albums, including their early singles hits. He had been with Canned Heat for more than three years. Assisted by advice from his stellar US bass player, Mayall recruited the rest of the musicians. The next was Harvey Mandel, guitarist. Mayall remembers: "I knew his work, especially the Christo Redentor album, and considered him to be a very original sounding player." Like Peter Green, Mandel had come from a Jewish family. He purchased his first guitar aged 16 and began practicing day and night, working out the guitar parts to Ventures records and blues recordings. "In Chicago I used to play every night. Guys like Mike Bloomfield, Paul Butterfield, Barry Goldberg and myself would jam with all the Chicago blues artists," Mandel later recalled. He sat in with Buddy Guy, Otis Rush, B.B. King, Albert King, Howlin' Wolf and Muddy Waters. He soon joined Barry Goldberg and Charlie Musselwhite's bands, but Mandel's playing was anything but conventional, combining distortion with multi-string bending and sustained feedback. Mandel recorded three instrumental LPs as a leader before joining Canned Heat in late July 1969. When Taylor left the Heat in May 70, he took Mandel with him.

Mandel's playing style was entirely different from the likes of Clapton, Green or Taylor, and while hard to describe, it is easy to recognize. His string-bending balanced start-stop phrases with a mellifluous melodic sense. His powerful riffs appealed to Mayall, who was always looking for something fresh. In the studio, Mayall was able to integrate Mandel by balancing the sound levels; in concert, it was far more difficult, as volume and feedback remained essential elements of Mandel's style. Rounding out the band was violin wizard

Don 'Sugarcane' Harris. Harris, an admired pioneer of the electric violin, had enjoyed an amazing career that went back to the beginnings of rock 'n' roll. More recently, in late 1969, he had been hired by Frank Zappa to contribute to his latest solo project 'Hot Rats' His characteristically stinging accompaniment to 'Willie the Pimp' bears witness to his wonderfully gritty sound. Mayall took his new unit into Larrabee studios in Los Angeles to record a new album, aptly named 'USA Union'. It was produced by Mayall and featured ten new songs. The album was released in October 1970 to mixed reviews in the States, but rose to number 22 and stayed for over five months in the US charts; it got to number 30 in Britain. Mayall's music had come a long way since his days with Decca, the dark, lonely, wailing blues sound giving way to more cheerful, up-beat sound.

Now, after nearly a decade on the road, Mayall was trying to take life at a slower pace. At the beginning of 1970, he was near to physical exhaustion. He stopped maintaining a regular music group, choosing to employ suitable musicians whenever he wanted to record or tour. He had planned to keep the 'USA Union' band together only for about nine weeks, but in fact it lasted until the summer of 1971. The all-new American band embarked on a five-week tour of North America on September 11.

In November 1970, Mayall came up with 'Back to the Roots', another ambitious project in the form of a double album. It was recorded in about 10 days in mid-November, with Mayall using his latest band, but augmented by Eric Clapton, Mick Taylor, Johnny Almond, Steve Thompson, Keef Harley, Jerry McGhee and drummer Paul Lagos. Mayall: "The initial idea was to gather together all the major musicians who have played throughout my career, but the immensity of this task overwhelmed putting it fully into effect." Although many other famous ex-Bluesbreakers weren't asked to contribute, Mayall managed to create a unified album using overdubbing techniques. The lavishly presented double LP reached number 31 in the UK (Mayall's last album to chart in Britain until 1993), and climbed to number 52 in the USA, but did not enjoy the success that Polydor and Mayall were hoping for. Mayall later admitted: "I'm not happy with the final mixing and I'm solely to blame. Having convinced all of these people to play, I wanted them all to be heard at once. I went a little overboard, and they sometimes cancelled each other out." In January 1988, Mayall took the master tapes to Pacific Sound in Chatsworth, California, to revive eight of the original tracks for a release entitled 'Archives to Eighties' which came out in April of the same year, with a greatly improved sound.

Putting the idea of 'chamber blues' firmly behind him, Mayall got Paul Lagos to return to the drum seat permanently in January 1971. A protégé of the great jazz drummer Philly Joe Jones, Lagos had played with Shuggie Otis, Leo Kottke and Little Richard, and had been a member of the psychedelic combo Kaleidoscope. The new five-piece undertook a two week tour of Europe in late February/ early March 1971, including making an appearance on Beat Club, German TV's equivalent to Britain's 'Top of the Pops'. The tour of Europe was followed by a tour of Britain, opening at Birmingham Town Hall on March 3. The following month saw the band cross-cross North America again, with prestigious dates at both Fillmore auditoriums. After some gigs in Germany in June, Mayall dissolved the band. Larry Taylor opted to stay on, while Mandel, Harris and Lagos continued to play together in other groups. Mandel went on to further develop the technique of fretboard tapping, and was to have a direct influence on outstanding musicians such as Stanley Jordan, Eddie van Halen and Joe Satriani, among others.

For his next project, Mayall stripped the group down to a trio, utilizing only Larry Taylor and guitarist Jerry McGee. Mayall knew Jerry already from the 'Back to the Roots' sessions, where he came in un-planned, as an old friend. McGee had been a member of the Candy Store Prophets, together with Taylor. They were in Bobby Hart's backing band, and also provided the instrumental support for the early Monkees recordings. McGee played guitar on the first two Monkees' albums. From 1968 to 1972, McGee was a member of the Ventures, a guitar-based combo. He had also played and recorded with Delaney & Bonnie and Nancy Sinatra before joining Mayall. The trio with McGee was more a studio project than a live band. Although they did play local gigs, they also managed to get an album out. Entitled 'Memories', it was recorded in early July at Larrabee in Los Angeles. McGee contributed some great guitar, sitar and steel dobro licks to give the sound an added dimension; it was also Mayall's last release without a drummer. The music is up to Mayall's usual standard, with Taylor and McGhee putting in virtuoso performances. Mayall produces some outstanding wailing harmonica on 'Play the Harp'.

In late August, Mayall was back in the studio again, producing an entire album for blues giant Albert King. Sessions took place at Wolfman Jack Studios on August 28. Mayall took bassist Larry Taylor along, and invited local jazz greats Blue Mitchell (trumpet) Clifford Solomon (saxophone), Ernie Watts (tenor sax) and Ron Selico (drums) to participate. Albert King brought along his cousin Lee on rhythm guitar and another friend, in turn, played the organ. Mayall himself contributed organ, piano, harmonica and 12-string guitar. The legendary blues guitarist and singer employed a unique style. Being left-handed, like Otis Rush, King would play a right-handed guitar upside down, which necessitated pulling down strings for bends and vibrato. King also used unorthodox tuning, and instead of using a pick, he would often push the strings down with his thumb on his Gibson Flying V. The Mayall-produced album was inspired, a three-way fusion of contemporary American city blues (from the Mississippi Delta), Los Angeles jazz, and British blues. The result was a blues record where the jazz aspect predominates. Mayall deliberately chose different keys to the ones King usually used. "By changing keys it makes you think differently", Mayall explained. "It kept him from clichés and he came out with some wonderful stuff." All tunes were King-Mayall collaborations, as Mayall remembers: "He'd go out for coffee and I'd work up the tune. By the time he came back, we'd have it all ready for him. He'd hear it and play along with it à la jam session, then he'd come up with some words and that would be it." Sadly, the tapes to this amazing record remained in the Stax vaults for 15 years before Fantasy records released them in late 1986 as 'The Lost Session". Mayall: "The intent was to make it different from the Stax sound. I accomplished that but Stax didn't release it."

Albert King appeared with Mayall again in the summer of 1982 for the Blues Alive concert, together with Buddy Guy, Junior Wells, Etta James and Mick Taylor. Producing this record marked a turning point in Mayall's career. It was the first time he had played with top jazz musicians such as Blue Mitchell and Clifford Solomon, and he invited them to join his next band. The agreed, as they had just quit the Ray Charles' Orchestra, together with Ron Selico.

Five days after the sessions with Albert King, Mayall found himself producing an album for James 'Shaky Jake' Harris, another black blues singer and harmonica player, this time on Crusade, a Polydor subsidiary. The record was interestingly entitled 'The Devil's Harmonica'. Harris had been playing harp since the age of five, and in the late 50s and early 60s, performed regularly in Chicago clubs with his nephew, the legendary Chicago guitarist Magic Sam. In 1962, he was part of the first American Folk Blues Festival to tour Europe. Recordings took place on September 2 at Larrabee studios. Freddy Robinson, also ex-Ray Charles, contributed guitar, while Mayall had Ron Selico alternate with Phil Parker on drums; Larry Taylor played bass, and Mayall added piano, rhythm and slide guitar to seven of the ten tracks. Interestingly, Mayall had hired Elliott Ingber to contribute guitar parts instead of McGee; the notable session man had recorded with Frank Zappa, Canned Heat and Captain Beefheart. In the latter's Magic Band his playing style interestingly earned him the nickname 'Winged Eel Fingerling'! 'The Devil's Harmonica' was a fine blues album without gimmicks or excessive production values, and still sounds contemporary. Unlike Chess records' efforts to modernise blues heroes Muddy Waters and Howlin' Wolf's sound, Mayall's sensitive production does not sacrifice Harris' identity. What a pity this rare and fascinating LP has never been released on CD! Mayall never again produced for the Crusade label.

The band that Mayall had put together for the Albert King and 'Shaky Jake' sessions was too good to let go, but Mayall also had European tour commitments looming. He therefore planned to return to LA to record a jazz-blues fusion project with the same soulful black musicians who had made such outstanding contributions to

❻ *The Bluesbreakers back together in 1982 with Mick Taylor, John McVie, Colin Allen and Mayall. What a shame they never made any studio recordings!*

❼ *The "Turning Point" chamber blues line-up in 1970 live in concert: Johnny Almond, Alex Dmochowski, Jon Mark and Mayall.*

❽ *Drums were back in 1971 with Paul Lagos in the "USA Union" band, featuring Larry Taylor, Harvey Mandel, Don "Sugarcane" Harris and Mayall.*

❾ *The famous blues summit in San Francisco, February 1–4, 1968
with Jimi Hendrix, Albert King and Mayall.*

🔟 *Mayall with his modified teardrop Baldwin/Burns guitar in 1970.*

JOHN MAYAL

12 new tracks by one of to

Produced by John Porter

AND THE BLUESBREAKERS
BLUES FOR THE LOST DAYS
y's most influential blues artists

-D.
dditional item).

SILVERT
RECORD

© 1997 Silvertone Record

❶ *A rare Silvertone advert from 1997.*

⓬ *Long-time buddies: Mayall with the legendary Buddy Guy backstage around 1992.*

his two most recent projects as producer. Also, the up-coming tour of Europe was scheduled to promote 'Memories', Mayall's forthcoming album, which was recorded with a three-piece. Obviously, it wouldn't make sense to promote the album with an entirely different band, so the fusion idea would have to wait until Mayall was back from Europe.

As sometimes happens in business, people get cold feet at the last minute and quit, which is precisely what guitarist Jerry McGee did. Again, Mayall had to look for another at short notice; the first concert was scheduled for September 12. Mayall received a recommendation from Chas Chandler for a Scottish guitarist named Jimmy McCulloch. McCulloch had been playing in bands since the age of 15, and when he joined Mayall, he was still only 18. Mayall hired him before hearing him: "I was told he was a guitarist who was technically good and not just a straightforward guitarist." Later, Mayall was all enthusiasm: "Jimmy is beautiful. He's eighteen... and plays fantastic guitar." On bass was Larry Taylor, and Mayall added drummer Keef Hartley, who was out of a job at the time. "We didn't even have a rehearsal before we started in Germany. It was just a case of plug in, see what happens", explained Mayall. After the tour, the musicians all went their separate ways.

The boyish McCulloch never appears on any Mayall record, with the exception of 'Hear Me Calling You', a slow blues that Mayall released 41 years later on 'Historic Live Shows, Vol. 1', but unfortunately it doesn't live up to McCulloch's huge talent. He went on to play with Stone The Crows, where he found himself with ex-Mayall stable mates Steve Thompson and Colin Allen. We went on to play with John Entwistle, Paul McCartney and the Small Faces, but on September 27, 1979, his life came to tragic end, overdosing on morphine and alcohol at his London flat; he was only 26.

In October 1971, Polydor released a first Mayall best-of album for the European market entitled 'Beyond the Turning Point'. This low budget sampler contained nine tracks from the first three Polydor albums and is one of the very few compiled by Mayall himself, who also designed the cover.

CHAPTER 7

Moving On

The jazz-blues bands, 1971–74

The European tour over, Mayall returned to LA in early October to fulfil his intention to team up again with Freddy Robinson, Blue Mitchell and Clifford Solomon. His next musical foray was equally as dramatic as 'The Turning Point' but took him towards a fusion of jazz and blues. Retaining only Larry Taylor from the recent European tour, Mayall returned to the musicians he had played with on the solo LPs he had produced for Albert King and 'Shaky Jake' Harris earlier in the year. Instead of recruiting younger musicians and having to nurture them, Mayall now surrounded himself with mature jazz soloists capable of working with taste and invention from the barest of frameworks. Mayall was at the height of his commercial and artistic fame, and playing the biggest venues of his career. He could afford to pick and choose from the very best, some of whom were even slightly older than himself! Mayall was paying tribute to the many jazz and swing records he had grown up with. Bands such as Chicago and Blood, Sweat and Tears showed that jazz-rock was emerging in a big way, so it seemed natural to move towards a fusion of jazz and blues, especially as the blues have always been the mother of jazz. So Mayall's new band produced blues-based jazz, and its jazz-trained musicians played in a style known as 'hard bop' (today it's called 'acid jazz').

Guitarist Freddy Robinson and trumpeter Blue Mitchell became the cornerstones, staying from October 1971 to December 1973. On saxophone there were Clifford Solomon, Fred Clark and Red Holloway; on bass Larry Taylor, Putter Smith (for the March 1972 Australian tour only) and Victor Gaskin, while the skilful Ron Selico on drums completed the picture.

Freddy Robinson was self-taught; both his father and grandmother were blues lovers. While still in his teens, he joined Little Walter's combo, appearing on several historic Chess recordings. He went on to work with Jimmy Rogers, Junior Wells, Earl Gaines, Willie Dixon and Howlin' Wolf, playing lead on the latter's legendary 1960 Chess date that produced 'Spoonful', 'Wang Dang Doodle' and 'Back Door Man'. After moving to Los Angeles in 1968, he worked with the Ray Charles' Orchestra, and soon built up a reputation as an ace L.A. session man. With long time cohort Monk Higgins in charge, Robinson tasted chart success in 1970 with a superb instrumental entitled 'Black Fox'. During the early '70s, he recorded several solo albums for Enterprise, the Stax subsidiary, boldly blending blues, jazz and soul into his own distinctive sound. Unlike all previous guitarists in Mayall's band, Robinson played in a much jazzier style, using thicker strings without bending them a lot. His light-fingered fretwork had a warm, bluesy tone that was instantly recognizable. His instrument of choice was a 1961 Gibson hollow body Barney Kessel custom, played hitched up under his chin using a short strap. Besides contributing outstanding guitar, Robinson always sang one or two blues numbers in his wonderfully warm, soulful voice.

Blue Mitchell rose to prominence as a member of the Horace Silver Quintet in the early sixties. Originally discovered by Cannonball Adderley, Blue soon earned respect as a brilliant trumpet player. He joined the Horace Silver Quintet in 1958 and stayed for seven years. He recorded for Blue Note and produced infectious jazz that was shot through with funk, soul and swing. During the '60s, Mitchell played with Jimmy Smith, Bobby Timmons, Jackie McLean, Les McCann, Elvin Jones, Philly Joe Jones, Sonny Stitt, Stanley Turrentine, Richard Holmes, Yusef Lateef, Wynton Kelly, Johnny Griffin, Jimmy McGriff and Grant Green. Aware that opportunities for playing straight-ahead jazz were dwindling, Mitchell became a prolific session man for pop and soul in the late '60s, before deciding to tour with the Ray Charles' Orchestra from 1969–1971. In 1971, he not only joined Mayall's new band, but also began recording with Mainstream Records under his own name. He invited Mayall to guest on his debut album 'Blues' Blues', Mayall contributing harmonica to three tracks. On joining Mayall's band, Mitchell commented: "It was too good a gig to miss. The money's great. The atmosphere's beautiful. Such a relaxing gig." In Mayall's band, Blue Mitchell soon stood out for his clear, bluesy trumpet, swinging tone, and lyrical, melodic sound. Clifford Solomon brought the saxophone back to Mayall's sound. Formerly with Lionel Hampton, the jazz veteran had played tenor and alto with Ike and Tina Turner, Clifford Brown, Quincy Jones, Wes Montgomery, Art Farmer, Jimmy Witherspoon, Johnny Otis and Ray Charles. Drummer Ron Selico, who joined for a short stint a little later than the others, had played with James Brown, Shuggie Otis and The Mothers of Invention. Keef Hartley, the ex-Bluesbreakers stalwart and friend of Mayall's, replaced him.

The new group started touring the United States in October 1971, performing until the end of the year. None of Mayall's jazz-blues bands played old Bluesbreakers or 'Turning Point' songs, and neither did they do jazz standards (with the exception of Horace Silver's wonderful 'Filthy McNasty'!). Instead, they concentrated exclusively on improvised tunes, which meant they played a different show every night. Mayall: "Each number is completely improvised. I just go on stage knowing that everybody up there can play anything, so all I do is come up with the first chorus and a theme. Everybody listens and plays from that, checking it out, adding what they feel, and take it how they hear it on the second chorus, and it's often something that's a surprise to me. So I respond to that, and everybody responds to each other, and it can go anywhere!"

While on tour, the group made some live recordings in Boston (November 18) and at Hunter College New York (December 3 and 4). Like 'The Turning Point', Mayall was keen on using the live setting to capture the group's spontaneity. The resulting album, 'Jazz Blues Fusion', was spectacular and more jazz-oriented than anything Mayall had ever done, with free flowing, wailing solos over long, improvised accompaniments. Mayall had reinvented himself; the seasoned musicians he had assembled meshed together brilliantly. His new ensemble was free from any self-imposed, slavish devotion to traditional blues structures. The results created from Mitchell's jazz phrasing and Robinson's bluesy jazz guitar were simply breathtaking. Again, Eddie Kramer masterminded the live recordings, and Mayall produced them, including the sleeve artwork. 'Jazz Blues Fusion' was released to glowing reviews in April 1972 in the US and May in Britain, and turned out to be Mayall's last big hit, spending 18 weeks in the Billboard album charts.

The versatile Ron Selico left at the end of December 1971 to work with soul singer Eric Mercury, so Mayall asked ex-Bluesbreaker and good friend Keef Hartley to stand in during the tour of Australia in March 1972. At this point, Taylor also dropped out. Mayall commented: "Larry got sick at the end of February and has gone into retirement for two years to study string bass, something he's wanted to do for a long time. He's been on the road for 15 years and really needs the rest." To cover bass duties, Mayall got hold of Putter Smith, a friend of Larry's, who had played with Mose Allison and Mason Williams. The tour was a huge success, and from now on, Australia and New Zealand became regular destinations. Putter Smith was then replaced by Victor Gaskin, a New Yorker who had worked with Duke Ellington, Les McCann, Cannonball Adderley, Thelonius Monk, the Jazz Crusaders, Harold Rand, Monty Alexander, Dexter Gordon and Chico Hamilton. Gaskin also played bass guitar, but preferred double bass, possessing a special instrument with a peculiar shape that had been built in Canada during World War II. With new member Gaskin on board, Mayall's band toured Britain and Europe in April and May 1972. Of his singing abilities, Mayall felt moved to comment 28 years later in the liner notes to 'Rock the Blues Tonight': "I can't say I'm quite so thrilled with my vocal contributions which are, in most cases, excruciating and erratic to say the least. I can look back on those years now and realize I had much to learn about singing in live concert environments. Most times I led the band into uncharted ground and would improvise entire shows."

Back in the States, Mayall set up a gig at Los Angeles' Whiskey A Go Go for Monday, July 10, in order to record another live album. For this one-off gig, Mayall added Larry Taylor (he wanted to combine electric bass with Gaskin's acoustic), plus a trio of veteran jazz saxophone players including Ernie Watts, Charles Owens and Fred Jackson. The resulting album entitled 'Moving On' was even better than its predecessor, as more thought had gone into composition and structure. Mayall wrote all nine tracks, but the live recordings unfortunately turned out to be unusable due to sound interference, and the band had to do them all again in the studio. 'Moving On' was in fact a fake live album; Mayall cleverly managed to integrate the live atmosphere by lifting the crowd noise and overdubbing it onto the beginning and ending of each track. Mayall produced 'Moving On' and also provided the artwork. Released in December 1972 in the USA and January 1973 in Britain, it reached number 116 in the US charts. Although reviews were mostly good, it took until 2009 before this outstanding LP was available in digital format.

Saxophonist Clifford Solomon left to work with Johnny Otis in the summer of 1972, and was replaced by the lesser known tenor player Fred Clark, who came from a more R&B-oriented background, and had played with Sonny Thompson in the '50s. After this, he returned to R&B to play with Pee Wee Crayton and others. At about the same time, guitarist Freddy Robinson was invited to record with his mentor, Monk Higgins. The album was entitled 'Little Mama', a funky record if ever there was one. Robinson can be heard putting distinctly Mayall-inspired harmonica licks down on three tracks.

For 1973, Mayall had a new saxophone player in mind to complete his jazz-blues line-up. The man he was hoping to get on board was Red Holloway, who had played with the best in the business. As Jimmy Witherspoon once put it, "Red's the best damn horn. No one can touch those blues solos." Holloway had served as bandmaster in army bands, and from 1963 to 1966, he was in Brother Jack McDuff's band, which also featured the young George Benson on guitar. Between 1968 and 1982, Red worked as musical director, talent coordinator and house bandleader for the exquisite Parisian Room in Los Angeles, where some of the greatest artists in jazz regularly appeared. Holloway was swiftly recruited.

With Red Holloway now on board, Mayall decided to make his next album project a studio affair. 'Ten Years Are Gone' celebrated his tenth anniversary as bandleader. Blue Mitchell, Red Holloway, Freddy Robinson, Victor Gaskin and Keef Hartley recorded nine tracks at Los Angeles' Sunset Sound Studio between March and early May 1973. In addition, Mayall recalled Sugarcane Harris to guest on it. Also, Mayall handed production duties to Don Nix, who has since become a long-term Mayall collaborator. Nix was a singer, songwriter and author of the blues classic 'Going Down'. One of the lesser known figures in southern rock and soul, he had produced Freddie King, Albert King, Delaney & Bonnie and Jeff Beck. The resulting studio album included some fine tunes like 'Ten Years Are Gone', 'Driving Till the Break of Day', 'Drifting' and 'California Campground', while others were less impressive. Compared to 'Jazz Blues Fusion' and 'Moving On', this record was more sophisticated, incorporating elements of blues, jazz, gospel and rock. Freddy Robinson contributed the song 'Undecided', which he also sang; it was the first time someone other than Mayall had sung since the days with Peter Green.

For incomprehensible reasons, Mayall, Nix or Polydor decided to include four additional, rather tedious live recordings to make 'Ten Years Are Gone' a double LP. It was released in October in the USA and November in Great Britain, reaching number 157 in the US album charts. After having finished the new album, the band toured heavily throughout 1973; US dates included the Newport Jazz Festival as well as the Philharmonic Hall and Stony Brook University in New York City.

In 1973, Mayall was also invited to guest with veteran acoustic folk blues duo Sonny Terry and Brownie McGhee for their album 'Sonny & Brownie' on A&M. Sugarcane Harris, Jerry McGhee (no relation), and John Hammond also participated; sessions were held at Hollywood's Paramount Recording Studios. Mayall had already met Brownie McGhee back in 1956 at a session in Manchester when he sat in; this was probably the first American blues musician Mayall had ever met. Mayall contributed harmonica, guitar and piano to four tracks, and even sang a few choruses on the aptly titled 'White Boy Lost in the Blues'.

Shortly before the end of 1973, Mayall, who had turned 40 in November, decided to split up the group, commenting: "That band was good and easy to work with; it was fresh and challenging every night. Now, something like that could go on forever, but it's not really progress. So, time for a change." Mayall retained only Holloway on horns and flute for 1974. The New Year saw Mayall return to the electric, funky, blues-rock sound of old. As he was now rather out of touch with emerging musicians in the U.K., he decided to put together another all-American band. One of the first people he had in mind was guitarist Jesse Ed Davis, a full blooded Kiowa Indian from Oklahoma, who had played with Taj Mahal and Clapton and already recorded three solo albums. Mayall explained: "Jesse Ed showed up to join the band, rehearsed one afternoon, took a cash advance and never showed up again. He was a junkie, needing money." That was the end of that. However, after auditioning was over, it was clear that Mayall's new outfit had an interesting combination of instruments, with twin lead guitars, saxophone, bass and drums: "an entirely virgin set of Mayall sounds", as Mayall himself explained. After the jazz excursions, it was a return to straighter, funkier blues. The three other newcomers to Mayall's band in 1974 were guitarists Hi Tide Harris and Randy Resnick, and drummer Soko Richardson.

Hi Tide Harris could sing and play lead guitar and was already an established bluesman in the San Francisco area when he joined. During his lifetime, he played and recorded with soul singer Johnny Taylor, Lowell Fulsom, Jimmy McCracklin, Big Mama Thornton, Roger Collins, Bob Geddins, Shakey Jake Harris and Charlie Musselwhite. Contacted through Mayall associate Lee King (cousin of Albert and rhythm guitarist on Mayall's Albert King solo project), Hi Tide turned up and knocked Mayall out with his gritty style. At the time, he had just recorded a solo project entitled 'Watergate Blues'. Randy Resnick was the other man on lead. The pale, bearded guitarist had been playing for some ten years, and came from the Pure Food and Drug Act, where he played with former Mayall sidemen Sugarcane Harris, Harvey Mandel and Paul Lagos. His technique was bold, and there were things he did with his six stings and a pick that were totally fresh. The adventurous guitar prodigy had already pioneered fret board tapping as a playing technique in the 1970's, influencing Harvey Mandel. On live shows with Mayall, Randy had a special 'showcase' number to show off his extraordinary guitar skills. The interweaving of Harris and Resnick's guitars couldn't have been more apposite; it was immediately clear that their interplay would be the motor in the band. Mayall: "Both brought something different to the music. Hi Tide held down all the traditional blues licks, while Randy was the man with a brilliant technique and style. It worked very well for us." This was the first time Mayall had had a band with two lead-guitarists, but certainly not the last. As for the new drummer, Soko Richardson was a big, burly African-American percussionist who always wore a turban, and had been playing in various bands since he was nine years old. More recently, he had drummed for Ike and Tina Turner for ten years, but had also played with Terry Reid, Earl Hooker, Albert King and Bobby Womack, before former Mayall saxophonist Clifford Solomon recommended Soko to John. Bass player Larry Taylor returned to the Mayall ranks after a two-year hiatus, during which he had made a serious study of the acoustic (upright) or double bass. It brought a new amplitude to his playing, also because he now preferred to play on a Fender fretless, so his sound had also changed. A phone call from John made the right impression, and he was waiting at Mayall's place in no time, claiming: "Playing in a band like John's is the greatest thing in the world because it's musical freedom". Another plus was that, as the new band members all lived in close proximity to one other, they were able to rehearse quite a lot before touring and recording.

During March and April 1974, Mayall took his new sextet to the Angel City Sound Studios in Los Angeles to record his next album, 'The Latest Edition'. It also marked the end of Mayall's five-year association with Polydor. Musically, it was a fresh, new approach, breaking away from jazz-blues to a funkier, blues-rock style. There were even two producers, the more famous of which was Tom Wilson, noted for his work with Bob Dylan, Frank Zappa & the Mothers of Invention, Simon & Garfunkel and John Coltrane. Using a lot of vocal overdubs, Wilson produced a smooth album without sounding sugary or slick. 'The Latest Edition' still sounds very spontaneous. Mayall: "I've got a lot of affection for 'The Latest Edition'. The spirit of the performances and the songs were excellent. It remains among my favourites." In Europe, they released 'Gasoline Blues' (dedicated to the energy crisis) as a single, coupled with a number that sadly didn't make it onto the album entitled 'Brand New Band', a stand-out track with a lot of great solos. It seems likely that another fine Mayall tune was cut during these sessions entitled 'Al Goldstein Blues' (Goldstein was the founder of a US porn magazine), and was released later as the B side of 'Step in the Sun', a single released the following year. 'The Latest Edition' was released in September in the US and in December in Britain.

With recording now over, Mayall took his new band on the road for a British and European tour, starting in late April. On July 19, 1974, back in California, Mayall jammed with Eric Clapton and his band at their concert at the Long Beach Arena. This was the last time they were to play together until Mayall's 70th birthday concert on July 19, 2003. Tours of Japan, China, Australia and New Zealand followed in early October; interestingly, no US gigs were planned.

Towards the end of 1974, Mayall decided to call it a day. He discharged Hi Tide Harris and Randy Resnick, his two guitarists, as well as Red Holloway, retaining only his rhythm section. After five years and nine albums, Mayall's recording contract with Polydor had also expired. During his time with Polydor, Mayall had recorded mainly original songs, and avoided covers. Of all 102 tracks released on Polydor, Mayall wrote 94 of them. On only eight tracks are band members credited as co-writers or writers. Mayall's Polydor years were commercially his most successful, so he didn't have any trouble finding another recording contract, and signed for ABC Records shortly afterwards. Time moves inexorable on, and Mayall was resolved to move with it.

CHAPTER 8

Evolution and Neglect

The ABC and DJM years, 1975–81

Mayall was now integrating not only jazz and funk elements into his music, but also rock 'n' roll and country influences as well; he even went so far as to recruit female lead and backing singers, absolutely unique when you consider the stripped-down, macho, electric blues-rock of the Bluesbreakers tradition. The years 1975 to 1981 are generally considered to be the low point in Mayall's career, a conclusion that, at the very least, is pretty wide of the mark. Although it's true that several albums from this period failed to chart, much of Mayall's music from the late '70s retains its fascination, thanks to the amazing standard of the musicians he was able to find and hire. Much of Mayall's success so far had been based on the element of surprise, as Mayall himself was well aware of: "Everybody accepts that element in my musical set up. You could say they expect the unexpected. It allows me a tremendous amount of freedom, and the trust that audiences all over the world have in me is really astounding." Mayall's new band in 1975 was a seven-piece, and signalled another dramatic evolution in sound. The most striking feature was the decision to include female vocalist Dee McKinnie. For the first time, Mayall's distinctive voice had the benefit of female accompaniment. On lead guitar now was Rick Vito, who could also sing, plus Jay Spell on keyboards. Mayall retained Larry Taylor on bass, Soko Richardson on drums, while Sugarcane Harris returned to fill out the sound, despite Taylor's misgivings. Spell hailed from Memphis, and had played with Tower Of Power, Don Nix, Eddie Floyd and Eric Mercury before joining Mayall. Dee McKinnie sang in Spell's band, and with Mayall, she mostly sang duets with John in her sweet, bluesy voice. Vito had played and recorded with Matrix, The Wright Brothers, Troy Newman, Delaney & Bonnie, Dobie Gray, Little Richard, John Prine, Todd Rundgren and Bobby Whitlock. Larry Taylor recommended Vito to Mayall. Vito recalls: "I went to see the original Fleetwood Mac with Peter Green at the Electric Factory in Philadelphia at the end of December 1968, and forty years later, I'm still in awe of his performance that night. Peter was a master of taste and tone, sang great songs amazingly well, and was obviously the guiding force behind his band. He was just about everything I wanted to be as a musician. I'm still working on it!" Vito's choice was proof of Mayall's reputation as an outstanding talent-spotter; the guitarist played wonderfully fluent, country-tinged blues, and was the perfect choice.

Mayall was now with ABC Records, who issued six LPs during his turbulent three-year tenure with the label. Although ABC had many good blues musicians under contract, they never really promoted Mayall enough, and became increasingly disinterested in his productions. Mayall remembers: "They released the six albums sort of privately, never really promoting them. They weren't in the stores for more than a couple of minutes. Throughout all this I was still making a pretty good living on the live circuit. Albums to my mind were not a career tool, but represented whatever band I had at that time." Mayall's debut album with ABC was called 'New Year, New Band, New Company', an apt title. The main difference came from the spark provided by Dee McKinnie, whose vocals lifted Mayall's performance to a new level. Spell on piano and clavinet provided neat counterpoint to Vito's spirited, flowing guitar runs. As usual, the gatefold cover was designed by Mayall, and included the lyrics of all ten songs. Released March 1975, it made the Billboard charts at number 140, but was Mayall's last album to chart for many years. McKinnie wasn't too well received by Mayall fans, who declared that his work had become 'soft' and lost its 'edge'. ABC issued 'Step in the Sun' as a single, taken from the album, and coupled it with 'Al Goldstein Blues', a very rare track, probably recorded in spring 1974 with Polydor. Unfortunately, this amazing song has never been re-

released, although it would have made a fantastic bonus track for the digital release of 'New Year, New Band, New Company' in 1993.

The new band started gigging in the US in early 1975. For a few concerts, guitarist Mick Radford replaced Rick Vito; Radford had played with Chuck Berry, Albert Collins, Maria Muldaur and Ocean, and fitted in very well. In late summer of 1975, the band moved to New Orleans to record their next LP. 'Notice to Appear' traded the country feel of 'New Year, New Band, New Company' for sophisticated New Orleans funk. This sudden departure had been triggered by Mayall's management and ABC records, who advised Mayall to collaborate with a producer. Their inspired choice, R&B legend Allen Toussaint, had a decided impact on Mayall's trademark sound. Toussaint was one of the architects of New Orleans soul-funk, and renowned as a producer, songwriter, pianist and singer. He wrote many hits in the 60s, and in the following years, the likes of Dr. John, Z.Z. Hill, James Cotton, Albert King, Etta James, Paul McCartney, Paul Simon, Robert Palmer, Patti Labelle and Frankie Miller travelled to New Orleans to take advantage of his exceptional skills as producer. To record under Toussaint's expert supervision, however, the producer usually transposed his guests' talents into a different style, often writing the majority of the songs himself. While Mayall was initially thrilled by the prospect of collaborating with Toussaint, the terms of the arrangement were never clearly defined. With the best of intentions, Mayall installed his band at Sea-Saint Studios. Unfortunately, the creative partnership failed to materialize. For the first time in his career, the bandleader was relegated to just vocal duties. On 'Notice to Appear', Toussaint contributed three-quarters of all songs. "I was exported to New Orleans with the band," Mayall recalls. "It was a very laborious and unusual thing for me to be involved in. On paper, the idea sounded fine. But I tend to work very quickly in the studio; the band knows what to do and we get it done. Allen's way of working was very different. We would be waiting for hours, and sometimes days, for him to come downstairs and show his presence. Then he would just sweep in with these wonderful ideas. His instructions were very specific; you do this, you do that, play it note for note. We were really just pawns in this whole thing. It was frustrating. My guys were questioning me as to why I had stranded them in New Orleans. They kept looking at me wondering when they would be going to work. We were there way too long, and had to bail out. We had concerts lined up. After we left, Allen continued working on the album with his own musicians. Dee and I were later brought back to do the singing." Toussaint rallied to pull the album together in Mayall's absence. Drawing on the skills of his vaunted regulars, including the celebrated pianist and organ player James Booker, tracks such as 'Hale to the Man Who Lives Alone' and 'Lil Boogie in the Afternoon' were delightful swamp funk. 'Notice to Appear' turned out to be a good album, but Mayall admits: "It was really an Allen Toussaint album. Nonetheless, I was and remain a big Toussaint fan, but it was one of those things... I wish I had understood what was expected of me and the band before we started." 'Notice to Appear' was the first album without a picture of Mayall on the front, wasn't well received by fans, and failed to chart.

After having toured the States and recorded two albums with his new band, Mayall took them on a tour of Europe in the autumn of 1975. As it was not possible to take Jay Spell, Ronnie Barron replaced him. Another excellent find, actor, soul singer and keyboard player Barron had played with New Orleans' best such as Smiley Lewis and Sugar Boy Crawford before teaming up with friend Mac Rebenack (Dr. John). Together they came up with the idea of blending cajun, voodoo and New Orleans blues, together with the recent psychedelic sounds, and became Dr. John and the Night Trippers! Barron was even said to have contributed vocals to 'Sweet Virginia' for the Rolling Stones in 1971. During their month-long European tour, the band played mainly to full houses, and even found time to perform TV recordings for the BBC's 'Old Grey Whistle Test' on October 21. These sessions were released in 2007 on the CD 'Live at the BBC'. When the tour was over, Spell replaced Barron, who went on to have a solo career.

In May 1976, Mayall took his band into the studio to record tracks for 'A Banquet in Blues', his next album, together with many musicians hired specially for it. These not only included ex-Mayall men such as John McVie, Blue Mitchell, Red Holloway, Jon Mark, Johnny

Almond, Alex Dmochowski, Sugarcane Harris and Ronnie Barron, but also many LA jazz luminaries such as Larry Gales on bass, Roy McCurdy on drums, Buck Clarke on percussion, Benny Powell on trombone, and Novi Novag on viola. "People were always putting proposals forward for me to do reunion albums with the people I had played with" Mayall recalls. "The LP 'A Banquet in Blues' was my shot to pick all my favourite people and, track for track, make a varied album, not just in songs and tempo, but personnel as well." Produced by Mayall, it turned out to be a mixed bag with three outstanding songs: 'You Can't Put Me Down', 'Table Top Girl' and the atmospheric 'Lady'. 'Fantasyland' clocked in at 14 minutes and was by any standards overindulgent, and the disco backbeat on 'Seven Days Too Long' was jarring, to say the least! What was bluesman Mayall up to? Released in August 1976 with artwork by Mayall, it was not well received by critics and blues fans and did not chart on either side of the Atlantic.

Mayall was then invited to guest on a recording by actor Keith Carradine, who had just won an Oscar for his song 'I'm Easy', a feature of Robert Altman's film 'Nashville' the previous year. Alongside studio instrumentalists Lee Ritenour, Larry Carlton and Earl Palmer, Mayall played harmonica and e-piano on the funky shuffle 'Been Gone So Long'.

In spring 1976, Roy McCurdy replaced Richardson, although the latter would return for another stint with Mayall at the beginning of 1977. McCurdy will always be best known for his important contributions to Cannonball Adderley's Quintet from 1965 to 1975, but he had also gained a reputation playing with the Jazztet (1961–1962), Bobby Timmons, Sonny Rollins (1963–1964) and Art Farmer. Clearly, Mayall had the knack of picking musicians of the front rank. The 6-piece group with McCurdy started a US-tour to support 'A Banquet in Blues', but never played outside the United States. Around September 1976, Mayall decided to break up the band, retaining only bass player Larry Taylor and Jay Spell on keyboards.

Mayall's next venture was a big band. He gathered together ten musicians for a US tour starting in October. With bass and keyboards covered, Red Holloway was back on tenor sax, while the new guitarist was Gary Rowles, who had played with Love, Cottonwood, Flo & Eddie, Richard Torrance and Leon Russell. Frank Wilson was brought in drums, supported by percussionist Warren Bryant. Ann Patterson contributed tenor and alto saxes and oboe. Mayall employed two ladies on backing vocals, Pepper Watkins, who had sung with Tower Of Power, and Patty Smith (not the beat poet pioneer), who had sung with Barry Goldberg and the Blue Oyster Cult. Mayall recorded the big band at the Roxy in Los Angeles on November 24, and for this, he decided to add four more horns to augment the sound, with Red Holloway conducting. The resulting live album entitled 'Lots of People' was a far better effort than Mayall's previous ABC albums. The live set kicked off with the superb 'Changes in the Wind', followed by 'Burning Down', 'A Helping Hand', the breathtaking 'I Got to Get Down with You', and the fast driving 'He's A Travelling Man'. The remaining three songs were culled from previous Polydor albums, and the indestructible 'Room to Move' was back in the set. Unfortunately, 'Lots of People', released April 1977, did not chart, but remains a powerful musical statement, and is very collectable. At the end of November 1976, Mayall broke up the band, saying: "I wasn't satisfied with the horn section and wanted to go back to the drawing board. I missed the days of the quartet." So his next group was a straight four-piece, as in the days of the Bluesbreakers. In February 1977, Mayall lured back bassist Steve Thompson and drummer Soko Richardson, but the new guitarist was James Quill Smith, who had worked with Dr. John and Three Dog Night, and had impressed Mayall from the first. Augmented by Jody Linscott on percussion, Mayall took his new unit to Los Angeles' ABC studios in March 1977 to record an album entitled 'A Hard Core Package'. Probably Mayall's strongest effort to date for ABC, it sounded like the old Bluesbreakers, and was released in August 1977, but unfortunately failed to chart. The album title was an allusion to Mayall's interest in collecting early pornography and erotica. When Mayall's father died in 1971, he inherited a huge collection of post cards, photographs, books and limericks dating back to Victorian times. Mayall became a serious collector and later contributed to several famous erotic magazines.

From April to June 1977, the new quartet went on a three-month European tour, followed by dates in the summer in the US, including a gig at The Bottom Line in New York on July 11, which was broadcast live on KBFH radio. Around this time, Mayall was invited to guest on 'Born Loose', a number on Rod Stewart's new LP 'Foot Loose & Fancy Free', to which he added some fine accompaniment on harp.

1978 started with an extensive US tour. Impressed by the success of his new quartet, Mayall wanted to make a live recording of the band. 'The Last of the British Blues', the result, is an excellent, gritty-sounding disc, but was unfortunately his last for ABC. Recordings took place during spring 1978, collecting live performances in Baltimore, Cincinnati and New York. Seven female backing vocalists, including Pepper Watkins, were later overdubbed in the studio. 'Tucson Lady', the opener, was an absolute highlight, and Mayall provided the cover artwork again. Not long after the release of 'The Last of the British Blues', ABC was sold to MCA, who soon discontinued producing it. The demise left Mayall without a recording contract, but he found a new home on the lesser-known DJM label a few months afterwards.

The most significant event of 1978 took place over the Labour Day weekend, when, together with guitarist James Quill Smith, he was invited to guest with Harvey Mandel, due to play at a big outdoor festival at Stone Lake, Wisconsin. Harvey had an attractive lady singer in his band named Maggie Parker, and it was love at first sight. Mayall: "We met there on stage and we've been together ever since. She hit me on the head with her tambourine to show her excitement!" Maggie Parker and Mayall were later to marry on January 8, 1980 in England.

The late 70s was a tough time for blues musicians. Disco was at its height, and blues music was out of favour; 'Saturday Night Fever' dominated the cinemas. As Mayall put it: "The disco boom blew it all away, people overlooked the blues." In addition, the recession had hit the record industry hard, and artists of the calibre of Etta James, Taj Mahal and Canned Heat were suddenly without record contracts. Mayall seemed to have worn out his fan base with his restless experimentation in personnel and sound. He was lucky to find support in British music magnate Dick James, who had amassed a fortune with his music publishing deals with The Beatles and Elton John. James had recently formed DJM Records, a small but independent British label, which seemed perfect for Mayall. Having signed up Mayall, DJM immediately sent him into the studio to record a new album in January the following year. Unfortunately, DJM management had specific ideas about it. Mayall remembers wistfully: "In order to get the deal, DJM required that we hire a big name producer. So, vast sums of money were misspent on doing that. It was just absolutely crazy. There were all of these top-of-the-line studio musicians from New York and California waiting around as the budget just kept climbing and climbing. In the midst of it all, I didn't even get to play any instruments on it. I just did my vocals. It was dreadful, an expensive disaster. I don't know if I alone was responsible, but the label went bankrupt fairly soon after." The album in question was the aptly named 'Bottom Line', recorded January 1979 in unknown studios in New York (tracks 1 to 6), and Los Angeles (tracks 7 and 8). Former Bob Dylan producer Bob Johnston handled production, and forty-one musicians were involved, none of them members of Mayall's band! Mayall commented: "Like Allen Toussaint, Bob Johnson wasn't good for me. Both were more interested in their own credits than in my music, and wanted to push through their own musical ideas." Despite the great musicians, the over-slick production came in for criticism, while loyal fans considered it an embarrassment. The title track, co-written by Leon Pendarvis and Mayall, is an electrifying, funky tune, but the other seven songs are all pretty lacklustre. 'Bottom Line' was released in May 1979.

By the beginning of 1979, Mayall had his next band together, this time an eight-piece with two female singers, a keyboardist, a sax-player, bass and drums, plus guitarist James Quill Smith from his last unit. The singers were Kathryn Fields and Maggie Parker, on keyboards was Chris 'Hambone' Cameron and on saxophone and flute was Christiaan Mostert. The band's new bass player was Angus

Thomas, who came from Harvey Mandel, while Ruben Alvarez filled the drum stool. Most of these gifted young musicians were unknown, and Mayall had given them all a lucky break by employing them. For most, it was their first-ever professional job. Mayall took his new unit on a tour of Europe in May 1979, but it was a difficult time; at some venues, they were almost booed off the stage because of the hostile reception to their recently released 'Bottom Line' LP.

Back home in the States, singer Kathryn Fields was immediately replaced by Rebecca Burns, who had sung backup on Mayall's 1977 album. Using the band from the recent tour, Mayall lost no time in booking a studio to record the next LP, which he was to produce himself. 'No More Interviews' consisted of nine new songs, and was recorded in July at Kendun Studios in Los Angeles. Released in November, it was typical Mayall. The only cover was the LP's opener 'Hard Going Up', one of the highlights and even better than Little Sony's original. Further highlights were the slow 'Sweet Honey Bee', the powerful 'Stars in the Night' and the driving 'Take Me Home Tonight', sung by drummer Ruben Alvarez. Rick Vito and Ronnie Barron also made contributions. Although this was a fine album and earned some rave reviews, it remained a minor seller, and has never been released on CD, which is a great pity. 1979 proved to be a pivotal year for Mayall, both personally and professionally. Disco and punk dominated the mainstream, and Mayall struggled to keep his career afloat; the popularity of blues music was at an all-time low. Personally, however, his relationship with Maggie Parker was blossoming, and became a huge source of strength for Mayall; since the early 1980s, Parker has taken an active and skilful part in managing her husband's career.

Terrible misfortune hit Mayall and his family on Sunday, September 16, 1979. After a long dry spell, a forest fire, nothing uncommon in the Hollywood area, raged out of control and spread to the usually peaceful Laurel Canyon. The inferno started at around two in the afternoon on the canyon's southwest flank. Almost immediately, huge flames were menacing Grandview Drive, built shoulder to shoulder with homes possessing some of the best views. The wildfire came so quickly that most escaped with just the clothes they were wearing. Within minutes, 23 houses at Grandview and adjoining Colecrest Drive were burning uncontrollably. Mayall and his loved ones were all able to escape, but he lost all his possessions in the fire, including photographs, recordings, books, memorabilia, and the diaries that he had meticulously kept for the last twenty-five years. These were an irreplaceable source of first-hand knowledge on the explosive rise of the British blues boom. Mayall himself later commented: "I lost everything. Nothing left except the foundations. That was a big shock. You get wiped out. You just start completely from scratch, especially if you're the sort of person who collects everything. But you know, life goes on and you have to deal with it. It took three years to rebuild the house. The worst loss was my diaries that I'd written since 1947. I still get pangs about losing those, and photographs and tapes of live gigs from the '60s, such as when Hendrix sat in." These dairies were thoroughly done (like Bill Wyman's for the Rolling Stones), and would have been fascinating to read today. John sifted through the black ash that could have been his books or guitars, his diaries or piano. The house had gone up like matchwood, but those on either side weren't even singed. Despite the fire taking his entire earthly possessions with it, Mayall remained stoic and determined to recover. Built on the foundations of the old, the new house was completed in 1982. Right after the fire, however, the Mayall's stayed over at John McVie's house, which may have given him the idea of reforming the Bluesbreakers at some point in the future. The urgent problem was that Mayall was underinsured, and needed to make a lot of money to rebuild his home. He had to downsize his band to five as he couldn't afford seven musicians on the payroll. After just nine months and one album, he sacked five from his band in September 1979, retaining guitarist James Quill Smith and Maggie Parker, and then undertook a gruelling world tour that would have exhausted a man half his age. While in Australia in 1981, he did 42 shows in forty-nine days, travelling hundreds of miles between shows daily. Road warrior Mayall was still doing the same kind of month-long no-days-off tours thirty years later, in his seventies! Soko Richardson rejoined on drums, and Mayall recruited newcomer Kevin McCormick to play bass. The new quintet was tightly knit and promised to be one of Mayall's most dynamic. The band started to recapture the sound and energy of the early work that established Mayall as a major force on the British blues scene. They played most concerts in North America, but also toured Australia. Larry Taylor returned to replace Kevin McCormick on bass; it was the last time he would play with Mayall.

Back home in California, the band entered Media Art Studios at Hermosa Beach in July 1980 to record 'Road Show Blues', his third and last album for DJM. Seven tunes were recorded, augmented by two live tracks, cut at the Golden Bear Club in Huntington Beach, this time with Christiaan Mostert on sax and flute. The title track was written by Maggie Parker, while 'John Lee Boogie' was dedicated to veteran American blues man John Lee Hooker, one of Mayall's formative idols, with whom he had toured Britain in summer 1964. (It took until 1998 for Mayall and Hooker to record together.) Another of Mayall's heroes, J.B. Lenoir, was honoured by the Chicago blues classic 'Mama Talk to Your Daughter', a song that Mayall had already recorded in 1966 with Peter Green. The two live tracks were the pulsating 'Mexico City' and a rousing cover of Jimmy Reed's 'Baby What You Want Me to Do', already a staple of the live shows, sung together with Maggie Parker. 'Road Show Blues' was a pleasant enough album with unspectacular sound quality, produced by Mayall and released April 1981. It remained Mayall's last studio album for seven long years, in fact until 'Chicago Line' in 1988. Like ABC, DJM did not do very much to promote Mayall's work, and soon all three albums on the label were deleted. After Dick James' death, Polygram acquired the DJM catalogue, but the new owners were not interested in Mayall. While he still thrived on the concert circuit, performing more than 127 shows a year, by 1981 he found himself without a recording contract. While the band was mainly working in America, Mayall struggled to find a new label. In August 1980, after the recording of 'Road Show Blues', Maggie Parker stopped touring and Mayall's group continued as a quartet, cross-crossing Europe in autumn 1980, including communist-controlled Poland for the first time. In early 1981 there followed a giant tour of Australia with 42 shows in forty-nine days. In April 1981, Mayall decided to call it a day and disbanded the group. James Quill Smith, whom Mayall once described as "the best guitarist I've had since Eric Clapton", had been with the band for more than four years. Unlike Eric Clapton, Peter Green, Coco Montoya and Walter Trout, this highly gifted guitarist sadly never had much of a solo career afterwards.

CHAPTER 9

The Return of the Bluesbreakers
The Memphis bands and Mick Taylor, 1981–84

From the mid-1970s, Mayall's popularity began to fade; his records were trashed by the critics and ignored by the public. He was even regarded by some fans as a has-been, his days of glory long gone. Mayall had most likely driven some fans away with his ceaseless musical experiments, regarded by many as moving away from his blues roots. By 1981 he found himself without a recording contract, and his musical career slipped into near obscurity. The early 80's were a particularly bad time for blues artists in general, as most record companies were affected by the recession. Consumer interest in the blues began to wane in the periodic ebb and flow of contemporary fashion. The blues had become decidedly unfashionable, and so, with the public interest at an all-time low, Mayall had to struggle to keep his recording career afloat. He remembers: "There was a bad patch because my record deal ran out, and it was very difficult for blues people to get deals. Disco was in full force. So I was doing a lot of roadwork, but it was a bad period for getting an album out. There's absolutely no connection, over the years, between my records and the popularity that I've had in clubs. That side of it has been good all along. In terms of our live shows, we've been constantly in the public eye. I was always in work. I never really had a dull period when there's not been enough work. There was no need to work 300 days a year, like back in the early days." Mayall entered a slow decline; he was still playing roughly 120 live dates a year, and could always make a good living out of live concerts, but he saw his recording career dwindle and finally die after several label changes. Furthermore, the abstemious musician who'd once fired sidemen for having a drink before a show now developed his own alcohol problem, a taste for drink that remained unquenched for several years. "Throughout the 70s, I performed most of my shows drunk," he admitted later to Down Beat. In order to restore his reputation and rebuild his career (it would be wrong to talk about a comeback, for Mayall had never been away), he was aware that he had to return to his roots. This required him to restore the Bluesbreakers name (he had been performing under his own name for more than 12 years), recruit British musicians with whom he had played during the '60s, give up drinking for good and find a new recording contract as a means of publicising credible blues recordings. The resurgence would come step by step. He managed to banish the bottle within three years, but gathering the right musicians to try and re-create the magic of the '60s would take longer.

When the Bluesbreakers returned, the band was in fact Memphis-based. Mayall recalls: "My good friend producer Don Nix was to come up with the suggestion that I fly out to Memphis and get together with some of his local musicians." Mayall's new six-piece comprised of guitarist Don McMinn, who'd previously worked with Memphis Slim, and the legendary former Stax session man Bobby Manuel on rhythm. Memphis-born piano wizard Larry Raspberry was also recruited, together with bass player Jeff Davis and drummer Mike Gardner, whom Mayall knew very well from Jimmy Buffet's 1977 Coral Reefer Band.

This band immediately went into Memphis' Daily Planet Studios in May 1981 to record a ten-track album; Don Nix produced it and also wrote three of the ten songs. With the sessions completed and mixed, Mayall shopped his self-financed record around the US, unsuccessfully looking for a label willing to release it. Four years later, five tracks could be found on the tiny Australian AIM label entitled 'The Return of the Bluesbreakers', but it took nine years before One Way Records released it in a package entitled 'Cross Country Blues'. Highlights were the slower numbers such as Nix's wonderful 'The Same Old Blues', which has since become a blues standard (covered by no less than Freddie King), and Mayall's 'Rise Again', while other songs, influenced by rock 'n' roll and the Memphis setting, were less convincing.

The band gigged locally but also came to Europe to complete 25 dates in Italy and one at the Nyon Festival in Switzerland. Unfortunately, on July 31 in Ischia, rhythm guitarist Bobby Manuel quit the band, forcing them to finish the remaining commitments as a four piece. On August 3, in Via Reggio, the tour manager ran off with the concert takings, and at their last gig in Elba on August 4, there was no sound equipment as the company responsible had cleared off the night before! After only three months, the Memphis Bluesbreakers had come to a sad and sudden end. For the rest of the year, Mayall didn't maintain any band. In November, he played alongside his idol Muddy Waters at the Roxy in Los Angeles, and then fronted a New Year's Eve party hosted at Gossips club in London. Mayall's eldest son Gary helped run the venue, and Mayall was backed by Diz & the Doormen, with Alexis Korner as special guest. Gary Mayall recalled: "The year ended on an all time high, with an unforgettable New Year's Eve party. My dad was in town, and at fairly short notice I booked him to play live, backed by the best, authentic New Orleans R&B band in town, Diz & the Doormen. Alexis Korner joined the bill as special guest, and 700 people queued to get in. It was the busiest night Gossips had ever seen, with a line stretching right around the block. John and the band played an awesome set, Alexis sang a beautiful rendition of Sam Cook's 'Bring It On Home', and together they blasted the roof off!"

Mayall travelled to Harrogate in Yorkshire to marry Maggie Parker on January 8, 1982. Maggie remembers: "John's eldest son Gaz, and John's mentor, Alexis Korner, came up from London; my mother and aunt got there all the way from Chicago. We hired a bus to take our party to the Registry Office, and then on to The Sportsman's Arms, a 17th Century coaching house in the English village of Pately Bridge, in the North Yorkshire countryside. While the storm raged, we celebrated around a cozy fire and cut the cake, starting our new chapter as husband and wife. It was magical."

Mayall continued to pursue his idea of assembling the Bluesbreakers with original members, motivated not so much by nostalgia and fond memories but by sheer need. He later recalled: "The problem was that the business was run by people who weren't interested in the blues." In 1981 Clapton was a global superstar and unavailable, Peter Green was battling with mental health problems and still very fragile, so Mick Taylor seemed the obvious choice. Taylor, now 33, had left the Rolling Stones in late 1974, toured with the Jack Bruce Band and Alvin Lee, and cut a superb solo debut for CBS in 1979. Unfortunately, the legacy of his five years with the Stones had left Taylor with a ferocious drug habit. Taylor remembered: "People are always asking me whether I regret leaving the Rolling Stones. I make no bones about it—had I remained with the band, I would probably be dead. I was having difficulties with drug addiction and couldn't have lasted. I was using anything I could get. It began as an occasional recreational thing. But by the time I returned to London in 1973, I'd become more and more dependent. I was using every day." Bass player John McVie was also enticed back after 15 years; he described it as a 'welcome sabbatical' from the highs and lows of Fleetwood Mac, and drummer Colin Allen returned after 13 years away. The Bluesbreakers enjoyed acclaim from critics and fans as they criss-crossed the US. Having warmed up by playing a few concerts in California in January, the band continued with an extended tour of Hong Kong, Australia, New Zealand and Hawaii until February 21. They played three more gigs in Berkeley, Oakland and Santa Cruz from May 20 to 22.

As far as the set list was concerned at this time, the band mostly relied on well known favourites from 60s albums like 'Crusade' as well as songs played by Mayall's last few bands such as 'An Eye for an Eye', 'Rock It in the Pocket', 'Black Cat Moan' and 'Road Show', the latter with Maggie Mayall on vocals. Freddie King's instrumental 'The Stumble' had, of course, been Peter Green's showcase. Mick Taylor's version took a different approach, with some powerful guitar/piano interplay. Exceptions to the rule were some exciting new compositions such as 'The Dark Side of Midnight' (a wonderfully driving blues shuffle), 'I Should Know Better' (an outstanding minor key tune, co-written by Mick Taylor, with Mayall on organ and harmonica), 'Lookin' for Willie' (a funky mid-tempo blues), 'You Never

Can Be Trusted' (a powerful shuffle), 'Howlin' Moon' (a nice slow blues with refreshingly different chords, lyrics by Maggie Mayall and breathtaking slide guitar by Taylor), plus the two rock 'n' roll numbers, 'Ridin' on the Santa Fe' and 'She Can Do It'.

From June 2 to 20, the band went on an extended US tour of twenty concerts, covering the east coast and mid-west. The two shows played at the Wax Museum in Washington on June 17 were recorded, the idea being to release a live album, but the time still wasn't right. The US tour culminated with a blues summit at the Capitol Theatre in Passaic, New Jersey, on June 18, 1982, where Mayall and company were joined by blues legends Buddy Guy, Junior Wells, Albert King, Etta James and Sippie Wallace for a special show. This was captured on video as 'Blues Alive', basically a Bluesbreakers reunion concert combined with an American folk blues festival! The Bluesbreakers perform 'An Eye for an Eye' before the great Etta James takes over on the Jimmy Reed standard 'Baby, What You Want Me To Do', one of her live highlights. For the next couple of tunes, the Bluesbreakers were joined by two big names in Chicago Blues, Junior Wells and Buddy Guy, who often appeared as a team at the time. The Albert King performance is followed by an all-star jam, but the undisputed star of the show is Mick Taylor, who is in top form. In its longest version, the movie lasts 90 minutes, but there must be many outtakes. It took more than two years for footage from this outstanding concert to be released (October 1984), by which time Mayall was touring with Coco Montoya. Eagle Records eventually released 'Blues Alive' on DVD in 2002, now entitled 'Jammin' with the Blues Greats'. In 2011, Blues Boulevard Records released it on CD calling it 'In the Shadow of Legends'. Right after the show on June 18, John McVie departed after only five months, officially because of Fleetwood Mac commitments, but actually because he had been drinking and was caught 'juiced up' at several gigs. McCormick replaced him for the last two shows on the US east coast. The decision to fall back on ex-Bluesbreakers was fine as far as touring was concerned, but the time was not yet ripe for a new recording contract. About the Washington live recordings, Mayall commented: "I was shopped around to no avail. Despite the high calibre of performances by world-renowned musicians, it seemed that no one wanted to take a chance on signing me for a new deal. We toured America and Australia for six months, after which nothing really happened."

To replace McVie permanently, Mayall turned to Steve Thompson again, who had been away for nearly four years, and James Quill Smith on guitar. The Laurel Canyon line-up was now complete, so Mayall took them on a two-week tour of Italy until December 10, with Maggie Parker taking vocal duties on some numbers. The band toured Europe from May 20 to June 14, continuing the forward momentum. The new song 'Italiano Style' was constantly on the set list, and 'Catfish Blues' had become 'Muddy Waters Blues' in memory of the great man who had passed away on April 30. The tour kicked off in Wiesen, 50 km south of Vienna, over the Whitsun holiday weekend, with the Peter Green Band, Roy Harper, Barbara Thompson's Paraphernalia, Stan Webb's Chicken Shack and Larry Coryell on the same bill. The Bluesbreakers headlined at the end of the third day. Only one live track survives from this tour, recorded in Concarneau, France, and issued in 2006 on the 'Exclusive Live Rarities' CD, entitled 'French Toast'. Soon after the tour was over, Mayall disbanded the group, but was back with Mick Taylor again just six months later.

In the summer of 1983, Mayall was invited to participate in a TV Special with Bonnie Riatt, the stunning redhead who could play exquisite slide guitar and sing beautifully. Mayall met Kal David for the first time, Riatt's superb guitarist, who would join Mayall's band about a year later. Mayall and Riatt became good friends, but have unfortunately never recorded together.

In October and November 1983, Mayall joined Canned Heat as a guest for a two-month U.S. tour. Mayall commented: "After the Mick Taylor/John McVie/Colin Allen exercise, after which nothing really happened, I went out solo for a while with a revised edition of Canned Heat as a backing band, which was a lot of fun. It was there that I met Walter Trout who impressed me a great deal." The 1983 line-up was Walter Trout and Mike Halby on guitar, Ernie Rodriguez on bass and Fito de la Parra on drums. Unfortunately, no recordings survive of this fabulous combination. On November 29, Mayall turned 50 and celebrated his half-century at the Central Club in Los Angeles, where Coco Montoya happened to be on stage with a local band. Montoya remembers: "When they told me John Mayall was there, I dedicated a real bastardized version of 'All Your Love' to him. Unknown to me, the guy running the board made a mix for John. A little later, John gave me a call." Montoya's tenure with Mayall is covered in depth in the next chapter.

At the beginning of 1984, Mick Taylor was free of commitments, so Mayall re-recruited the stellar guitarist for another four months of tour dates, together with Tim Drummond on bass, known to Mayall from the 'Bottom Line' sessions in 1979. Mike Gardner returned to play drums after an absence of two and a half years. They embarked on a two-week US tour from April 5, starting with six club dates in the LA area on January 19. At these warm up concerts, Mayall allowed Walter Trout to sit in on guitar. As we know, Trout had previously toured with Mayall as a member of Canned Heat. After four months, more than twenty gigs and no recordings, the band was done. Mayall commented: "The problem with this line up was that everybody lived in different countries and states, which eliminated the possibility of weekend gigs. This led to the final break up, and my search for local musicians who would be available at any given time." Tim Drummond continued touring and recording, while drummer Mike Gardner returned to Memphis to front his own band.

After his last tour as a Bluesbreaker, Mick Taylor went on the road with Bob Dylan and pal Colin Allen. He later moved to New York City and formed a series of blues and fusion groups. In the latter half of the '90s, he returned to England to play blues festivals with a touring band. In 1998 Taylor issued 'A Stone's Throw', his second solo album in three decades. Taylor also made himself available for reunion projects such as Mayall's 70th Birthday Concert in 2003. During their second period together in the '80s, Mayall never released a studio album with Taylor because of the lack of interest, despite the fact that hardcore Stones fans would have bought it, if only because of Taylor's presence, such was the esteem in which he was held. In 1982 Taylor's royalties were stopped for the six albums he had recorded with The Rolling Stones (from 1969 to 1974), but a reconciliation of some kind or other must have taken place, as since November 2012 he has appeared alongside Jagger and company on stage several times, contributing his superlative licks to 'Midnight Rambler' and other classics.

For Mayall, the tours with Mick Taylor were the springboard to revitalizing his career. Public reaction had convinced him that he should return to his original dynamic, driving blues sound. This meant a definitive end to all musical experiments. Around March 1984, Mayall also stopped drinking for good, and his career immediately improved.

CHAPTER 10

Reformation, Reinvention and Rejuvenation
The Bluesbreakers Reform, 1984–93

Buoyed by the enthusiastic reception to the re-formation of the Bluesbreakers, Mayall wanted to select young Los Angeles musicians to give the band a new lease of life. "With Mick Taylor living in England, it seemed obvious that a new edition of the Bluesbreakers should be formed in order to continue the flow of creativity. So that's why I got the L.A. guys together in a band in 1984 and made a fresh start," said a rejuvenated Mayall, now free from the alcohol addiction that had plagued him over the last few years. The LA-based Bluesbreakers comprised of Coco Montoya and Kal David, two lead guitarists, and the rhythm section of bassist Bobby Haynes and drummer Willie McNeil. The Los Angeles musicians were hand-picked and carefully groomed, just like their British predecessors had been in the '60s. Mayall recalls putting the band together thus: "When the decision came to get the Bluesbreakers together in LA, Coco Montoya was the first choice of guitar player. He had been a bartender at the club where Mick Taylor, John McVie, Colin Allen and myself had had our first rehearsal in January 1982, but I didn't know what a fine blues guitar player he was until I heard him locally. He had left a strong impression on me the night I heard him performing at The Central Club in L.A." If the truth be told, Montoya actually started out as a drummer, and had this to say about his background: "I grew up playing rock and roll, and in high school I did the usual jobs, playing drums in bands in Los Angeles. Then one day I went to a concert featuring Creedence Clearwater and Iron

Butterfly. Albert King played between the two groups and I had never heard of him. He picked up his guitar and did 'Watermelon Man'. That was the first time I heard music that came from the heart. That revolutionized my whole life and showed me what music and guitar playing really were about. It went right into my soul. It grabbed me so emotionally that I had tears welling up in my eyes. Nothing had ever affected me to this level. I knew that that was what I wanted to do." Meanwhile, Montoya kept on playing drums very successfully with top bluesmen like Freddie King. His biggest break was when 'Iceman' Collins hired him in 1972: "Albert asked if I wanted to learn to play blues because, if so, I should stick with him, he would teach me. What a great gift he gave me! I stayed with him for around five years and he was like a father to me." Now Montoya began doubling on the guitar, and Collins went out of his way to teach him what he knew. Montoya remembers he never took formal lessons from the master of the Telecaster: "It was more from just hanging in the hotel rooms. He would grab his guitar and I would pick up one and we'd play for hours. He'd play that beautiful rhythm of his and just have me playing along. I just learned by listening, all by ear. I just play it the way I hear it. He was always saying, 'don't think about it, just feel it.'"

In November 1983, Montoya was jamming in a Los Angeles bar when Mayall walked in. Montoya launched into 'All Your Love' as a tribute, which so impressed the British bluesman he took a tape of the performance home with him. In June 1984, Mayall called Montoya: "I want you to come down and play and see how things work." Montoya knew he could not pass up this chance of a lifetime, and soon afterwards joined the Bluesbreakers. It's true to say Montoya plays with an emotional intensity few guitar players possess; he is left-handed, but plays right-handed guitars upside-down, i.e. with the low 'E' string at the bottom, just like Albert King, Otis Rush or Jimi Hendrix could. Usually, left-handed players used left-handed guitars, with the low 'E' string uppermost, i.e. nearest to the player's thumb. During his first years with Mayall, Montoya played a Gibson Explorer, which featured a pointed design and a strong, typical Bluesbreakers sound, later switching to a custom Toru Nittono Stratocaster-style instrument, whose special sound became his calling card. Montoya was also an excellent slide guitarist and an outstanding singer, possessing a strong but soulful voice. And like the great guitarists in whose footsteps he was now following, Montoya's scalding chops suggested huge potential. Montoya recalls: "With John Mayall, we played everywhere. My guitar advanced very fast with him, simply because of the pressure of being in that band and following Eric Clapton, Peter Green and Mick Taylor. John always wanted us to play like ourselves and not copy the records. I learned a lot from him." Given that the Bluesbreakers were known for the quality of their musicians, Montoya had their massive reputations to deal with as well. "When playing a song like 'Have You Heard', I had to play like Eric Clapton. If we were doing 'Oh, Pretty Woman', I wanted to be Mick Taylor. John eventually sat me down and explained that he hired me to be me. He said, 'What the hell, Coco, you played all the time with Albert Collins and you forgot what the rule is.'" Mayall recalls : "If I hire a musician, I try to let him be himself, because if a guy is playing what he feels rather than what he is told to, he'll do a better job."

The other player was Kal David, who'd briefly played with Mayall a year earlier in that all-star TV special with Bonnie Raitt. As a teenager, David had been in the Exceptions, alongside bass player and singer Peter Cetera, who later joined Chicago and sang many of their hits. Later, David formed the Fabulous Rhinestones, and became featured guitarist for Etta James and Robbie Dupree. He played a magnificent Gibson Firebird, which is still the instrument he is most associated with. Like Montoya, David was also a fine singer, blessed with a voice that laid bare his soul, and fully matched the blazing intensity of his guitar playing. For his new bass guitarist, Mayall chose Bobby Haynes, recommended by Red Holloway. Haynes had toured with Percy Mayfield, and then worked with T-Bone Walker and Big Joe Turner. His jazz career began with Dexter Gordon before he joined Chico Hamilton for two years, moving on to the Jazz Crusaders, Papa John Creach, Paul Butterfield, Marvin Gaye, Bobby

Womack, Lou Rawls, and Ike & Tina Turner. Haynes played a Fender Precision with the Bluesbreakers, switching to a new Steinberger XP2 bass for lightness a few years later. Willie 'Dred' McNeil, the young new fellow on the drum stool, was a friend of Jason, Mayall's son. In an interview in early 1985, Mayall aired his views on the matter: "One of the great things about reforming the Bluesbreakers, and especially in having two guitar players is that we're able to recreate and rejuvenate most of the early '60s Bluesbreakers tracks that were so popular. Reason being that on the Clapton ones, for instance—most of those classic tunes—Eric would play the rhythm guitar and he would play the lead guitar. So, in actual fact, there were basically two guitars playing in order to make those songs sound the way they did. Now with two guitar players in the band, we find that we can cover most of the first Bluesbreakers album, much to everyone's delight. So we play a lot of the old favourites and a lot of the new ones, too."

After three days of rehearsal at Mayall's Laurel Canyon house, the bandleader took his new unit on an Italian tour from June 14 to July 3. After the last show in Trieste on July 3, they rushed to Canada to play the Montreal Jazz Festival the following day. The one-hour show was recorded and broadcast. 'Parchman Farm', one of the ten songs recorded, was released in 2001 on a 4 CD set celebrating 20 years of the Montreal International Jazz Festival, 1980–2000. It's a long version with a superlative Kal David solo, testifying how well this line-up could cook up a storm playing live. In July 1984, Mayall took his new 5-piece into Los Angeles' Sunswept Studio to record nine songs for the next record. This was Mayall's third attempt to release a new album, yet he still couldn't find a label; it took ten long years before it was released, in a collection entitled 'Cross Country Blues' in April 1994. Compared to the 1981 Memphis studio album, the sound quality was slightly inferior, but the interesting song material and excellent musicianship more than make up for it.

For the rest of the year, the group did about twenty concerts in the USA, featuring songs from the unreleased album such as 'My Baby', 'Lonely Feelings', 'Ridin' on the L&N', 'Maggie's Boy' and 'Italiano Style', combined with older numbers like 'Parchman Farm', 'Steppin'

Out', 'Tears in My Eyes', 'Fly Tomorrow' and 'Room to Move'. In January 1985, they toured Scandinavia and Germany, followed by a US tour in February and four Canadian dates in April, after which drummer McNeil quit. Mayall quickly picked up Keith John to replace him for the next four US gigs in May.

After a year on the road, David left for good in May 1985 to be replaced by Walter Trout. Trout had had a disrupted home life, which forced him to turn to music for solace. In his late teens and early twenties, he played with numerous New Jersey bands, and his first big break was with Louisiana Red in 1969. For a while, Trout only played the harmonica and sang, but joined Canned Heat in 1981 as a guitarist and never looked back. Although his presence gave the band a new lease of life, the band unfortunately had a reputation for hard drinking and even harder drugs. Trout stayed for four years, which had a detrimental effect on his substance abuse. "I drank to escape the pain of my youth and the pain I was feeling," he explained later. "I was running from a lot of my past. I took as much as I could get." Joining the Bluesbreakers was an ambitious step: "I felt really honoured to follow in the footsteps of Clapton, Green and Taylor. It was funny because in the late '60s in America a lot of white kids learned about the blues through British acts like John Mayall. The Bluesbreakers albums were very popular. So, to play the songs that I had grown up listening to was a great honour; I had a ball. When I joined Mayall's band, I went to his house and we rehearsed for one day. The next thing I knew we were in Czechoslovakia playing to 20,000 people every night!"

Trout arrived with drummer Joe Yuele, who had been recommended by Montoya. Yuele had started playing drums at 14 and joined his first band, the Vee Jays, a year later. The turning point came in 1974, when he joined the Juke Rhythm Band in Los Angeles. They specialized in Chicago blues and were kept busy backing touring blues greats such as Albert Collins, Lowell Fulsom, Big Joe Turner, George 'Harmonica' Smith, Big Mama Thornton, and many more. In 1976, Yuele toured the United States with Dobie 'Drift-A-Way' Gray, Simon Stokes & The Nighthawks and the Coco Montoya Blues Band, before joining Mayall and breaking all records by staying for 23 years! Trout found himself sharing the spotlight with Montoya, something that wasn't always easy, although he affectionately remembers: "For four years as duelling guitarists in Mayall's band, Coco and I toured the world. We did over 1000 shows together. Coco is undoubtedly one of the very best guitar players and singers out there, and someone who has my deepest love and respect." New live and studio albums followed. To celebrate the sense of renewal, the 51-year old bandleader decided on a clean-cut new look with shorter hair and for the first time in many years, no beard! Around this time, Mayall also started using a new guitar, a Rickenbacker 660/12 black solid-body 12-string, hand-carved and exquisitely decorated with turquoise and shells. It took pride of place on the sleeves of both "Behind the Iron Curtain' and 'Exclusive Live Rarities'.

In 1985, Mayall immediately took his new band on a European tour from May 28 to June 10, with two dates in Bratislava, five in Hungary and three in Berlin. The open air concert on June 6, in Szeged, Hungary, was taped and Mayall released it as 'Behind the Iron Curtain' the following year on the GNP Crescendo label. After 'Road Show Blues', it was the first Mayall album in five years, but the sound quality could have been better. Only seven songs were released of the sixteen performed. Mayall explains: "I had the audio tape to take home with me as a souvenir, and the energy on it, I could see there was enough in there to make an album. I played it to a local record company, GNP Crescendo in L.A. They instantly liked it. So it led in a roundabout way to reaching a larger audience in Europe. And it was the start of it all. That got a German company interested and led us getting the record deal with Entente later on. Step by step, we were getting back in the mainstream of known record companies." For the rest of 1985, the Bluesbreakers played mostly US dates, including New York's famed Carnegie Hall on June 29, plus a trip to play in Buenos Aires on October 12.

On October 25, Mayall was invited to participate in an all-star jam at LA's Irvine Meadows Amphitheatre; among the musicians were Bo Diddley, Chuck Berry, Ron Wood, Carl Wilson and Mitch

Mitchell, to name only a few. The show was filmed and later released as 'Bo Diddley and Friends'. As can be seen, the Bluesbreakers line-up with Montoya, Trout, Haynes and Yuele lifted the band to a whole new level, and luckily for Mayall, remained unchanged for nigh-on four years. The mid-80s saw a renaissance of interest in blues music, spearheaded by brilliant musicians such as Stevie Ray Vaughan, Jeff Healey and Robert Cray. Interest in Mayall's work soared, and the Bluesbreakers enjoyed high profile tours and good album sales.

From February 1 to March 1 the following year, the band played 30 concerts in 29 days on tour in Europe. Montoya now played a Gibson Explorer, and Trout his Stratocaster, but with a more rock-oriented style, using the volume knob to create violin-like sounds. Trout explained: "The volume swells was a trick I got from watching Roy Buchanan as a kid." Europe was followed by concerts in the USA and Canada, then it was back to Europe in July for the summer festivals, including Montreux on July 8. It was the first time Mayall had played in this part of Switzerland, and although concerts at this prestigious festival were normally taped for broadcast on radio or TV, no live recordings of Mayall in Montreux have ever been issued. Including their tour of Australia from October 15 to November 9, the Bluesbreakers played about 120 concerts in 1986.

1987 started with a short tour through the southern states of the US before returning to Europe for more gigs. Two entire concerts were filmed, one in Vienna on March 22, where Mayall performed the two rare songs 'How Come' and 'She's My Lover'. The other, in East Berlin on April 5, was filmed and broadcast a year later on East German TV. This show is especially memorable for a life-saving incident. The Bluesbreakers were doing the East Berlin show alongside the Santana Band and by this time, Trout was getting through a bottle of Jack Daniels a day. After seeing him playing 'all juiced up', Santana took him aside, and in a heartfelt conversation told Trout in humble but unequivocal terms that he was squandering his God-given gift. Santana told him he greatly appreciated his talent and was deeply concerned about his self-destructive lifestyle. At the time, Santana was closely following Indian mystic and visionary Sri Chinmoy, who promoted a teetotal, vegetarian lifestyle with meditation and sport. Suddenly, Trout had an epiphany, or moment of profound insight. Trout recalls: "After that I went to Mayall and said, 'You'll never see me drunk on stage again.' And that was when I stopped." Shortly afterwards, Trout checked in to rehab to get off drugs and alcohol for good. In 1990, Trout dedicated the song 'Sweet as a Flower' (on the LP 'Prisoner of a Dream') to Santana, in gratitude for helping to get him back on the straight and narrow.

On this European tour, the interplay between Montoya and Trout reached new heights: on 'Room to Move', the Bluesbreakers' closing number, the two guitarists would seamlessly weave the riff from Clapton's 'Layla' into their solos. Meanwhile Mayall, like Ray Charles and others at the time, had succumbed to the charms of the synthesizer, using all of its gimmicks to augment the band's sound. Three concerts in Frankfurt, Bonn and Münster were taped, with the intention of releasing another live album. Called 'The Power of the Blues' it was released on Entente, a small German label owned by Frank Eyssen in Hannover. Compared to 'Behind the Iron Curtain', this had far better sound quality, and also included two new original songs, 'Wild About You' and 'Racehorse Man'. This wonderful live album is always worth listening to. Mayall commented later: "Both live albums were a foot in the door. They put up the cost of our studio album, and led to us doing 'Chicago Line', and things have grown back up from then. 'Chicago Line' was picked up by Island Records and then Island had one of their own, 'A Sense of Place'. But it's a rocky world out there. The main thing is that the band has been, through it all, very constant; we've done our quota of over a hundred shows every year since '84 and it's just been building and building. But we put a lot into these shows, and it pays off if you're conscientious, and not just happy to rest on your reputation."

Back in the US, the Bluesbreakers played at the legendary Jazz and Heritage Festival in New Orleans, did some shows at the Ritz in New York City with Mick Taylor sitting in, and then at the Channel Club in Boston one day later. In New York, star drummer Bernard Purdie replaced Joe Yuele on 'She Can Do It' just because he was so keen to play alongside Mayall and Taylor. In December, a short Italian tour saw the year out.

In January 1988, Mayall and Yuele re-recorded eight of the original eighteen tracks on Mayall's 1970 release 'Back to the Roots' at Pacific Sound Studios in Chatsworth, California. Released by Polydor in April 1988, it was entitled 'Archives to Eighties'. March and April 1988 saw the Bluesbreakers playing concerts in Europe again, this time mainly concentrating on the German-speaking areas. One concert, on March 16, was later broadcast on August 18 as a TV special. 23 years later, the one-hour show was released on CD and DVD entitled 'Live in Germany 1988', and although the guitar solos are fine throughout, Mayall's harmonica was not working properly, and detracts from the listening enjoyment. Early April found the Bluesbreakers at Peter Maffay's Red Rooster Studio in Bavaria, where they recorded 'Chicago Line', Mayall's new studio offering. Produced by Tony Carey, Maffay's Californian keyboard player, it is the only Bluesbreakers' studio album featuring Walter Trout. It was released in July on Entente Records, with Mayall paying tribute to his American blues roots by supplying an attractive collage to the gatefold sleeve. Of greater significance is the fact that it was Mayall's first studio album for seven years. Mayall: "'The Power of the Blues' sold well enough to justify a new studio LP on Entente records. But before I went into the studio I made sure I had in my contract the rights to that package for American release. I called up my contact at Elektra Records, who was a big fan of mine from years ago, only to find out that he'd left and he'd gone to Island and was now the A&R man at Island Records. They gave me his number and we reacquainted ourselves. I sent him the tape and within two days, Island said, 'Yes, we want it.'"

In July 1988, Mayall travelled to Germany where he was featured guest on Peter Maffay's 'Lange Schatten' tour from August 17. Mayall fans were decidedly confused, as Maffay's unspectacular music and rather clichéd German lyrics had little in common with the blues; he is known only in German-speaking countries. Nevertheless, it was good money and provided the opportunity to win over a new audience who, it could safely be presumed, knew next to nothing about the blues. Apart from contributing harmonica and guitar to some of Maffay's tunes, Mayall played four to five of his own songs, including his signature 'Room to Move'. After 35 sold-out concerts in eleven weeks, Mayall returned to California.

The Bluesbreakers started 1989 with a tour of Scandinavia in January, during which Mayall became so ill that he was bed-bound. Now that he was clean, Trout took over for the rest of the tour, a fact that persuaded him that it was time to start a solo career of his own. He later told Guitarist Magazine how it happened: "I was in the Bluesbreakers and I wasn't thinking of leaving or anything. But we were playing a club in Denmark one night and John got incredibly sick, so sick in fact that he wanted to cancel the gig. So we talked to the promoter and he said he was going to lose a lot of money—was there any way that the band could go on without Mayall? Anyway, he announced to the crowd that John wouldn't be playing tonight, but the band would, so anyone wanting their money returned could have it. As it happened, only about 100 people left—which meant there were still over 600 in the crowd—so I got up and I fronted the Bluesbreakers for that night, singing all the tunes and playing a lot more guitar than I normally did, which seemed to go down really well with the fans. But it happened that in the crowd that night was a guy from John's record company, as well as the promoter that was booking him. When I came off the stage the record company asked me if I would like to do my own album, and the promoter said I should put my own band together, and come back to Denmark. So it happened just like that, and I sort of fell into it." Trout completed another tour of Europe with Mayall, working until May 1989, but remembers with gratitude: "It was great to work with John—it was probably the best period of my musical career. So many players before me had used the Bluesbreakers as a kind of a musical university, studying then moving on. We used to have a phrase for John—we called him the benevolent dictator. He's a very joyful, happy man with a great sense of humour who was always a pleasure to work for and to be around, but you have to do your job. He wants you to get up and play your best every night—and he's very good at drawing that out of you. I think John's biggest talent is being a bandleader and that's a considerable talent in itself. It's a talent that Duke Ellington and Count Basie had, a special quality to bring the best performances out of their players. John's music is very spontaneous—even if you rehearse it things can change totally when you get on stage. You have to watch him all the time 'cause he has little signs with his hands or eyes that he uses to conduct the band when he wants to change something. It's quite a special skill. After four years of working with John I've tried to adapt that to suit my own band, maintaining the spontaneity."

At first, Mayall wanted to replace Trout with 'Sugarcane' Harris, the ace violinist who had played with Mayall between 1970 and 1975, but his dependence on drugs had made him unreliable, and he sadly never showed up for the tour, although Montoya says he was tremendous at rehearsals. With only Montoya on guitar now, the Bluesbreakers played a memorable date at the Great Woods Blues Festival on June 25 in Mansfield, Massachusetts, with Stevie Ray Vaughan and Johnny Winter on the same bill.

At the end of 1989, Mayall recorded eleven songs for 'A Sense of Place', the new album on Island Records, with R.S. Field producing. Mayall wanted to give it a touch of the Louisiana sound, so celebrated slide guitarist Sonny Landreth was invited to contribute. Landreth played Cajun-style with the slide over his pinkie to allow more room for his other fingers, and his wonderful sound dominates the album. Montoya is heard on only six songs, as other session musicians flesh out the sound, including Cid Sanchez and Debbie Davies on guitar. Only one track is a Mayall composition, the piano boogie-woogie 'Send Me down to Vicksburg', which Mayall had recorded in May 1981 for the Memphis Bluesbreakers album. Standout takes include the opening number, a wonderful version of the J.B. Lenoir tune 'I Want to Go', 'Sensitive Kind', a typical J.J. Cale ditty, the biographical 'I Can't Complain' written by Mayall's wife Maggie, and Don Nix's 'Black Cat Moan'. This release made clear that Mayall wasn't drawing inspiration exclusively from African-

American blues sources, but from rock and country influences as well. 'A Sense of Place' was released in May 1990, Mayall's first release to make the Billboard album charts for fifteen years. Emerging artists such as Jeff Healey and Gary Moore had been popularising the blues, and Mayall had the marketing clout of a major label behind him, getting his records into the shops at long last. During the sessions, Rick Cortes replaced Bobby Haynes on bass, but Freebo (Daniel Friedberg) took over for the remainder of the year (Cortes returned in 1991). Freebo had played with Bonnie Raitt, the Edison Electric Band, the Blues Busters, Buddy Guy, Maria Muldaur and Ringo Starr, and his instrument of choice was a striking MusicMan Stingray five-string fretless.

From May 9 to 15, the quartet did a short tour of Japan. One of the Tokyo shows provided the live version of 'Tears Came Rollin' Down', released at the end of 2006 as part of the 'Exclusive Live Rarities' CD on Eagle. On June 2, a Japanese TV crew filmed the concert at the Bottom Line in Manhattan, which was released in October 2004 on DVD, but without Mayall's blessing. Shortly after came an appearance on BBC's 'Rock Steady', a televised concert of three songs at Camden Lock in London on June 5. Another series of concerts in America followed before the BBC asked for them back in mid-July for a radio session. The band stayed in Europe, touring from September 18 to October 20, and it was around this time that Mayall hatched a plan to record a new studio album with Eric Clapton, backed by the Fleetwood Mac rhythm section of John McVie and Mick Fleetwood! Unfortunately, Eric's record company Warner Brothers, vetoed it immediately. Mayall later told Guitar magazine in early 1993: "I can't touch base with Eric; he could touch base with me if he wanted to, but he's totally guarded. I've no contact whatsoever. I've tried over the years, but it doesn't work. I met him about three years ago at somebody's party, and we chatted briefly but it was just polite conversation. And prior to that it was seventeen years since I'd seen him! I think a lot of it has to do with the fact that so many people want the alliance to come back—you know, John Mayall and Eric Clapton playing together again. It's like a legacy that comes with the territory, and he does everything he can to prevent it happening. Although his management and record company did agree to him doing something at Island Records, a kind of reunion album. Mick Fleetwood said yes and John McVie said yes and their managers said yes. Eric apparently said yes but then the Warner Brothers' accountants said no! The correspondence went on for weeks and weeks. But it was way out of my price range. They wanted a ridiculous amount of money, which was probably cheap for his level, and it was going to his favourite charity—it wasn't anything that was going into his pocket. But it was still way outside our budget." So that was the end of that, at least for now.

Towards the end of 1990, Mayall was forced to replace Freebo, as it was obvious that he and Montoya didn't get along. The bandleader charged Joe Yuele with finding him a new bass player, and as the drummer had played with Cortes and liked his groove, he was asked to join. Cortes had played with most of the New Orleans soul and blues greats including 'Zigaboo' Modeliste and Leo Nocentelli, Andy J Forest, Ivan Neville, Razin' Cain and Little Queenie & the Percolators. When he joined Mayall's band in 1991, he preferred to play five-string basses. As one of his sponsors was Seymour Duncan, his various instruments were fitted with an interesting range of prototype pickups! With Mayall, however, Rick used his superb 1964 Fender Precision bass, and also provided stunning vocal harmonies with Montoya. The stellar line-up of Cortes, Montoya and Yuele remained stable for the next three years.

On February 8, the Bluesbreakers appeared on the Johnny Carson Show, augmented by a full and fantastic-sounding horn section. Unfortunately, the performance has never been released. May 3 found Mayall and his Bluesbreakers playing at the New Orleans' Jazz Heritage Festival, in good company with B.B. King, Taj Mahal, John Lee Hooker, Clarence 'Gatemouth' Brown, Earl King, John Mooney and Marva Wright. The band toured Australia again in spring 1991, and then crisscrossed the European continent from Greece to Norway to attend the summer music festivals. August 17th found the Bluesbreakers at the Newport Festival in Rhode Island on the

US east coast. In December, Mayall visited Los Angeles' Studio Dee to add some fine harmonica on 'Superman Man' and 'Bad For Me', songs that were released much later on Maggie Mayall's solo effort 'Dig This'. The sessions included Rick Vito and James Quill Smith on guitar, and Lenny McDaniel on piano, bass and drums.

1992 started with a series of concerts in the Midwest, after which Mayall flew to the UK to play a special show on February 20, backed by his eldest son and his band at Gossips, the London music club, before the Bluesbreakers toured Europe and the US over the entire summer season. Back in the States again, the band retired to the Clubhouse recording studio in Burbank, California, to record 'Wake up Call', their next release. Mayall had secured a recording contract with Silvertone Records, at the time the largest independent music label in the world. Robbie S. Field and Dave McNair had produced 'A Sense of Place' for Island Records, and their services were recruited again for 'Wake Up Call'. Mayall commented: "They really have this great touch. This time around we just worked together so well. It was such a relaxed and easygoing thing, but very creative. I was really sorry when it finished and that doesn't happen often. A lot of it has to do with producer R.S. Field—who I only know as Bobby, a great guy from Nashville who's really into the blues. He had a lot of good ideas. It sounds tight because of the strength of the rhythm section. They are so together." The guests were of the highest calibre: Buddy Guy and Albert Collins on guitar, Mavis Staples' beautiful Stax soul voice, and guitarist Mick Taylor, veteran Bluesbreaker in his own right. Mayall: "Guest artists like that are not just out of the blue; they're people I've known for years and years." Buddy Guy performed a memorable cover of Junior Wells' 'I Could Cry'. Albert Collins, the Texan 'Master of the Telecaster' is heard playing guitar on the two Mayall songs 'Light The Fuse' and 'I'm A Sucker For Love', but for some strange reason is not listed on the sleeve. Mick Taylor adds lead on 'Wake Up Call' and 'Not At Home'. Maggie Mayall sings a moving duet with her husband on the album's closer, the Jimmy Reed classic 'Ain't That Loving You, Baby'. The twelve tracks contain a wider variety of musical influences than the name 'Bluesbreakers' might imply.

Mayall claims that six other songs were recorded during the 'Wake Up Call' sessions: he re-recorded two for his next release, and the other three surfaced on a Silvertone compilation released in 1998. 'Wake Up Call' was released April 5, and sold around 250,000 copies, notching up a week in the UK album charts, Mayall's first since 1971! It was also nominated for a Grammy as Best Contemporary Blues Album, but sadly failed to win. The superb 'Wake Up Call' and its predecessor 'A Sense of Place' helped position Mayall at the very centre of the on-going blues revival.

March 1993 saw the Bluesbreakers tour the US again, accompanied by Buddy Guy, who had meanwhile also signed to Silvertone. A tour of German-speaking Europe followed, with 19 dates. The four shows starting May 12 were promoted as Blues in the Summer with Pete York and Mose Allison. At the Montreal Jazz Festival on July 3, Mick Taylor contributed some superlative guitar; the Bluesbreakers then played in Nyon, Switzerland on July 24, and at the Cambridge Folk Festival in England on August 1. One concert on September 13 at Austin City Limits, Texas, was filmed. In October, the quartet toured in the Far East, including Hong Kong and Singapore in early October.

Montoya had now been playing with Mayall for nine years, longer than any other guitarist before. Albert Collins, his friend and confidante, had meanwhile been diagnosed with cancer, and during a visit, Montoya was told to move on and do his own thing. Mayall also understood the time was right, as Montoya remembers: "Both Albert and John pushed me out of the nest nice and easy." In planning his departure, Montoya put in a good word about his replacement. "I think John already had him in mind, but I said, 'You know, Buddy Whittington would probably be the one to get.'" Montoya's words proved amazingly prophetic, as this great Texan guitar slinger joined the Bluesbreakers and went on to stay for fifteen years!

Montoya went on to a successful solo career with his soul/R&B approach, and his 1994 release 'Gotta Mind To Travel' became an instant favourite with blues fans, immediately ranking him among the best in the scene. Like many of Mayall's sidemen, Montoya learned a lot from his former boss, and remembers affectionately: "John is very meticulous about how he wants things to be, he has vision and knows what he wants to do. Once he sees things he goes for it and he cannot be detoured. He directs very well and that is just one of many talents he has. Mayall taught me how to be organized."

CHAPTER 11

Staying Power

The Bluesbreakers with Buddy Whittington, 1993–2008

When Montoya left the Bluesbreakers in November 1993, Mayall already knew who his replacement would be, but the superb Cortes/Yuele rhythm section he wanted to keep. His new guitarist of choice was Texan Buddy Whittington. Texas has produced many outstanding players: T-Bone Walker, Freddie King, Albert Collins, Johnny 'Guitar' Watson, Johnny Winter and Stevie Ray Vaughan immediately come to mind. Mayall discovered Whittington in 1991, when the Bluesbreakers were booked at a club in Dallas called Dallas Alley. Whittington's band opened for the Bluesbreakers, and Mayall was mightily impressed with his finesse. Now was the right time to recruit him.

Whittington started playing guitar at eight after listening to his sister's Beatles, Rolling Stones and Bluesbreakers records. At 14 he was already a part of the Dallas/Fort Worth music scene and playing in the clubs along Jacksboro' Highway. At high school, Whittington was in a band called Short Change that opened for southern rockers Point Blank, whom he later joined. Although he became versatile enough to play anything from country to rhythm and blues classics to rock 'n' roll, his main love was the blues. During the early 80's, he formed his own group The Sidemen, who became well known in and around Texas. During his 15 years with Mayall, Whittington brought a powerful new dimension to the Bluesbreakers sound, not only on lead, but also through his excellence on rhythm and slide guitar. Whittington's style was highly distinctive, using his 1963 Fender Stratocaster or Lentz (modelled after the Fender Telecaster) plugged into a Dr. Z amp. His searing tone is typically Texan. He explained:

"It's that Les Paul-through-a-Marshall tone that Eric refined in '66. It can't be topped! It's that perfect Gibson-Marshall 'thang' we're all striving for!" Whittington also had a soulful bluesy voice and was also an accomplished songwriter. Mayall commented years later: "Buddy is my all-time favourite. He's the most complete guitar player I've ever worked with. I mean he can play anything. And after all these years, he's still full of surprises every night. He has got such a unique style and power that I would hate to have to compare his contribution to the Bluesbreakers to any of his illustrious predecessors. Buddy is a class by himself." Whittington and Yuele stayed for fifteen years, although many bass players were to come and go in the next few years. Drummer Joe Yuele had also become an invaluable asset as tour planner, taking over travel arrangements, car rental and driving. He also took charge as musical arranger, and recruited most if not all new Bluesbreakers members from 1990 till 2008.

May 1994 found the Bluesbreakers at studios in Burbank and Hollywood to record 'Spinning Coin', Mayall's second release for Silvertone. The new album contained eleven songs, produced and engineered by the same team as 'Wake up Call' and 'A Sense of Place', R.S. Field and Dave McNair. Mayall raved about them: "Dave Mc Nair and Bobby Field, who have joined me for the third time in a row now, they just have such incredible ears, they just have that magic touch. The intention of this one was to present the Bluesbreakers as they are today. So it's just the four of us. It's very special and a lot more intimate in that respect." It included five new Mayall originals, and among the highlights are 'Double Life Feelings', 'Voodoo Music', 'When The Devil Starts Crying', and 'Remember This', while other songs have more of a country feel about them, thanks to Whittington's versatility. 'Spinning Coin' was released on February 13; on both CD and LP covers you could see that Mayall had grown another beard.

Between recording sessions, the quartet toured Europe in summer 1994, with occasional support by Marla Glen and Jeff Healey. They mostly performed songs from 'Wake Up Call', as their Madrid concert, which was broadcast on Spanish TV, confirms. Two tracks

Backstage in Zurich in April 1988 with the author. Photo: Edi Schwager

The Bluesbreakers with Eric Clapton in 1966. All smiles except for John McVie!

⑮ *A mature Mayall, posing for a publicity shot.*

⑯ *(right) The expanding Mayall family celebrating Christmas at home in 199*
from the top Zak, Maggie, the newborn Sammy and Joh

🔴 *A striking-looking Mayall in 1969, around the time of "Turning Point".*

18 *The creative "Diary of a Band" line-up in late 1967, with Dick Heckstall-Smith, Mick Taylor, Keef Hartley, Keith Tillman, Chris Mercer and Mayall.*

19 *Starting from scratch again in 1982 with the revitalized Bluesbreakers: John McVie, Colin Allen, Mick Taylor and Mayall.*

❷⓪ *An athletic twelve-year-old Mayall with his granddad in 1946.*

john   jerry   larry

❷① *Fred Leeson, Mayall's granddad, in 1962. They were close, and Leeson guided the young Mayall*

❷② *The young bluesman: Mayall in 1956 aged 22, with beard and cigarette*

*24 In 1954 serving
the allies in Korea,
aged just 20.*

*Mayall's famous tree house in Cheadle Hulm in 1950, at the back
23 Acre Lane. Sadly, both the tree and house are long gone.*

You're in the army now! The 19-year-old Mayall in the Royal Engineers in 1953.

26 *Three of Mayall's earliest guitars, all heavily sculptured and customized.*
The first is his Weldons semi-acoustic, the famous nine-string, the second a Burns Bison
(also pictured on the "Diary of a Band" cover),
and the third is a Fender Stratocaster Mayall used for 11 years from 1968 on.
All were lost in the Laurel Canyon fire.

from this were later released in 2006 on 'Exclusive Live Rarities'. Two other important events happened in 1994: Mayall was awarded the British Blues Connection 1994 Scroll Of Honour, and on his 61 Birthday, November 29, Maggie gave birth to their second son, Sammy.

In 1994 the Bluesbreakers were supporting red-hot Texas boogie and blues rockers ZZ Top, playing about twelve dates across the American Midwest, starting in Cleveland and ending in Wichita, Kansas. Billy Gibbons even invited Mayall to tour with them again, and re-join in the autumn, but Mayall declined, as he wanted to take his son Zak camping. This decision was incomprehensible to both Whittington and Yuele, as the drummer later admitted: "Billy Gibbons is a great guy and very approachable. We were all able to get friendly. We had a great time being part of the show and were very disappointed when John again turned them down when asked to stay on the tour." Mayall embarked on a five-week US tour in March & April, followed by another tour of Europe. From April to May 1995, the Bluesbreakers played 42 concerts. More US dates followed. On September 21, Mayall was invited to the House of Blues in Hollywood for an election fund-raiser to help re-elect Clinton and Gore. The Blues Brothers with Jim Belushi were the house band, and Mayall was asked to sit in, playing harp. Bill Clinton also accompanied them on his saxophone, while on Jay Leno's chat show, Al Gore was asked what his favourite birthday gift was, declaring it to be a box set of John Mayall CDs, a gift from his wife. Talk about friends in high places!

In October Mayall had to make another change. Bass player Cortes wanted to be a proper daddy to his young daughter, which naturally involved being at home more, so Mayall had to let him go. Afterwards, starting his own Internet-based consulting company enabled Cortes to play music without leaving town for long periods, an ideal situation for a family man. John 'JP' Paulus replaced Cortes, on the recommendation of drummer Yuele: "John Paulus and I had been band mates and good friends for twenty years. So JP joined the band." Paulus was born in Miami and trained by jazz virtuoso Jaco

Pastorius; he had also played with Bobby Caldwell, the American singer/songwriter, but had grown up listening to Mayall's records, saying: "He was responsible for getting me into the blues. Real Blues. I kind of thought I knew the blues but John showed me."

From May 25 to June 1, the Bluesbreakers were headlining on a Mediterranean passenger cruiser at an event called 'The Blues Cruise'. Amazingly, the event had been advertised as follows: "Pompeii, the Blue Grotto, the Bluesbreakers and Buckwheat Zydeco, all in the same day! Seven days of breathtaking scenery and legendary places, seven nights of live blues parties and dancing. Only on the ultimate rhythm & blues cruise! It's blues heaven! An entire week with all your favourite artists. Bring your instrument and jam all night long, every night! All you can eat gourmet meals, complimentary wine with lunch and dinner. Blues workshops and autograph parties." And not only the Bluesbreakers were on board, but also Buckwheat Zydeco, a leading figure of the dance music of southern Louisiana's French-speaking Creoles, Luther Allison, piano playing swamp blues queen Katie Webster, Austin's singer/pianist Marcia Ball, as well as Louisiana Red and John Mooney, among many others. What a line-up!

Soon it was time to record another album. From October 1 to 16, the Bluesbreakers went to studios in Calabasas to record 'Blues for the Lost Days', produced by John Porter. Mayall: "He suggested bringing Tommy Eyre in to do some keyboards on six tracks, in conjunction with me. I hadn't seen Tommy in years, not since I produced that Aynsley Dunbar Retaliation album in 1969." Interestingly, Eyre's contributions on the organ were played in a style characteristic of Mayall himself. Eyre is perhaps best known for his work with Joe Cocker; he arranged and played the distinctive Hammond organ on Cocker's chart-topping cover of the Beatles' 'With A Little Help From My Friends', adding more than a touch of class to it, and you can also hear him on Gerry Rafferty's global hit 'Baker Street'. There were eight session musicians in total on 'Blues for the Lost Days', including Clifford Solomon and Red Holloway on tenor saxophones, George Bohanon on trombone, and Darrell Leonard on trumpet. The new release brought a welcome return to jazzier sounds, with tunes like Eddie Harris' 'How Can You Live Like That?', and the addictive swing of 'Stone Cold Deal'. Even the title track had a distinctly jazzy touch. 'Blues for the Lost Days' displayed much better song material than 'Spinning Coin'. Released on March 31 to critical acclaim, it reached number 9 on Billboard's Top Blues Albums charts. Critics praised it as one of the best Mayall albums for twenty-five years, calling it "an excellent modern blues album", and "a well produced, creative, varied and reasonably entertaining set." The fiercely traditional 'Living Blues' magazine, however, gave it a distinctly unflattering review, their critic PJ Klemp writing: "In the liner notes to Blues For The Lost Days, John Mayall explains that this album represents an acknowledgement of fellow blues artists who have influenced his music for the past third of a century. During that period the prolific Mayall and his Bluesbreakers helped found the British blues revival, and he has contributed to it by turning out on average of an album a year. Often faulted for having too little imagination, Mayall has based his career on conventional blues arrangements, sometimes with pronounced jazz influences. His latest release is consistent with the rest of his work, as his band does a workmanlike job with some distinctly uninteresting material, though anyone looking for the latest hotshot guitarist to wear a Bluesbreakers uniform will be disappointed. Mayall takes care of the harp, a little guitar, some of the keyboards, and the singing—with the same roughness he has shown for three decades. Unfortunately, Mayall's whining voice makes the weakness of his lyrics more obvious. Song writing is a problem throughout, particularly when he addresses such trite themes as war (it's horrible), street crime (it's a shame), his mother (he loves her), and his wife (ditto). 'All Those Heroes' and 'Blues for the Lost Days' reveal equally predictable attitudes towards his blues predecessors—Mayall worships them, of course, but the cataloguing of their names grows tedious and almost as hollow as the mawkish nostalgia for those lost days. When he covers songs by Eddie Harris or Billy Washington and Fred Stryker, the results are still unimpressive. In the rendition of 'Sen-Say-Shun', Buddy Whittington's guitar playing captures a lot of Freddie King's jittery funkiness, but none of the fluidity in his lyrical style. When even King's classic instrumental track and a horn section can't save 'Blues for the Lost Days', it's clear that this release is flat." Bearing in mind that 'Living Blues' is a Mississippi-based magazine for blues purists, it's not surprising that Mayall fell out of favour with them. 'Blues for the Lost Days' was his third and final album for Silvertone.

The following year, the Bluesbreakers appeared at the 19th annual Blues Festival at Long Beach, California. This took place in early September at the Labour Day weekend and included a historic reunion of British blues musicians, the . breakers being joined on stage by Mick Taylor, Peter Green, Kim nonds, Chris Dreja and Jim McCarty (of the Yardbirds), plus Keith Emerson on keyboards! "We've got a limey brigade on stage tonight!" quipped Mayall at the start, although the 64 year-old bandleader showed himself highly adept at guiding them through a wide range of material. After a long period of mental illness, this was Peter Green's first American concert in 28 years, and probably the most anticipated of the entire festival, but Green's reticence showed that he still had a long way to go. He appeared distant at times, and his singing voice sounded groggy, but on moody instrumentals like 'Albatross' and 'The Supernatural', Green filled the air with sweet, sad, beautiful sounds, not only reminding us of what he had been, but what he could be again. Mayall later commented: "It sure felt good to see him picking up the guitar again, but to tell you the truth, he worked so quietly that I just didn't hear very much of his playing. He's definitely not his old self, of course, but it's nice that he's healthy and working again."

In the meantime, Mayall had signed with Eagle Records, founded in April 1997 by three former colleagues of Castle Communications, the British company that had released the Mayall compilation 'The Collection' in 1986, containing material from the Decca vaults. Mayall's relationship with Eagle proved much more durable than with any other label. Eagle not only promoted the new studio albums, but also re-released older Mayall material on a regular basis.

To record 'Padlock On The Blues', the first album for his new label, Mayall had prepared 13 songs, eleven of which he had written himself. He and his wife Maggie took care of production, and Eagle's generous budget enabled Mayall to hire guest musicians of the calibre of John Lee Hooker, Ernie Watts Tommy Eyre and Coco Montoya, plus a horn section. The sensation was the collaboration with blues legend John Lee Hooker on 'Somebody's Watching' and 'Bad Dream Catcher', with the Bluesbreakers having to make a special trip to San Francisco to record at Hooker's favourite studio! 'Padlock on the Blues' is a solid album of quintessential, guitar-based blues-rock, but there are also some Latin and jazz-tinged grooves, which reinvigorate the sound. It was released on April 23, and garnered some positive reviews, but sadly didn't chart.

Mayall closed 1998 by appearing with Buddy Guy and Koko Taylor at a benefit concert for the Delta Blues Museum in Clarksdale, Mississippi, on November 14. After a busy touring schedule throughout the spring and summer of 1999, September brought another change: after four years, bass player Paulus' stint with the Bluesbreakers came to an end. A short time afterwards, he joined Canned Heat on Larry Taylor's recommendation, and he still plays with them from time to time. Once again, it was Yuele's job to find a suitable successor, so he decided to give his pal Greg Rzab a call. At the time, Rzab was playing with Buddy Guy, so when Buddy fired his entire band, the timing could not have been better. Rzab had played with Otis Rush, but was also busy working with Albert Collins, Luther Allison, Willie Dixon, John Lee Hooker, Robert Jr. Lockwood, Hubert Sumlin and Junior Wells, many of the original Chicago blues musicians who have now passed away. Then followed a twelve-year stint in Buddy Guy's band. In 1994 Rzab was invited by Mick Jagger to audition for the Rolling Stones, hoping to fill Bill Wyman's shoes, but the remaining Stones picked Darryl Jones instead.

By the year 2000, Mayall had started Private Stash Records, his own exclusive label, selling CDs and DVDs on the Internet and at concerts. John's wife Maggie was helping to run their homepage. In an interview with French magazine Soul Bag, Mayall commented: "These are supplementary albums for those who never can get enough. These CDs are not of any interest for the record companies, because they don't have enough commercial potential, but they do bring pleasure and joy for those who love our music, supplying them with something they would like to listen to." Over the years, Private Stash has released a wide range of live material for hardcore fans; please see the discography for more details.

Throughout May, the Bluesbreakers toured the UK, accompanied by Peter Green's Splinter Group. All 31 venues were sold out, and a gala-type climax to the final show took place at London's Albert Hall, where last-minute tickets were reportedly changing hands for £250! Sadly, Green's health was too fragile to allow him to sit in with the Bluesbreakers on a regular basis, something many fans were naturally longing to see. The UK tour also saw a change in the bass department, as Rzab, who had only been with Mayall for eight months, suddenly quit. It was around May 22. "Greg walked out on us because he had an offer to join the Black Crowes," was Mayall's comment. Immediately, Yuele called his friend Neil Simpson of the Climax Blues Band, and asked him to finish the tour, which he was happy to do. "Neil did a fabulous job!" Mayall said afterwards.

'Boogie Woogie Man' was the title of the next release, a 100 % solo effort by Mayall and his first since 1967, but this was far from being another 'Blues Alone' release. Most tracks are solo piano boogie-woogies, with the exception of 'Another Man' which is a Mayall harp feature. Mayall commented: "A few years ago, I began to incorporate a boogie-woogie solo segment into our nightly concert set list. This was a chance for me to pay some homage to my earliest heroes."

Back in the States, Yuele recruited Greg Boaz on bass, but he only lasted a few weeks before Mayall replaced him with Hank van Sickle, who amazingly became the longest-serving bass-player in Bluesbreakers history! Van Sickle grew up listening to Thelonious Monk, Bill Evans, Stan Getz, Oscar Peterson, John Coltrane and Miles Davis; he had immersed himself in the classic 50s Chess recordings of Little Walter, Sonny Boy Williamson, Muddy Waters, Jimmy Rogers and Howlin' Wolf. There was also the blues-rock influence of the 'British Invasion' as typified by Mayall, The Rolling Stones and Cream. After moving to California, his many contacts allowed him to freelance, showcasing his ability to play in different styles. Between tours, Van Sickle continued to be in demand as a session player, especially with legendary jazz organist Jimmy Smith. Mayall later praised his new joiner: "In my opinion, the measure of a great bass player in the realm of the blues is one who lays down good solid bass patterns in the rhythm section, and who works in total harmony with the drummer to work as one entity. It's not the flashy playing of someone who would rather be a lead guitarist, but someone who lays a foundation for the front line instruments to build on. Ever since Hank Van Sickle has been in the band, the Bluesbreakers have never sounded better."

Mayall's next recording was an ambitious project entitled 'Along For The Ride', recorded in early October in Calabasas, California. The album assembled a veritable who's who of top-flight musicians, including many famous ex-Bluesbreakers. 'Yo Yo Man' featured Peter Green, John McVie and Mick Fleetwood, the founding members of the original Fleetwood Mac, playing together for the first time since Green quit the band thirty years earlier. The only Mayall original is 'California', a jazzy thing originally found on 'The Turning Point' in 1969. This new version sounds wonderfully fresh with Red Holloway on tenor sax, while Davy Graham, Britain's folk blues legend, adds a little Jon Mark-style groove on acoustic guitar. Elsewhere, the guitars of Peter Green and Steve Miller blend together surprisingly well, while Whittington is often relegated to playing rhythm. 'She Don't Play by the Rules' features a tasty Mick Taylor solo. 'Along for the Ride' was released on April 23 and reached Nr. 4 in Billboard's Top Blues Albums charts, although the record was perhaps more rock than blues. Having so many stars and luminaries tended to reduce their impact, and perhaps people were expecting too much and the results were a little disappointing. In Blues Revue, critic Hal Horowitz wrote: "Mayall tries too hard to create sparks. Some of it works and some of it doesn't. Steve Miller and Steve Cropper are both relegated to practically inaudible rhythm guitar, and the reunion of Peter Green, John McVie and Mick Fleetwood on 'Yo Yo Man' lies disappointingly limp. The great Otis Rush seems lost as he shares the vocals on his own 'So Many Roads', and there is no guitar."

In 2001, Mayall enlarged the band by adding keyboard player Tom Canning, who had played on 'Wake up Call' and 'Along for the Ride'. The year also saw Mayall publish a book containing all 292 of his recorded lyrics. It was entitled 'History of a Bluesman through his Songs', a delight for all hardcore fans.

From February 19 to March 13, Mayall took his five piece to studios in Calabasas, California, to record 'Stories' the tersely named new release, produced in collaboration with David Z. The band recorded fourteen new songs, six of them Mayall originals, and three by Bluesbreakers past and present. Highlights include 'Kids Got The Blues', a Mayall-written blues-rocker, 'Pride and Faith', a wonderful jazzy shuffle with exciting chord changes, and 'The Mists Of Time', an organ-led minor-key blues. The new album came out on August 27 and, despite being one of Mayall's rockiest offerings, got to number one in the Billboard Blues Charts. Although 'Stories' is one of Mayall's best-sounding albums, from now on his priority would be finding aspiring young musicians to keep the music fresh. The album was promoted with yet more touring: first a fifteen-date US tour starting on September 7, followed by a thirty-nine date British tour supported by the Peter Green Splinter Group until December 4, a gruelling schedule that would put many younger acts to shame, as there were no days off. 'No Days Off' was also the name of the follow-up record, released April 2003. It was pretty much a live version of 'Stories', but fresher and more spontaneous than the studio effort, and is a must-have among collectors.

2003 began with short tours of Hawaii and Australia; the Bluesbreakers played the Basement Club in Sydney on February 12, and their performance was filmed and released on DVD as 'Cookin' Down Under' on Mayall's Private Stash label. This live concert is well worth checking out, especially the version of 'Hideaway', where Whittington transforms the instrumental into an amazing showcase medley of Freddie King tunes. The highlight of the year was undoubtedly the momentous 70 Birthday Concert on July 19 at King's Dock Arena in Liverpool, which saw the long-anticipated reunion with Clapton. Mayall remembers: "The initiative came from

UNICEF. They contacted my record label, and Eagle Records came to me a while ago with a proposition to have a high profile concert in support of UNICEF, which attracted me immediately because it was for a good cause, but also—and I'm not trying to hide that fact—it was a good opportunity to get in touch with Eric again. Since I last recorded with him on Back to the Roots in 1970, I've tried many times to contact him for various projects, but his record company had always vetoed the idea. However, this took so much advance planning that I wondered if it would ever happen." The incredible line-up was completed by ex-Bluesbreakers legends Mick Taylor on guitar, Henry Lowther on trumpet, and Chris Barber, another famous bandleader, on trombone. Rehearsals took place at London's Waterloo Sunset Studios on Wednesday the 16 July; they did a quick run-through in Liverpool on the day. It was a wonderful concert, and the extended Bluesbreakers backed Clapton as well as any band, if not better, an enduring testimony to the quality of Mayall's musicians. This piece of blues history was recorded and released as 'John Mayall & The Bluesbreakers And Friends, 70th Birthday Concert' and got to number 8 in Billboard's Top Blues Album charts. For more details, also on the DVD, please see the discography.

This was followed by US dates for the Bluesbreakers in August and September, at the end of which Canning left the band, choosing instead to continue backing his old employer, French 'Elvis' Johnny Hallyday, but he would eventually return to the fold in a few years' time. To top the year off, the BBC broadcast 'The Godfather of British Blues', an excellent hour-long documentary on Mayall's life and career, which was released by Eagle Vision the following year. The programme contained many rare interviews and concert clips; please see the discography for more details.

In July 2004 the Bluesbreakers toured Scandinavia together with 13 year-old Eric Steckel as special guest. Steckel's appearance at the Sarasota Blues Festival in Florida had been nothing short of sensational, and the teenager prodigy made a lasting impression on Mayall, who was always keen to support young talent. From October to November, the Bluesbreakers embarked on a UK tour of 35 dates, with Mick Taylor as a special guest throughout. Besides supplying his fabulous guitar licks on every number, Taylor also shared vocal duties, singing on 'Late at Night', 'Can't You Hear Me Knocking' and 'Blind Willy McTell'.

2005 saw the release of the next studio album of fifteen songs entitled 'Road Dogs', produced by Mayall and the Bluesbreakers. Mayall wrote thirteen, Whittington, Yuele and van Sickle the other two. Also recorded at Calabasas, California in early 2005, it was another solid blues workout. Joining in were ex-Bluesbreaker Tom Canning on organ and piano, Dale Morris Jr. on violin, and the young Eric Steckel, who added blistering lead guitar on 'Chaos In The Neighbourhood', a moving blues-rock lament. Released on June 14, 'Road Dogs' reached number four in Billboard's Top Blues Album charts. Mayall's lyrics came under fire again, with Blues Revue commenting: "15 slickly produced, hook-laden originals. Mayall's lyrics are generally concerned with self-reflection (with an ample dose of sermonizing as well). He seems to have given his words much thought—perhaps too much. Those who believe that brevity is the soul of wit might find his prolix lyrics a distraction."

On 19 May, the Bluesbreakers were playing a show in Malibu when Mayall surprised his drummer by presenting him with an engraved gold watch. He announced: "Joe Yuele has been playing drums for me for more years than all former Bluesbreakers drummers put together, and would seem to be eligible for a lifetime achievement award it there ever was one! No-one has propelled my previous rhythm sections with a steadier command of his instrument than Joe, and he continues to anchor the beat with an incomparable drive." Yuele had been laying down the rhythm for the Bluesbreakers for twenty years, a remarkable testament to the man's loyalty. On June 10, Buckingham Palace announced that Mayall, together with Brian May and Jimmy Page, had been awarded an OBE for services to music. On November 25, Mayall journeyed to London to accept the presentation from Prince Charles, the heir to the British throne remarking with typical Goon Show humour that he hoped that the award would give Mayall the incentive to keep on working!

A special US-wide tour of 32 concerts took place in the autumn of 2005 entitled the 'Rockin' Blues Revue', together with Robben Ford and Eric Bibb. Bibb, who opened the concerts, delivered a unique blend of finger style acoustic gospel-blues, and his rootsy performances generated universal acclaim. The Bluesbreakers were Ford's backing band. These were beautifully paced concerts, always ending in a big finale, with all the musicians playing together. In July the following year, Mayall and the Bluesbreakers were back in the studio to cut another new record, this time to honour one of Mayall's blues heroes, the late great Freddie King. King had been a huge influence on Eric Clapton, Peter Green, Stan Webb and Stevie Ray Vaughan, to name but a few. Called 'In the Palace of the King', it was recorded at LAFX in North Hollywood. "The Bluesbreakers have been associated with the music of Freddie King right from the beginning," explained Mayall. "So, it was a logical step for the band to record an album of songs written by him or associated with him. It became sort of a trademark with the Bluesbreakers in the early days to do one of his instrumentals: Eric with 'Hideaway', Peter Green with 'The Stumble', and then Mick Taylor doing 'Driving Sideways'. So it was kind of a tradition, and the style of his guitar playing is the one constant thing that runs through all the early albums. It has always been identified with the Bluesbreakers guitarists. And I thought he was one incredible singer and he was a strong influence on my vocal style." Mayall remembered the great man thus: "I think I first saw him at the Bag Of Nails where he was playing with Chicken Shack with Christine Perfect on keyboards and she let me sit in [this must have been around January/February 1969]. Freddie knew about my connection with all the British guitar players, so he was interested in meeting me, and used to come back to my flat and we'd listen to a lot of records there. I played him a bit of Eric Clapton and Jimi Hendrix, and he thought Eric was terrific, but he was quite a bit put off by Hendrix. He thought he was overplaying. I sat in with Freddie several times, not only in England, but in America too. He was a very imposing figure and a very smiley, affable, big man; when he walked into my flat he filled the place! We didn't know too much about his real career back in the States because all the visiting bluesmen were so revered here. It was impossible to imagine them at home in their own country hustling around trying to make a living, but largely ignored. But it was a racially divided country and he wasn't widely appreciated outside his own circle." Freddie King's career was tragically cut short on December 28, 1976, when he died of heart failure aged just 42 after playing a Christmas concert. Of the fourteen tracks on the album, only five come from King's classic King/Federal period from 1960–66; six others come from King's blues-rock phase when he recorded for Shelter (1970–73). Mayall wrote two tracks: 'King of Kings' and 'Time To Go', the latter a horn-drenched remake of King's slow blues 'The Welfare (Turns Its Back On You)' but with new lyrics. 'Cannonball Shuffle', composed by Robben Ford, was the only instrumental, but wouldn't it have been a better idea to let Buddy Whittington (also a native Texan) record his stunning medley of Freddie King classics instead? In between sessions, the Bluesbreakers did fourteen more U.S. dates. 'Palace of the King' was released on April 13 the following year, and reached number 3 in Billboard's Top Blues album charts, staying for a total of 12 weeks.

There was another UK tour of 37 dates for the Bluesbreakers starting on October 17, together with Stan Webb's Chicken Shack as special guests. At the gig on November 5 in Norwich, 14-year-old Oli Brown, a local guitar hero, joined The Bluesbreakers onstage, and completely wowed the crowd. Brown would open for Mayall's UK tour five years later. At the end of 2006, Eagle Records released a 5 CD set entitled 'Essentially John Mayall' to coincide with the fortieth anniversary of the Bluesbreakers' classic 'Beano' album. The boxed set was packed with rare and wonderful recordings from virtually every Bluesbreakers line-up. In January 2007, Decca released 'John Mayall and the Bluesbreakers Live at the BBC', which was frustratingly incomplete as it entirely ignored the period with Mick Taylor! Mayall had not been involved or informed, and Decca didn't even have the decency to send him a copy.

Gig-wise, 2007 started off with shows in the US in February and April, and continued with another European tour from July 5 with 30 concerts to cover the popular summer jazz and open-air festivals.

The Bluesbreakers played a total of 67 gigs in 2007, about 20 less than the previous year.

At the beginning of 2008, Mayall was led astray from his beloved Bluesbreakers. Mark Hummel had invited him to play at his harmonica 'blow out' series of concerts. These take place all over California every year, and have been a part of the music scene since 1991. Among other masters of the harp, blues greats such as Billy Branch, James Harman, Kim Wilson and Carey Bell have graced the festival in the past, so clearly, Mayall felt very honoured to have been asked. Mayall did eight concerts altogether, getting to know Lazy Lester, a legend for his fifties recordings for Excello, and Kenny Neal, the modern swamp blues master and multi-instrumentalist. The backing band consisted of Rusty Zinn on guitar, Bob Welsh on piano and guitar, R.W. Grigsby on bass and Marty Dodson on drums.

Having returned to the fold in February, Mayall and his band spent the next eight months on the road, criss-crossing California, South America and Europe in a series of gigs. Friday 24th October saw the last ever concert of this longest of all Bluesbreakers incarnations. Suddenly, Buddy Whittington, Hank van Sickle and Joe Yuele were out of a job. On the eve of his 75th birthday, Mayall decided to retire the longest-standing Bluesbreakers line-up of the lot. A few days later on November 10th, Mayall posted the following statement on his website:

"Dear Loyal Friends and Fans, as reports about the disbanding of the Bluesbreakers have been circulating since the end of the last European tour, I have to apologize for not announcing and confirming it sooner. Physically and emotionally it has been a tough decision to make. The main reason is that at age seventy-five I want to cut back on my usual heavy workload and also give myself freedom to work with other musicians if and when I feel like it. Needless to say this doesn't mean I'll be abandoning the blues but rather hoping to expand on it through guest appearances and in the company with other musicians. Meanwhile I can't thank Joe, Hank and Buddy enough for all the great contributions they've made to my musical journey thus far. It has been a great ride indeed."

Whittington, who over the years had energized Mayall's band with his blazing input on guitar, reacted prudently: "I can't speak for anyone else, but I am no longer employed by Mr Mayall. I don't think Joe and Hank are either. No hard feelings, I just think he wants to try something different and 'back off' off working a little at 75." However, drummer Joe Yuele felt the split was far from amicable, recalling: "When John sacked the whole band in 2008, we were very disappointed in his decision after being together all these years. Also what was disturbing to us was John telling us he broke up the band because he was quitting touring. In a short while we realized it was all bullshit! He was putting together a new band and didn't have the courage or the respect to tell us the truth."

CHAPTER 12

Good Old Rockin' Blues

2009 to Present with Rocky Athas

Mayall had this to say about the outstanding Whittington/van Sickle/Yuele band that lasted so long: "With the last line-up, we got as far as we could go. At the end, I wouldn't say that it got stale but I've missed the pepper and the bite. I thought that it was time for a fresh air supply; I wanted to shift up a few gears and feel more energy again." At an age when most people are taking it easy, Mayall assembled an all-new band that he fully intended to go on tour with. He clearly had no intention of retiring. Mayall has always said "Jazz and blues musicians' careers don't end except by death." As for plans for a new album, he commented in November 2008: "Eagle say they won't need another album 'till later next year' and by then it will be with the new band that I'll be debuting in the spring."

In February 2009 Mayall took part in another of Mark Hummel's "big blow" west coast harmonica tours before announcing the new band. It wasn't as easy finding recruits, as Joe Yuele wasn't around to help recruit talent anymore. All new joiners had to be friendly non-smokers; a good relationship was crucial for a settled life on the road. Mayall: "As a bandleader you have to be able to recognize early on who can work together before you put everyone in the room to play."

The new guitarist of choice was Rocky Athas, a friend of Whittington's. Mayall first got to know Athas when the Texan's band played support to the Bluesbreakers back in October 2002. Mayall was impressed enough to take Athas' phone number for future reference. As for the bass department, Mayall selected ex-Bluesbreaker Greg Rzab, and also told him to bring a drummer! Rzab took along Jay Davenport, also from Chicago, so they joined the band as an item. A last minute addition was ex-Bluesbreaker Tom Canning on keyboards. Mayall was very happy with his choice, as only Athas and Davenport were total newcomers.

Athas' childhood friend had been Stevie Ray Vaughan; they grew up together in the Dallas suburb of Oak Cliff and were also schoolmates. In 1974 Athas formed Lightning, his first rock band, which became one of the biggest draws in Texas nightclub history, but unfortunately they split up in the 80s. By the age of 23, Athas had been inducted into Buddy magazine's "Texas Tornados" as one of the top ten best guitarists in Texas. Athas was in highly respectable company, as previous winners had been Johnny Winter, Jimmy Vaughan, Bugs Henderson, Eric Johnson and Billy Gibbons; Stevie Ray Vaughan would receive his award two years later. Athas' growing fame wasn't limited to the Lone Star State; Irish band Thin Lizzy wrote "Cocky Rocky" after hearing Athas play one night at the Dallas club Mother Blues. Queen guitarist Brian May also witnessed Athas' performance, and was so floored by his finger tapping technique that he used it on the next Queen album. This was well before the emergence of Eddie Van Halen. Athas' career took another big step forward when he became lead guitarist for southern rockers Black Oak Arkansas, touring with them from 1996 for five years. In 2000, Athas worked with Buddy Miles on an excellent release called "The Blues Berries". When Athas joined Mayall, he was already a veteran, with a wicked tone and a thriving solo career. Unlike his illustrious predecessors, however, Athas didn't have a singing voice. Bass player Greg Rzab was back after a nine-year break, this time to stay a little longer. In the meantime, Mayall had forgiven the bassman for the stunt he pulled back in May 2000, when he suddenly pulled out of the Bluesbreakers' UK tour to audition for the Black Crows. "Star-Zab" was evidently too good a bass player to ignore, and because he had an excellent drummer with him in the shape of Jay Davenport, Mayall was happy to recruit both. The new band debuted live on March 20 in Cerritos, California at the Center for Performing Arts, the posters advertising "The John Mayall Band". It seemed Mayall had dropped the "Bluesbreakers" moniker for good. Then the band retired to the studio for just over a week from March 21 to record the new album, produced by Maggie Mayall and Michael Aarvold. "Tough" contained eleven new songs, eight covers and three Mayall originals. Among the best takes were "Tough Times Ahead", a lament about economic recession, "That Good Old Rockin' Blues", an anti-rap song, while "Slow Train to Nowhere" expressed the waste of alcohol addiction. "The Sum of Something" was a wonderful jazzy shuffle by Oregon-based singer/songwriter Curtis Salgado, and one of the album's highlights. "Tough" was released in September 2009, Mayall's first album in two and a half years, but compared to its predecessors, it was unexceptional and rather directionless. People had also been downloading free music for some time, and the industry was beginning to suffer from a serious financial crisis.

In a reversal of tradition at live shows, Mayall would begin all by himself before the band joined in. For the set, he would choose well-known songs from his massive back catalogue, such as "Oh, Pretty Woman", "Hideaway", "Have You Heard", "Chicago Line", "Parchman Farm", "Help Me", "Dream About The Blues" and "Room To Move". Why Mayall needed an entirely new band (essentially the Bluesbreakers in all but name) to play his older and more famous songs remains an open question. One possible answer is that he knew it would bring new life to the old classics, plus it was also what the public wanted. This was another superlatively good band: Athas sounded like the perfect blend of Clapton, Green and Taylor, Canning was superb on the organ, Davenport supplied super-tight drumming while Rzab laid down a solid groove and held the band together, acting as de-facto musical leader. In 2009 there were just 74 John Mayall Band concerts, not at all many by his usual busy standards. The following year would be a lot more hectic with 113 gigs, more than the last four years put together! Mayall had always preferred playing live shows and doing tours to studio work, saying: "The road is where all the creative work goes on." Studio recordings had increasingly become a duty. Talking about albums, Mayall said: "To me it ends when I finish the record and package it all up; I'm just interested in having an audience." For the first six months of 2010, the band toured the US, Australia, New Zealand and Europe, accompanied by Mayall's wife Maggie, who contributed her considerable talent by singing lead on "Howlin' Moon" and other songs. At this time, shows were two hours long, usually starting at 8pm with no support, with Mayall making an astonishingly fit and agile impression. Leaving his guitar at home, he now concentrated fully on playing organ and harp. On top of his keyboard, he had a file containing the lyrics to many songs which he often consulted, this occasionally leading to a belated start to his singing.

The next shock was Tom Canning's departure; he suddenly left on October 19 in the middle of the second European tour. Mayall commented: "With regard to Tom I don't know what his problem was. He just refused to sign a release for us to record live in London for that online deal, so he quit and was on a plane home next morning before breakfast. Strange, but the band has been much tighter and happier since." The tour in question closed by tradition with a concert in London on November 1. The show was recorded, filmed and later released on DVD and CD on Mayall's Private Stash label, entitled rather unspectacularly "Live in London". However, Mayall's original idea was to make it available using the Internet. On October 21, Mayall declared: "We are pleased to announce the first ever live stream broadcast of a John Mayall Concert! On Monday November 1st, you will be able to tune in to the London concert at Leicester Square from anywhere in the world." Sadly, the webcast was beset with accessibility problems and date changes, prompting Mayall to publish an apology on his website for his frustrated fans. Despite the technical and organizational problems, "Live in London" is a great album throughout, and superbly well recorded. One highlight is the scintillating version of "Room to Move" which features bass player Rzab quoting licks from Hendrix's "Third Stone from the Sun". Interestingly, the last time Mayall had done a live recording in London was the set captured at Klooks Kleek in December 1964, some 46 years earlier! Both albums include great versions of "Chicago Line".

2011 saw the band touring all over the US, Europe and Canada; the Canadian dates were so successful that the band had to return for eight more shows at the end of November. Around this time, critical voices started to emerge concerning Mayall's attitude towards his audience at live shows. In June, an Italian fan complained that Mayall objected to having an arm put round his shoulders during a post-gig photo opportunity; another comment posted in August accused him of coldly ignoring adoring fans while packing up his gear after a concert in Minneapolis. The fan wrote: "We see tons of live music all over the five state area, and only a couple of artists have not come back out to "meet & greet". Those artists usually leave a bad impression in our minds because of their failure to show appreciation to the very people that are enjoying and buying their music. Mr. Mayall ranked right up there with those types of artists, in our minds."

In September, Maggie Mayall used her website to declare that she and John had decided to end their relationship for good; Mayall's site had not mentioned this at all. Although most fans were still in the dark, it soon emerged that products on Mayall's Private Stash label were now available exclusively through CD Baby and amazon, but no longer carried by Maggie's homepage.

At their next UK tour in late October, emerging British blues rocker Oli Brown played support to the John Mayall Band. Brown, one of a new generation of blues musicians, had already built up a considerable following in Britain, his band winning best live act at the 2011 British Blues Awards, and his latest release, "Heads I Win, Tails You Lose", picking up the prize for best album. Amazingly, Blue Horizon founder Mike Vernon had handled production duties, just as he had in the old Decca days. Brown was also invited to sit in with Mayall during the tour. At their London show on October 29, Mick Taylor guested on three encores to complete a memorable tour. To round off the year, Mayall played a memorable concert at the Jakarta International Blues Festival on December 17, headlining with ex-Genesis guitarist Steve Hackett. As Athas had passport issues and was not able to attend the Jakarta show, Mayall recruited Oli Brown to take his place. At 21, Brown was about the same age as Clapton and Green had been when they started their "apprenticeship" with the Bluesbreakers in the mid-60s, so it seems here that history was repeating itself. Sadly, although the band completed 95 shows in 2011, there was no new album.

At the start of the New Year, Mayall attended Hummel's harmonica blow out, again as one of the guests, replacing Charlie Musselwhite for two shows. Until October 2012, they played shows throughout North America, together with white US blues pioneer and Grammy winner John Hammond. In November, in time for an extended European tour, Mayall released three new live CDs entitled Historic Live Shows Volumes 1, 2 and 3 on his Private Stash label. These contained 32 tracks spanning 28 years of music making, all from Mayall's vast archive. Such releases are a must for hardcore fans.

Mayall and his band did a total of 89 live appearances all over the USA, Canada and Europe in 2012, but the following year was not nearly as busy. Among the shortened touring schedule, highlights were Mayall's tour of Hawaii in May, with British blues icon Kim Simmonds of Savoy Brown as support, and the Sao Paolo concerts in the second week of June with Buddy Guy, Taj Mahal and Shemekia Copeland. Mayall remarked on his homepage: "We've had quite a few comments from fans on the leaner touring calendar for 2013. This is not because of any reluctance to tour on anyone's part, but just that they have a huge year coming up following John's 80th birthday in November, and many of the promoters wanted to hold off this year and go big next year! They are really looking forward to celebrating John's milestone year with all his wonderful fans!" As for news about the new album, Mayall wrote: "No plans yet for a new album. We are at the moment working on getting out of our contract with Eagle."

After Mayall had dissolved his contract with Eagle Rock, he joined Forty Below Records, an obscure, LA-based label who had released just four albums, all by lesser-known artists. However, as they were offering a special deal with Sony/Red covering distribution, Mayall was keen on signing. Another reason was that he had by this time collected together enough material for another studio album, his first in over four years. The band recorded "A Special

Life" at Entourage Studios in North Hollywood in early November, a healthy mix of songs by Mayall's idols, plus five original compositions. Musically, "A Special Life" was a fine album, with C.J. Chenier from Louisiana as the only guest musician. Son of great accordion legend Clifton Chenier, he specialized in Zydeco music, and contributes Cajun accordion and vocals to "Why Did You Go Last Night", a song written by his father. Other blues covers are the convincing "Big Town Playboy" by Eddie Taylor, a song Mayall performed a lot in the sixties, "Floodin' in California", a slow Albert King blues, and the Jimmy Rogers standard "That's All Right", played here more uptempo than the 1950 original. "Speak of the Devil" by Louisiana-based slide guitar wizard Sonny Landreth was another outstanding take, a song in the vein of Sonny Boy Williamson's "Don't Start me Talkin'". Officially released on May 13, "A Special Life" was available for Mayall's 80th Birthday tour of Europe.

On November 14, Mayall travelled to London to collect a Classic Album Award for his legendary 1966 Beano album, featuring Eric Clapton. At the awards ceremony at The Roundhouse, Black Sabbath guitarist Tony Iommi paid tribute to Mayall, saying: "I must say, it is so amazing to be in the same room as John Mayall because without him we wouldn't be here. Thank you!" The following year, the 80th Anniversary tour of Europe comprised 55 shows in thirteen countries, and was rounded off with a wonderful concert and celebration at Ronnie Scott's in London.

After roughly fifty years, it seems a complete travesty that one of the most important figures in the history of recorded music has not been inducted into the Rock and Roll Hall of Fame; the museum in Cleveland should really open an entire wing devoted to his achievements. At very least, Mayall is the greatest talent scout there has ever been for the blues. Not only did Mayall have the gift for knowing the real deal when he saw it, he was also smart enough to let his band members do their own thing when they signed on, instead of stifling their creative abilities to highlight his own. The only parallels that come to mind are bandleaders such as Muddy Waters, Art Blakey or Horace Silver. Now over 80 years old, the big question is how much longer Mayall can carry on making music. Let the man himself have the last word: "That will depend on good health. As long as I can give 100 % of myself, I'll be there. If the work is there and people to listen, the music will always be inspiring for me." What a wonderful legacy.

CHAPTER 13

Mayall's Voice and Instruments
John Mayall the singer, guitarist, keyboard
and harmonica player

MAYALL THE SINGER

If a blues musician is first and foremost a singer, then their voice is their main instrument. For a multi-instrumentalist and all-rounder like Mayall, however, this is obviously not the case, but this certainly does not mean he regards his voice as of secondary importance to his abilities as a guitarist, organist or harmonica player. For Mayall, then, singing and playing remain equally important. The truth to tell, Mayall was blessed with a unique and quite capable singing voice, perfectly able to communicate the range of emotions required by blues music. If you listen to the voices of Otis Spann, Jerry McCain or Ry Cooder, you will definitely find many moments that distinctly remind you of Mayall the singer. "I realize I don't have a black bluesman's voice," Mayall says, "But you work with what you've got. As long as I can get the emotion out and sing in tune, that's what I aim for, but I think I'm not always accurate, certainly in a live situation where you get carried away with the intensity of the music. So sometimes if you hear a tape, there's quite a few notes that you wish would be a little bit better in tune. But it is the emotion, really, that is most important." Mayall regards the blues as "technically imperfect" by definition, believing that a singer with a flawed voice can get away with those imperfections more easily than in other genres. "Someone who thought his own vocals were just terrible was Jimi Hendrix," Mayall says, "He was always going off: 'Oh, don't talk about my singing.' Like I say, it's wonderful that we have so many people who don't like their own vocals, who sound just great. I enjoy singing, so when I've done something, especially on record, that's a permanent thing that will last forever." In 1971, the music paper Sounds praised Mayall, commenting: "His voice, as always, has an edgy quality", while a year earlier another paper wrote: "Ladies find his curious voice, a kind of hernia-register amalgam of J.B. Lenoir tonality and Mose Allison phrasing, tough and sensual; guys find it tough and ballsy."

Criticism, however, has never been far away. In June 1974, the New Musical Express wrote this of Mayall: "His voice lay somewhere between the hungry howl of a hyena. and the mourning call of a grief-crazed Bedouin female!" Of his former boss, Eric Clapton reportedly once said "Mayall sings like your grandmother." Undoubtedly, Mayall was himself critically self-aware of his vocal limitations, and wrote this on the cover of his "Rock the Blues Tonight" release: "I can't say I'm quite so thrilled with my vocal contributions which are, in most cases, excruciating and erratic, to say the least. This aside, I can look back on those years now and realize I had much to learn about singing in live concert environments." Many artists, including Buddy Guy, have said they cringe at the sound of their own voice. Although during the sixties when he lived in London, Mayall was clearly not as good a singer as Mick Jagger, Stevie Winwood, Chris Farlowe or Georgie Fame, he was unquestionably better than Alexis Korner or Graham Bond, the other two leading lights of the British blues boom.

MAYALL THE GUITARIST

Although Mayall has helped promote the careers of very many exceptional guitarists, he has never been a particularly gifted player himself. When a music magazine interviewed him in the early seventies, he stated: "It's sort of strange that Guitar Player would want to interview me, because the magazine is usually reserved for people who play the guitar. I can hold one in my hands and pluck a few notes, but it's very hit and miss." Many years later, Mayall told another paper: "I'm such a limited technician on the guitar, but as time has gone on, I think I use it pretty effectively as a tool to express myself." His limitations as a guitarist are something he shared with Alexis Korner. His solos are often rather awkward and clumsy, but this is typical for a blues musician. John Lee Hooker and Lightnin' Hopkins also had their limits, and played with a certain ungainliness, but it is often just this quality which makes their guitar sound individual and charming. Asked about how he started, Mayall said: "T-Bone Walker was one of my favourites. I used to like Josh White, too, and Big Bill Broonzy. Teddy Bunn was another favourite of mine. All those things were about rhythm guitar, and I learned them all. I never really leaned into lead playing. It was a lot more of a rhythm thing, probably as a result of learning on the ukulele, strumming away, and that's why my lead guitar playing is probably not much more involved than John Lee Hooker's on a note-by-note basis; it's more about the feeling and the touch. I can't do the fast stuff, so I have to make up for it sparingly." In 1972, Mayall told Planet: "I don't like acoustic guitars, and it's probably fair to say I hardly ever use one—pretty well everything I've ever done has been on electric." Later, he told Guitar Player: "I don't really worry about instruments, because they're just tools. Stick an axe in my hand, and I'll see what I can do with it. It's as simple as that."

For these reasons, Mayall doesn't only play famous, high quality guitars like Fenders, but also Japanese-made Fender copies. His brand of choice is Squier, one of which is pictured on the cover of the "Stories" album, and most prominently on the "70th Birthday

Concert" cover. Mayall loves customising and lovingly decorating his guitars. This particular Squier Stratocaster copy he cut down and painted red, using the same paint as on the door of his house near Los Angeles! Carving and changing the shape of his guitars is one of Mayall's hobbies. In 1993, Mayall told Guitarist: "The 5-string was a solid-body Burns which I cut around and hand painted; none of them were really special makes. They're hybrids. The 9-string was my original 6-string guitar, which I bought in Japan when I was in the army. It was electric with an acoustic body (a Weldons semi-acoustic), and I originally wanted to make a 12-string out of it. So I started doubling them up from the E string on down, but when it got about halfway through, the neck started bending under the strain; it wasn't built to deal with it. So I took the sixth string off entirely, doubled up the first four and that left the fifth string on its own, which was about as much strain as it could take. With the 5-string you just take the sixth string off. I have that one tuned to open E because that's the one I use for bottleneck. Now I have a 12-string Rickenbacker (actually a modified 660/12, the guitar on the cover of 'Exclusive Live Rarities' and 'Behind the Iron Curtain'), and my regular guitar is a Japanese copy of a Stratocaster (the Squier mentioned above). And there again, I cut the body off that and did a new body which has no room for the knobs; I just have one volume control so the tone comes from the amp itself." In the sixties, Mayall played another solid-body Burns, a six-string Bison with four pickups, which he totally re-shaped; this he proudly shows off on the jacket of "The Diary of a Band" albums. An instrument Mayall used a lot during the late sixties was another radically modified Burns solid-body, shaped to look like a Vox Mark VI "Teardrop", and decorated with all sorts of ornamentation; it's the guitar that Mayall is seen playing on the cover of the US release of "Primal Solos", the front cover of "Thru the Years" and inside the fold-out jacket of "Bare Wires".

Pictures inside the "Turning Point" sleeve show Mayall playing a 12-string Fender XII (with strongly modified head), although the album sleeve mentions only a Telecaster 6-string as the Mayall's instrument of choice on the LP. In the late Sixties, Mayall purchased a Fender Stratocaster with a dark rosewood fingerboard, a guitar he also reshaped by sculpting 17 holes of various sizes into its body. This instrument is pictured on "Jazz Blues Fusion" and "A Hard Core Package". Mayall used it from 1968 on with the "Blues from Laurel Canyon" band, right up to 1979, when this guitar, together with his 9-string and the 6-string Burns, were sadly all destroyed in the house fire. After this disaster, Mayall hand carved another Fender Stratocaster in a similar way, as can be seen on the cover of "Road Show Blues" and on the CD single "Ain't No Brakeman".

On the cover of "In the Palace of the King", we see another Fender Stratocaster, customised in Mayall's inimitable way; interviewed by Guitar Player in December 1970, Mayall was asked if the Gibson Les Paul was his favourite. He answered: "Well, no. I didn't choose it. The guitar I had before that was a Fender, and it went out of tune. So I told my road manager to get me a new one... I don't know anything about these things." From 2009 on, he has been using a Vox V230 Tempest XII, a solid body 12 string with 3 pickups, of which Mayall purchased two, in light blue and sunburst, respectively.

AN OVERVIEW OF MAYALL'S ELECTRIC GUITARS

Instrument	Period Played	Pictures, LP Sleeves	Other Information
Weldons semi-acoustic, Mayall's famous 9 string (1)	around 1954 to 1967	The Blues Alone (front) Looking Back LP (back) The Blues Alone 2006 CD (back)	Mayall's first guitar, bought in Tokyo 1954 for $25. Converted to a 9 string. Painted, with John Mayall and Blues Breakers written on. Destroyed in 1979 fire
Burns solid-body, Mayall's 5 string, with 3 pickups (2)	around 1964 to 1967	Crusade (back) Lost and Gone (front) Earliest promo band photo with Eric Clapton 1965	Cut, decorated and hand painted, with John Mayall written on. Tuned to open E or C for bottleneck use

Instrument	Period Played	Pictures, LP Sleeves	Other Information
Burns Bison 6 string solid-body with 4 pickups (3)	around 1967/68	The Diary of a Band (front), So Many Roads, An Anthology 1964–1974 4CD box (front)	Entirely re-shaped, cut away, carved and engraved, with John Mayall written on. Destroyed in 1979 fire
Burns/Baldwin solid body "Teardrop" egg-shaped 6 string with 3 pickups (4)	around late sixties and 1970	Primal Solos LP, US-version (blue front), Thru the Years (front), Bare Wires (inside fold-out)	Totally modified to teardrop form like a Vox Mark VI, and decorated with ornamentation
Fender Stratocaster with dark rosewood fingerboard (5)	around 1968 to 1979	Jazz Blues Fusion (front) A Hard Core Package (back) Road Show Blues (back)	Entirely reshaped, 17 different holes in the body. Destroyed in 1979 fire
Fender Electric XII 12 string, with 2 split pickups (6)	around late sixties and seventies	Turning Point album inside booklet (CD) and folder (LP)	Slightly customized with modified head
Fender Telecaster (7)	around late sixties	(red and pic- tured on In the Shadows of Legends in 2004)	Mentioned on the cover of The Turning Point
Gibson Les Paul (8)	around 1970/71	Drivin' On, The ABC Years (inside booklet)	Unmodified
Fender Stratocaster with light maple finger-board (9)	around 1980 to 1995	Road Show Blues (front) CD-single Ain't No Brakeman	Hand-carved like guitar (5) but with a darker body and only 4 holes. Decorated with shells and turquoise
Fender Stratocaster sunburst with light maple fingerboard (10)	around 1982	(tour photos, Italy, November– December 1982)	Unmodified (later probably customised to become guitar 12)

Instrument	Period Played	Pictures, LP Sleeves	Other Information
Rickenbacker 660/12 black solid-body 12 string with 2 pickups (11)	around 1985 to 2002	Exclusive Live Rarities (front), Behind the Iron Curtain (front and back), Stories (inside booklet)	Hand-carved, modified and decorated with turquoise and shells. John Mayall written on.
Fender Stratocaster with light maple fingerboard (12)	around 1988 to 1993	Live in Germany 1988 Lange Schatten Tour 88 (inside booklet)	Radically modified, reduced and decorated with turquoise (originally probably guitar 10)
Squier Stratocaster with red body, white pickups and dark fingerboard (13)	around 1993 to 2003	Stories (back) 70th Birthday Concert	Radically modified, body cut to the minimum
Epiphone Wilshire with dark fingerboard (14)	around 2006	(tour photos, France, March 2006)	Minimized, with black head, body with pointed horns
Fender Stratocaster with dark rosewood fingerboard (15)	around 2006	In the Palace of the King (front and back of booklet)	Radically modified, minimized and decorated with turquoise
Fender Duo-Sonic II with 2 pickups and dark rosewood fingerboard (16)	around 2004 to 2012	(tour photos, Spain, July 2007), Rudy Rotta & friends (front cover)	Minimized, body and head modified, decorated with turquoise
2 Vox V230 Tempest XII 12 string solid-body guitar with 3 pickups, sunburst (17) and light-blue (18)	from 2009 on	Tough (inside booklet)	Both original and unmodified
Eric Johnson Stratocaster with 1 pickup and light maple fingerboard (19)	around 2014	A Special Life (front cover)	Cut body with 3D art, John Mayall written on, decorated with turquoise, shells, beads, coin, etc.

JOHN MAYALL THE KEYBOARD PLAYER

"I am a keyboard player first and foremost. The keyboard is number one, it has always been my main instrument and that's the one I get the most out of. It's a complete instrument; you can play chords, melody, everything on it," said Mayall, adding: "There's something from Albert Ammons and Big Maceo, but also from Horace Silver and Bobby Timmons in my piano playing." John Mayall's boogie-woogie influenced piano style is instantly recognizable, and always has a cheerful element in it. Listen to the piano playing on "Bear Wires" on Canned Heat's "Livin' the Blues": this is unmistakably Mayall! In the early days of the Bluesbreakers, Mayall purchased a Farfisa Compact organ, which that he often paired with a Hohner Cembalett, a smaller keyboard that he perched on top of the Farfisa. Just before Clapton became a Bluesbreaker in April 1965, Mayall replaced the Farfisa with the more powerful and better-sounding Hammond M100, which he immediately emblazoned with the words "John Mayall" in big letters on the back. This is organ you can spot on the "Beano" album, on "Bare Wires" and on the UK version of "Primal Solos". It's a fantastic instrument and a trusted companion on stage, but huge, heavy and unwieldy, not easy to transport while on the road. A brand new Hammond A3 eventually replaced the M100 in the spring of 1968. The following year, Mayall invested in an electric piano, most likely a Fender Rhodes that he used exclusively on his first US tours, especially during the jazz-blues years. Towards the end of the seventies, a Hohner Clavinet D6 was his keyboard of choice on stage. During the early eighties with the reunited Bluesbreakers featuring Mick Taylor, Mayall used a Yamaha piano keyboard next to his Hammond. As soon as synthesized keyboards were available from the early eighties, Mayall had several: a Roland, a Korg T3, a Kurzweil PC88, a Juno 1, and later a Yamaha S90. For his US tours in 2011 and 2012, Mayall used a Roland RD-700GX.

AN OVERVIEW OF MAYALL'S KEYBOARDS

Instrument	in use around	special
Farfisa Compact organ	1963 to 1965	Heard on the first live album
Hohner Cembalett	1963 to 1965	"John Mayall plays John Mayall"
Hammond M100 organ	1965 to 1968	Pictured on "Beano" and "Bare Wires"
Hammond A3 organ	1968 to 1980s	
Electric piano, probably Fender Rhodes	from 1969 on, USA	During his jazz-blues period
Hohner Clavinet D6 keyboard	around 1979	With the "No more Interviews" band
Yamaha piano keyboard	1980s	During the Mick Taylor reunion
Roland keyboard	1980s	
Korg T3 keyboard	1990s	
Kurzweil PC88 keyboard	after 2000	At the 70th Birthday Concert
Juno 1 keyboard synthesizer	after 2000	
Yamaha S90 keyboard	after 2000	
Roland RD-700GX keyboard	from 2011 on	

JOHN MAYALL THE HARMONICA PLAYER

"The harmonica is a lead-instrument, really, but it has tonal qualities and mouth noises which sets it apart from other instruments," Mayall once declared in an interview. Mayall is rightly famous for being an excellent, highly experienced harmonica player, greatly respected by many colleagues, including Mark Hummel. Mayall has always played diatonic blues harmonicas, never using chromatic ones. His playing was deeply influenced by Sonny Boy Williamson II (Rice Miller). Mayall has always been extremely proficient at playing first position (straight harp), second position (cross harp), and third position (slant harp) on his harmonicas, which means he can play three different keys on every mouth organ. At gigs, he always takes his various harmonicas: a minimum of 12 Hohner Super Vampers (with ten holes), one for each key, and one or two Echo Vampers (with twelve holes). When Hohner stopped producing Vamper harps, he changed to Hohner Marine Band harmonicas. To enable himself to play harmonica and keyboards (or guitar) at the same time, Mayall built a shoulder harness, designed to carry 12 harmonicas. Later he replaced this bulky contraption with a gun holster stuffed with harmonicas, an idea he took from other players such as George "Mojo" Buford.

CHAPTER 14

Bandography
John Mayall Bands

PRE-BLUESBREAKERS
(1952–1962)

FIRST SOLO EFFORTS 1952–1953, singing songs by Josh White, Leadbelly & Big Bill Broonzy
* **John Mayall** vocals, guitar ↺

THE DREAMLAND BOYS March 1955
* **John Mayall** vocals, guitar ↺
* **Mart Rodger** clarinet, vocals ↺

TRADITIONAL JAZZ BAND (name unknown) 1955
* **John Mayall** electric guitar ↺
* **Cephas Howard** trumpet (⊃ later formed *TEMPERANCE SEVEN*)
* Unknown trombone
* **Mart Rodger** clarinet ↺ (from the *DREAMLAND BOYS*)
* **Roger Woodburn** banjo
* **Peter Ward** drums ↺

THE FEATURED FIVE 1956, played traditional jazz
* **Johnny (!) Mayall** electric guitar ↺
* **Pete Brown** trombone
* **Martin Rodger** clarinet ↺ (from the above trad. jazz band and the *DREAMLAND BOYS*)
* **Nev Mathews** upright bass

- Pete Ward drums ☯

MARTIN ROGER'S HOUNDS OF SOUND September 1956 &
January 1957, also played trad. jazz
- Martin Rodger clarinet (from the 3 above bands ☯ to
  ZENITH SIX in January 1957)
- John Mayall guitar, piano, vocals, co-leader ☯
- Derek Atkins trumpet
- Alan Hare trombone (also leader of the *BLUE NOTE
  JAZZMEN*)
- Janet Bazley banjo or Frank Booth banjo, guitar
- Norman Sleiter bass
- Gordon Becket drums

JOHN MAYALL'S POWERHOUSE FOUR
(1955–1958)

JOHN MAYALL'S 1ST BLUES BAND, all from art school
- John Mayall vocals, harmonica, guitar, piano ☯
- Ray Cummings guitar ☯ then
  Bill Schulz tenor sax, in 1958
- Ricky Blears bass
- Peter Ward drums (from the above trad. jazz band, joined the
  BLUESBREAKERS in 1963), then Chick Taylor drums from
  1958 on

RECORDINGS: 7 live tracks on CD *TIME CAPSULE* recorded 1957
at Manchester Art College
CONCERT LOCATIONS: Manchester, Macclesfield and Liverpool.
In summer 1956, Mayall played a session with Brownie McGhee at
his flat in Longsight, Manchester

THE BLUES SYNDICATE
(1962)

JOHN MAYALL'S 2ᴺᴰ BLUES BAND, for a few months
- **John Mayall** vocals, harmonica, electric keyboard, guitar ☺
- **Ray Cummings** guitar (from the *POWERHOUSE FOUR*)
- **John Rowlands** trumpet
- **Jack Masarak** or **Mazerick** alto sax
- **Hughie Flint** drums (jazz-schooled, joined the *BLUESBREAKERS* in 1964)

RECORDINGS: 9 live tracks on CD *TIME CAPSULE* recorded 1962 at the Rex Ballroom, Wilmslow
CONCERTS: The Blues Syndicate played most of their 11 concerts in 1962 in and around Manchester, usually at the Bodega Jazz Club or the Clarendon Hotel, or at the Village Hall and Rex Ballroom in Wilmslow, often opening for jazz bands or Alexis Korner's Blues Incorporated.

THE FIRST BLUESBREAKERS
(1963–1965)

Encouraged by Alexis Korner, Mayall moved to London and formed his first *BLUESBREAKERS* in 1963. The bands worked semi-pro (all members had day jobs) until spring 1964. The Bluesbreakers played in and around London at the Marquee or the Flamingo Club during weekdays; at weekends, they drove up to Stoke, Manchester and Hanley, among other places, to play concerts.

BLUESBREAKERS # 1. January to July 1963

- John Mayall vocals, harmonica, keyboards, guitar ◡
- ◡ Davy Graham guitar (from *ALEXIS KORNER'S BLUES INC.*, was already established and had recorded ◡ A folk blues legend. Died December 15, 2008) then
  ◡ Sammy Prosser guitar ◡ then
  ◡ John Gilbey guitar (◡ joined the *SAVAGES*)
- ◡ Ricky Brown bass (from *CYRIL DAVIES R&B ALL STARS*, until March 1963 ◡ to *BRIAN AUGER'S TRINITY, STEAMPACKET, GEORGIE FAME*) then
  ◡ Pete Burford bass (◡ later to *MANFRED MANN* and back in band # 6) then
  ◡ John McVie bass ◡ (from April 1963 on. Previously with the *KREWSADERS*, a Shadows type band before joining the Bluesbreakers)
- ◡ Sam Stone drums ◡ then
  ◡ Brian Myall drums (until March 1963 ◡) then
  ◡ Keith Robertson drums ◡ (from April 1963 on)

BLUESBREAKERS # 2. July 1963 to April 1964

- John Mayall vocals, harmonica, keyboards, guitar ◡
- ◡ Bernie Watson guitar (he had been with *SCREAMING LORD SUTCH & THE SAVAGES, CLIFF BENNETT* and *CYRIL DAVIES* before ◡ turned to classical guitar)
- John McVie bass ◡
- Keith Robertson drums (for two or three weeks ◡) then
  ◡ Peter Ward drums (previously with Mayall in the *POWERHOUSE FOUR* until end of 1963 ◡) then
  ◡ Martin Hart drums (from January to April 1964 ◡ formed the *MARTIN HART TRIO* then played with *GEORGE RICCI*) then
  ◡ Hughie Flint drums ◡ (from April 1964 on, played with Mayall in *BLUES SYNDICATE* 1962)

RECORDINGS: 1ˢᵗ single **MR. JAMES/CRAWLING UP A HILL**
in March & April 1964 for Decca
CONCERTS: club dates in and around London; intervals at the
Marquee with Manfred Mann for £15 a night

BLUESBREAKERS # 3. May 1964 to April 4, 1965
In May 1964, the Bluesbreakers turned professional
- **John Mayall** vocals, harmonica, keyboards, guitar ◖
- ◖ a series of unsuitable guitarists to replace Bernie Watson ◖
  ◖ **Roger Dean** guitar (from *BOB XAVIER & THE JURY*
  [with Albert Lee], *RUSS SAINTY & THE NU-NOTES, JOHN
  LAYTON, BOBBY VEE*, the *OUTLAWS* and the *CRICKETS* ◖
  joined *RUSS SAINTY* again, then to *RONNIE JONES & THE
  BLUE JAYS*, the *TUMBLEWEEDS, COUNTRY FEVER, MICK
  GREENWOOD BAND, PJ PROBY, LEAPY LEE BAND*, the
  *FLIRTATIONS, SHEER ELEGANCE, the PLATTERS, THREE
  DEGREES* and the renowned *JOE LOSS ORCHESTRA* for 14
  years. Died August 3, 2008)
- **John McVie** bass ◖
- **Hughie Flint** drums ◖
- **Nigel Stanger** tenor & slide sax, Dec. 7, 1964 for live recording
  (from the *ALAN PRICE SET*)

RECORDINGS: the live album **JOHN MAYALL PLAYS JOHN
MAYALL** in December 1964 and 2ⁿᵈ single **CROCODILE
WALK/BLUES CITY SHAKEDOWN** in February 1965 for Decca,
plus **MY BABY IS SWEETER** and probably **ANOTHER MAN DONE
GONE** later released on the album with Clapton
CONCERTS: besides playing one-nighters around the country, this
band backed three US bluesmen on their UK tours:
- **John Lee Hooker** vocals, guitar, on his first tour of England
  (25 dates) in June & July 1964 (e. g. June 3, Cellar Club,
  Kingston, Surrey, plus June 16 Magdalen College, Oxford
  and June 26 Alexandra Palace, London, both billed with the
  Rolling Stones). Hooker died June 21, 2001.

- **Sonny Boy Williamson II (Rice Miller)** vocals, harmonica, on two or three UK concerts (exact dates unknown). Williamson died May 25, 1965.
- **T-Bone Walker** vocals, guitar, on his UK tour: March 5 to 30, 1965 (around 21 dates). Walker died March 16, 1975.

THE BLUESBREAKERS WITH ERIC CLAPTON (1965–1966)

BLUESBREAKERS # 4. April 6 to August 29, 1965
- **John Mayall** vocals, harmonica, keyboards �
- � **Eric Clapton** guitar (previously with the *ROOSTERS, CASEY JONES & THE ENGINEERS* and the *YARDBIRDS.* � On August 30, Clapton left for Greece to play music in the sun with the *GLANDS.* Rejoined the Bluesbreakers in early November 1965)
- **John McVie** bass �
- **Hughie Flint** drums �

RECORDINGS: the singles for Immediate *I'M YOUR WITCHDOCTOR / TELEPHONE BLUES* in June 1965 plus five tracks for BBC radio. Also *IF YOU GOTTA GO, GO NOW* with *BOB DYLAN*, recorded on May 12.
CONCERTS: club dates in and around London, England, Wales, plus the Uxbridge Blues Folk Festival June 19, 1965 (on the same bill with The Who, Spencer Davis Group, Solomon Burke, Long John Baldry and others.

BLUESBREAKERS # 5. September 1 to November 4, 1965
- **John Mayall** vocals, harmonica, keyboards, guitar �
- � **John Weider** guitar (joined Sept. 1, from the *MOMENTS,*

the *TONY MEEHAN COMBO* and *JOHNNY KIDD & THE PIRATES* ☉ Sept. 6, to *JIMMY WINSTON'S REFLECTION* before playing guitar and bass with the *ANIMALS* in 1968/69 and then with *FAMILY*) then

☉ **John Slaughter** guitar (on loan from *CHRIS BARBER'S BAND*, Sept. 7 & 8 only ☉ then

☉ **Geoff Krivit** guitar (joined early September, from *JIMMY POWELL & THE FIVE DIMENSIONS* who backed *CHUCK BERRY* in February 1965 ☉ October 27, to *DR. K's BLUES BAND*, later to record with *FAIRPORT CONVENTION*) then

☉ **Peter Green** guitar (for only one week, about 3 gigs in late October/early November ☉ to return in summer 1966) ☉ plus more guitarists, including John McLaughlin

- **John McVie** bass (☉ fired for drining October 3, back in December 1965) replaced by ☉ Jack Bruce bass, harmonica, vocals ☉ (from October 8 on, previously with *ALEXIS KORNER'S BLUES INC.* and the *GRAHAM BOND ORGANIZATION*)
- **Hughie Flint** drums ☉ (**Chris Winters** occasionally substitutes for Flint)

RECORDINGS: for BBC radio: five tracks with Geoff Kribet and Jack Bruce

BLUESBREAKERS # 6. November 6, 1965 to July 17, 1966
- **John Mayall** vocals, harmonica, keyboards ☉
- ☉ **Eric Clapton** guitar (back from Greece, rejoined November 6, 1965 ☉ left July 17, 1966 to form *CREAM*, later with *BLIND FAITH, DELANEY, BONNIE & FRIENDS, DEREK & THE DOMINOS*, before forming his own bands)
- **Jack Bruce** bass, harmonica, vocals (☉ left November 21, 1965, after only six weeks to join *MANFRED MANN*, then formed *CREAM* with Eric Clapton, later with the *TONY WILLIAMS LIFETIME, WEST, BRUCE & LAING* and various *JACK BRUCE BANDS*. Died October 25, 2014) then

◑ **Keith "Lee" Jackson** bass (from November 22 to December 3, 1965 ◑ to *JONATHAN KING'S HEDGEHOPPERS*, then *GARY FERR & THE T-BONES* and the *NICE*) then
◑ **John Bradley** bass (from December 4 until December 23, 1965 ◑) then
◑ **Pete Burford** bass (from December 24, 1965 for one week, from *MANFRED MANN* and the **BLUESBREAKERS # 1** ◑) then
John McVie bass ◑ (returned end of 1965)
- **Hughie Flint** drums ◑

RECORDINGS: the singles **ON TOP OF THE WORLD** and **DOUBLE CROSSING TIME** in November & December 1965 for Immediate, plus the live tracks recorded November 7, 1965 at the Flamingo Club in London, issued on **LOOKING BACK** (Stormy Monday) and **PRIMAL SOLOS** (5 tracks) with Jack Bruce on bass. In February 1966 the single **BERNARD JENKINS/LONELY YEARS** for Purdah records. Around March 1966 the **BLUESBREAKERS WITH ERIC CLAPTON (THE BEANO ALBUM)** for Decca. Also four tracks with **CHAMPION JACK DUPREE** in early November 1965, released on the Decca albums **FROM NEW ORLEANS TO CHICAGO** and **RAW BLUES**, plus radio recordings for BBC (9 tracks)
CONCERTS: club dates in and around London and England. On April 18, 1966, **MICK TAYLOR** played guitar during the second set of a gig in his home town Welwyn Garden City, substituting for Eric Clapton. On May 13, 1966, **GINGER BAKER** sat in on drums for a session in Oxford.

THE BLUESBREAKERS WITH PETER GREEN (1966–1967)

BLUESBREAKERS # 7. July 18 to September 25, 1966
- **John Mayall** vocals, harmonica, keyboards, guitar ☺
- ☺ **Peter Green** guitar, vocals ☺ (previously with *BOBBY DENIM & THE DOMINOES*, the *MUSKRATS* and the *TRIDENTS* on bass, and with *PETER BARDEN'S LOONERS* and *SHOTGUN EXPRESS* as a guitarist)
- **John McVie** bass (☺ fired for excessive drinking in early September) then ☺ **Steve Usher** bass (from *BLUE MONKS*, September 12 to about September 25 ☺)
- **Hughie Flint** drums (until September 4, ☺ went on to play with *ALEXIS KORNER'S FREE AT LAST, CHICKEN SHACK, SAVOY BROWN, GEORGIE FAME & THE BLUE FLAMES, ALAN PRICE FLOATING BAND, RONNIE LANE, MANFRED MANN, Mc GUINESS FLINT*, the *BONZO DOG BAND, GALLAGHER & LYLE, TOM NEWMAN, CHANTER* and the *BLUES BAND*) then ☺ **Micky Waller** drums (from September 12 on, previously with *FLEE-REKKERS, CYRIL DAVIES, LONG JOHN BALDRY & THE HOOCHIE COOCHIE MEN, MARTY WILDE & THE WILD CATS, BRIAN AUGER & STEAMPACKET* ☺ around September 25, to *GEORGIE FAME*)

RECORDINGS: none are known to exist with this line up

BLUESBREAKERS # 8. September 30, 1966 to early April 1967
- **John Mayall** vocals, harmonica, keyboards, guitar ☺
- **Peter Green** guitar, vocals ☺
- ☺ **John McVie** bass ☺ (back again)
- ☺ **Aynsley Dunbar** drums (previously with the Liverpool bands *LEO RUTHERFORD, MERSEYSIPPI JAZZ BAND, DERRIE WILKIE & THE PRESSMEN, THE FLAMINGOS, FREDDY STARR*, the *EXCHECKERS, STU JAMES & THE MOJOS* ☺ after leaving in early April 1967, joined the *JEFF*

BECK GROUP, then formed his own groups *AYNSLEY DUNBAR RETALIATION* and *BLUE WHALE*, before he played with *FRANK ZAPPA & THE MOTHERS OF INVENTION, FLO & EDDIE, JOURNEY, UFO, WHITESNAKE, SHUGGIE OTIS, JOHN LENNON, DAVID BOWIE, LOU REED, JEFFERSON STARSHIP, ERIC BURDON, MOTHER'S ARMY* and many more)

RECORDINGS: the single ***LOOKING BACK/SO MANY ROADS*** in September 1966. The album ***A HARD ROAD***, the single ***SITTING IN THE RAIN/OUT OF REACH***, plus outtakes released on ***THRU THE YEARS*** and ***RAW BLUES***, as well as the EP ***JOHN MAYALL'S BLUESBREAKERS WITH PAUL BUTTERFIELD***, all in October & November 1966. The Bluesbreakers single ***CURLY/RUBBER DUCK*** without Mayall in February 1967. The tracks ***PLEASE DON'T TELL/YOUR FUNERAL AND MY TRIAL***, as well as ***EDDIE BOYD AND HIS BLUESBAND FEATURING PETER GREEN*** in March 1967. Plus BBC recordings (at least ten tracks)

CONCERTS:
- **1966:** among many dates in England: December 10 at the Ram Jam Club in Brixton with the Jimi Hendrix Experience supporting!
- **1967:** A tour of Sweden (1st outside Britain) February 19–27 (twelve gigs in seven days). Then did a short UK tour with **Eddie Boyd** (vocals, piano) between March 12 and 22.

BLUESBREAKERS # 9. Early April to June 11, 1967
- **John Mayall** vocals, harmonica, keyboards, guitar ☺
- **Peter Green** guitar, vocals (☺ left June 11 to form *FLEETWOOD MAC*, then recorded under his own name and later with *KOLORS* and the *SPLINTER GROUP*)
- **John McVie** bass ☺
- ☺ **Micky Waller** drums (back again for a few gigs ☺ later joined *JEFF BECK, SPIRIT OF JOHN MORGAN, STEAM-HAMMER, ROD STEWART, SILVER METRE, PILOT, MIKE*

HUGG, TONY ASHTON, RON WOOD & RONNIE LANE and
the *DELUXE BLUES BAND*, died April 29, 2008) then
Ｕ **Mick Fleetwood** drums (for about a month from early April
on. Previously with the *SENDERS*, the *CHEYNES, BO STREET
RUNNERS, PETER B'S LOONERS* and *SHOTGUN EXPRESS* Ｕ
fired May 10, 1967, joined Peter Green's *FLEETWOOD MAC*
in June, then *ZOO* and in 2008 the *MICK FLEETWOOD
BLUES BAND*) then
Ｕ **Keef Hartley** drums Ｕ (joined May 13, 1967. Previously with
the *THUNDERBEATS, RORY STORM & THE HURRICANES*
(where he replaced Ringo Starr), *FREDDIE STARR & THE
MIDNIGHTERS* and the *ARTWOODS*)

RECORDINGS: The single **IT HURTS ME TOO/DOUBLE TROUBLE**
with Mick Fleetwood on drums in April 1967. Also the two live tracks
THE STUMBLE and **DOUBLE TROUBLE** that surfaced in 2006 on
the CD **EXCLUSIVE LIVE RARITIES**. The Mayall solo album **THE
BLUES ALONE** with Keef Hartley on drums in May 1967.
CONCERTS: first concerts in Northern Ireland: May 8 & 9, 1967.

THE BLUESBREAKERS WITH MICK TAYLOR I
(1967-1968)

BLUESBREAKERS # 10. June 20, 1967 to September 3, 1967
- **John Mayall** vocals, harmonica, keyboards, guitar Ｕ
- Ｕ **Mick Taylor** guitar Ｕ (previously with the *STRANGERS*,
the *JUNIORS & the GODS*)
Ｕ **Terry Edmonds** rhythm-guitar (from *TONY KNIGHT'S
CHESSMEN*, for one week, before joining Ｕ *FERRIS WHEEL*)
- **John McVie** bass (Ｕ left on September 3 to join *PETER GREEN'S
FLEETWOOD MAC*. Returned in 1982 to play with Mayall

and Mick Taylor for five months)
- **Keef Hartley** drums ◑
- ◑ **Chris Mercer** tenor sax, baritone sax ◑ (from the *BLUE MONKS*)
- ◑ **Rip Kant** baritone sax (◑ until August 13, 1967, vanished from the music scene) then
  ◑ **Dick Heckstall-Smith** tenor sax, soprano sax ◑ (joined August 25, previously played with the *JOHNNY BURCH OCTET, ALEXIS KORNER'S BLUES INC.* and *GRAHAM BOND ORGANISATION*)

RECORDINGS: The *CRUSADE* album, recorded July 12, 1967 (Terry Edmonds had already left)
CONCERTS: 1967: Among others, the south eastern Blues Festival on July 1 in Blackheath and the 7th International Jazz and Blues Festival in Windsor on August 13, on the same bill with Fleetwood Mac (1st ever gig), Cream (1st ever gig), Aynsley Dunbar Retaliation (1st ever gig), Jeff Beck, Chicken Shack and many others. A concert in Malmö, Sweden and a TV show in Copenhagen on August 26.

BLUESBREAKERS # 11. September 4, 1967 to April 21, 1968
- **John Mayall** vocals, harmonica, keyboards, guitar ◑
- **Mick Taylor** guitar ◑
- ◑ **Paul Williams** bass, vocals (from *WES MINSTER FIVE, ALEXIS KORNER* and *ZOOT MONEY'S BIG ROLL BAND* ◑ left October 29, 1967, to join the *ALAN PRICE SET*, the *PAUL WILLIAMS SET*, then joined *AYNSLEY DUNBAR'S BLUE WHALE, JUICY LUCY, ALLAN HOLDSWORTH, TEMPEST I*, the *I.O.U. BAND, BLUE THUNDER, COLOSSEUM* and the *BLUES PACKAGE*) then
  ◑ **Keith Tillman** bass (joined October 30, 1967, previously with *RALPH DENYER'S ROCKHOUSE BAND, STONE'S MASONRY* and *AYNSLEY DUNBAR RETALIATION* ◑ left February 25, 1968 to play with *DAVE KELLY, JOHN DUMMER, SWEET PAIN, MAINSQUEEZE* and *BO DIDDLEY*.

He returned early 1969 for some tour dates) then
↻ **Andy Fraser** bass (from February 25 to April 21, 1968.
He was only 15 when he joined and previously with
LAWLESS BREED ↻ formed *FREE* after quitting, then played
with *TOBY*, *ALEXIS KORNER*, the *SHARKS*, the *FRANKIE
MILLER BAND* and recorded three albums with the *ANDY
FRASER BAND*. Died 16 March, 2015)
- **Keef Hartley** drums (↻ to *GRAHAM BOND*, then *JETHRO
TULL* before forming the *KEEF HARTLEY BAND*; returned
to Mayall in 1971)
- **Dick Heckstall-Smith** tenor sax, soprano sax ↻
- **Chris Mercer** tenor sax, baritone sax ↻
- ↻ **Henry Lowther** cornet, violin ↻ (joined February 23, 1968,
previously played with *MANFRED MANN*, the *JAZZ POETRY
GROUP*, *GROUP SOUNDS FIVE* and his own *HENRY
LOWTHER QUARTET*)

RECORDINGS: The single ***SUSPICIONS*** in September 1967, the two
live albums ***THE DIARY OF A BAND*** from October to December
1967, the single ***JENNY/PICTURE ON THE WALL*** (with Peter Green
and Keef Hartley) in December 1967, plus radio recordings for BBC
in October 1967 and March 1968 (at least 22 tracks)
CONCERTS: 1967: September 30–October 10: A tour of
SCANDINAVIA (S, DK, SF), then dates in England and Ireland, a
tour of Holland (November 4–9), where the tracks for the ***DIARY
OF A BAND*** albums were recorded. **1968:** Their 1st US-tour, for five
weeks from January 9 to February 12 (with Keith Tillman on bass),
they played in New York (Café Au Gogo, 13 dates), Detroit (Grande
Ballroom, 1 date), Los Angeles (Whisky à Go Go, 4 dates) and in
San Francisco (Fillmore West & Winterland: 7 concerts, 4 with Jimi
Hendrix and Albert King on the same bill. Some of these Frisco
concerts were professionally recorded but never released on Decca).
Another tour of England, Denmark and Sweden from March 9–17
(without Henry Lowther), plus Scotland in April.

THE BLUESBREAKERS WITH MICK TAYLOR II (1968–1969)

BLUESBREAKERS # 12. April 23, 1968 (in the studio from April 3) to July 12, 1968

- **John Mayall** vocals, harmonica, keyboards, guitar ⊙
- **Mick Taylor** guitar ⊙
- ⊙ **Tony Reeves** bass (previously with *NEIL ARDLEY*, the *PETER LEMER QUINTET*, *GROUP SOUNDS FIVE* and the *NEW JAZZ ORCHESTRA* ⊙ to *COLOSSEUM*, *GREENSLADE*, *CHRIS DE BURGH*, *CURVED AIR* and *SANDY DENNY* later on)
- ⊙ **Jon Hiseman** drums ⊙ (previously with the *NEW JAZZ ORCHESTRA*, *NEIL ARDLEY*, the *MIKE TAYLOR TRIO*, the *PETER LEMER QUINTET*, *HOWARD RILEY* and the *GRAHAM BOND ORGANISATION*, *GROUP SOUNDS FIVE* and *GEORGIE FAME*)
- **Chris Mercer** tenor sax, baritone sax (⊙ went to play with *WYNDER K. FROG*, the *KEEF HARTLEY BAND*, *JUICY LUCY*, *GONZALES*, *FRANKY MILLER'S FULL HOUSE*, *CHRIS FARLOWE*. As a studio musician, his sax can be heard on more than 50 recordings)
- **Dick Heckstall-Smith** tenor sax, soprano sax (⊙ also to *COLOSSEUM*, later to form his own group *MANCHILD*, then played with *BIG CHIEF*, *TOUGH TENORS*, *MAINSQUEEZE*, *3-SPACE*, *DHS$*, the *DE LUXE BLUES BAND*, the *HAMBURG BLUES BAND* and the *SENSATIONAL KING BIZKIT BLUES BAND*. He died from cancer December 17, 2004)
- **Henry Lowther** cornet, violin (⊙ joined the *KEEF HARTLEY BAND*, then also became a studio musician playing on about 50 different albums. He later joined the *KENNY WHEELER LARGE ENSEMBLE* and reappeared on John Mayall's 70th Birthday concert in July 2003)

RECORDINGS: BARE WIRES, the two outtakes *KNOCKERS STEP FORWARD/HIDE AND SEEK* recorded in April 1968, plus the two live tracks *LOOK AT THAT GIRL/START WALKING* recorded May 25, 1968 at Falmer College in Brighton, released on *PRIMAL SOLOS CONCERTS: 1968* among others the Monsterkonzert at the Hallenstadion in Zurich, Switzerland on May 30 & 31 with Jimi Hendrix, Traffic, the Animals and Move on the same bill, and at the Amsterdam Concertgebouw on June 21 (six concerts in Holland from June 21–23). After disbanding his 7-piece group in July 1968, Mayall took a three-week vacation in Los Angeles to prepare for *BLUES FROM LAUREL CANYON*, to record two tracks with *CANNED HEAT* for their album Living the Blues, and to jam with the Heat at LA's Whiskey à Go Go.

JOHN MAYALL BAND # 13. August 9, 1968 to May 23, 1969
- John Mayall vocals, harmonica, keyboards, guitar ☉
- Mick Taylor guitar (☉ quit May 24, 1969 to join the *ROLLING STONES*. He left the Stones in December 1974 to become a member of the *JACK BRUCE BAND*, then formed the *MICK TAYLOR BAND*, toured with the *ALVIN LEE BAND* in 1981 and returned to the Bluesbreakers in 1982)
- ☉ Steve Thompson bass ☉ (was a virtual beginner when he got his first professional job with Mayall)
  ☉ Tony Reeves bass (January 10, 11, 21, 22, 1969 to stand in for Thompson who was ill ☉)
  ☉ Keith Tillman bass (replaced Thompson on the Swiss tour January 13–19, 1969☉)
  ☉ Jerome Arnold bass (to stand in for Thompson on January 21, previously with *HOWLIN' WOLF, PAUL BUTTERFIELD* and *BOB DYLAN*, then settled in London and led the *JEROME ARNOLD BLUES BAND* ☉)
- Jon Hiseman drums (☉ left August 25, 1968 to form *COLOSSEUM*, later with *WOLFGANG DAUNER, TEMPEST*, then *BARBARA THOMPSON'S PARAPHERNALIA* (his wife's band) and the *UNITED JAZZ & ROCK ENSEMBLE*)

◖ **Colin Allen** drums (joined August 26, 1968, previously with *ZOOT MONEY'S BIG ROLL BAND, DANTALION'S CHARIOT* and *GEORGIE FAME* ◖ left to play with *BRIAN AUGER, STONE THE CROWS, FOCUS, ROD STEWART, DONOVAN* and *MICK TAYLOR'S LIVE BAND*, before rejoining the Bluesbreakers with Mick Taylor in 1982)

RECORDINGS: The album ***BLUES FROM LAUREL CANYON*** recorded August 1968. Four tracks with *SHAKEY JAKE HARRIS* for his album ***FURTHER ON UP THE ROAD*** recorded in LA, October 1968. The three live tracks: ***WISH YOU WERE MINE*** recorded December 1968 in Sweden, issued on ***PRIMAL SOLOS***, ***HELP ME*** recorded February or March 1969 at Fillmore East, NYC, on ***EXCLUSIVE LIVE RECORDINGS***, and ***PARCHMAN FARM*** recorded May 9, 1969 in Birmingham, released on ***THE MASTERS***, plus BBC recordings (ten tracks).

- *CONCERTS, 1968:* 2nd US tour (incl. Canada) from Sept 6 to Oct 31 incl. Fillmore East, NYC on Oct 25 & 26, using Canned Heat's van and equipment, while the Heat toured the UK with Mayall's bus and PA. Played a UK tour in Nov., Scandinavia from Nov 29 to Dec 8 (13 concerts), and Scotland Dec 13–15 (4 concerts).
- *1969:* 7 Swiss dates Jan 13–19, plus TV appearance. Another US tour (incl. Canada) February 18 to May 3, including Fillmore East, NYC March 1 and the Palm Springs Pop Festival, plus GB & Denmark (5 dates) in May.

JOHN MAYALL BAND # 13*. May 30, 1969, for one night only!
- **John Mayall** vocals, harmonica, keyboards, guitar ◖
- ◖ **Keith Relf** guitar (*RENAISSANCE*, ex-*YARDBIRDS* ◖)
- **Steve Thompson** bass ◖
- ◖ **Jim McCarty** drums (*RENAISSANCE*, ex-*YARDBIRDS* ◖)

---

* As the new band (# 14) wasn't ready, Mayall asked Keith Relf and Jim McCarty of Renaissance to join him for the two shows at the Kulttuuritalo, Helsinki, Finland at May 30, 1969

Mayall created this concert poster in gouache in 1956 for The Featured Five, his second trad jazz band

28 *In the garden of his Laurel Canyon home at 8353 Grand View Drive, Los Angeles, in 1970.*

Live on stage around 1969. Notice Mayall's still uncustomised Fender.

30 *Newly wed! Mayall aged 22 with his bride Pamela in May 1956 at their modest flat in Longsight, Manchester.*

31 *The Mayall family in April 1965: Mayall, Pamela and their children Gary, Tracy and Jason.*

Mayall and wife Pamela in October 1965 with their children Gary, Tracy, Jason nd new arrival Benedict, a Nigerian baby they had recently adopted.

Mayall with the late, great B.B. King and Bluesbreakers Joe Yuele, Buddy Whittington and John Paulus (from ft to right) in Manchester, April 1999, at the close of another tour. They all look very tired except for Mayall!

34 *Mayall with t[...] first Bluesbreakers [...] feature a horn secti[on] in London, autum[n] 1967: Mick Taylor, Ch[ris] Mercer, Keith Tillma[n] Keef Hartley and Di[ck] Heckstall-Smi[th] (from left to righ[t)]*

35 *34 years after "Hard Road": John Mayall with Peter Green.*

36 *Musicians who featured at the Monsterkonzert, posing in front of the Hotel Stoller in Zurich, May 31, 1968.*

B.B. KING

— WITH VERY SPECIAL GUESTS —

JOHN MAYALL & THE BLUESBREAKERS

(All shows except Cardiff, Southend and Belfast)

TUE 20TH APRIL
CARDIFF ST DAVID'S HALL
01222 878444

WED 21ST APRIL
SOUTHEND CLIFFS PAVILION
01702 351135

FRI 23RD APRIL
NEWCASTLE TELEWEST ARENA
0191 401 8000

SAT 24TH APRIL
GLASGOW CLYDE AUDITORIUM
0141 287 7777

MON 26TH APRIL
SHEFFIELD ARENA
0114 256 5656

TUE 27TH APRIL
BELFAST WATERFRONT HALL
01232 334455

WED 28TH APRIL
BIRMINGHAM ACADEMY, NIA
0121 200 2222

THU 29TH APRIL
MANCHESTER EVENING NEWS ARENA
0161 930 8000 / 0161 832 1111

FRI 30TH APRIL
BRIGHTON CENTRE
0870 900 9100

SAT 1ST MAY
BOURNEMOUTH INT. CENTRE
01202 456456

B.B. KING
His Definitive Greatest Hits

34 track CD/MC
Released April '99

24HR NATIONAL CREDIT CARD HOTLINE 14

㊲ *B.B. King and Mayall: the poster for their joint UK tour, spring 1999.*

THE LAST UK BANDS
(1969–1970)

JOHN MAYALL BAND # 14. May 27, 1969 to June 2, 1970

- John Mayall vocals, harmonica, guitar ☉
- ☉ Johnny Almond tenor sax, alto sax, flute (previously with *NITE SOUNDS, WALLY JOHNSON, TONY KNIGHT'S CHESS MEN*, the *ALAN PRICE SET*, the *PAUL WILLIAMS SET, ZOOT MONEY'S BIG ROLL BAND*, and earlier Mayall recordings ☉ left with Jon Mark to form *MARK-ALMOND*. Died of cancer in Hayward, CA, 18 November 2009)
- ☉ Jon Mark acoustic guitar (used to accompany *MARIANNE FAITHFULL*, recorded with *GERRY LOCKRAN* and was with *SWEET THURSDAY* ☉ left with Johnny Almond to form *MARK-ALMOND*. Moved to New Zealand in 1980 to continue his musical career)
- Steve Thompson bass, until mid-January 1970 (☉ couldn't continue because of health problems. Later played with *HEAVY JELLY, STONE THE CROWS, JESSE ED DAVIS, ALVIN LEE, KEVIN COYNE* and the *MICK TAYLOR BAND* before returning to Mayall in 1977 and again in 1982) then ☉ Alex Dmochowski (a.k.a. Alex Paris) bass, from mid-January 1970 (previously played bass with the *AYNSLEY DUNBAR RETALIATION, HEAVY JELLY, NEIL CHRISTIAN'S CRUSADERS* ☉ after Mayall, played and recorded with *PETER GREEN, GRAHAM BOND* and *COUNTRY JOE McDONALD*, then joined *FRANK ZAPPA'S MOTHERS OF INVENTION*. Mayall featured Dmochowski in 1976 on *A Banquet in Blues*)
- ☉ Duster Bennett vocals, guitar, harmonica, bass drum, hi-hat; played US and UK tours and selected shows from February 12 to June 2, 1970. Bennett was already known as a British one-man blues band before joining Mayall. He played most of the set with the band, and also had a song or two of his own. ☉ After these tours he reverted to a solo career. Bennett tragically died in a car accident on March 26, 1976)

RECORDINGS: The live albums *THE TURNING POINT* recorded July 12, 1969 at Fillmore East in NYC, *LIVE AT THE MARQUEE* recorded June 30, 1969 in London, and *THE MASTERS* recorded June 1969 in Plymouth, Hull and York, also re-released on *THE TURNING POINT SOUNDTRACK/LIVE 1969*. The studio album *EMPTY ROOMS* recorded on different dates in autumn 1969 at studios in London, New York and Los Angeles. All recordings feature Steve Thomson on bass. Two live tracks from German TV on *THE LOST BROADCASTS* DVD recorded Jan. 31, 1970, with Alex Dmochowski on bass. Three more live tracks recorded Jan. 1970 in Germany on *HISTORIC LIVE SHOWS VOL. 1*, plus three further live tracks recorded for French TV early June 1970, released on DVD *SWEET LITTLE ANGEL*. No regular recordings with Duster Bennett exist. *CONCERTS:*

- *1969:* Olympia in Paris on June 2, then 4 dates in Germany and Austria in early June, followed by UK dates from June 10 to July 1, including the Bath Festival of Blues on June 28 with Fleetwood Mac, Ten Years After, Led Zeppelin, Nice, Chicken Shack, Colosseum, Keef Hartley Band, Blodwin Pig, Taste, Savoy Brown and Champion Jack Dupree. US tour from July 5 to October 25 with concerts at the Newport Jazz Festival July 5, and the Fillmore East NYC dates July 11 & 12, where *THE TURNING POINT* was recorded. Fillmore in San Francisco Aug 19–21. Fillmore East NYC Oct. 3–4. Then a British tour from Oct 31 with 23 dates, including Royal Albert Hall in London on Nov. 20.
- *1970:* A 30-day tour of Europe from Jan. 2 to early Feb (DK, N, S, D, A, NL, B, including a show for Beat Club on German TV recorded Jan. 31, with Alex Dmochowski on bass) plus Paris (Olympia) on Feb. 1. Another tour of USA & Canada from Feb. 12 to April 26 including Fillmore East NYC March 13–15 and Fillmore West in San Francisco, April 16–19. A tour of Britain May 1–18, then Germany & Austria May 20–28 (8 dates), the Netherlands May 29–31, France in early June (including a live TV show from Lyon for French TV with Duster Bennett).

JOHN MAYALL BAND # 15. June 27, 1970
- John Mayall vocals, harmonica, guitar ☉
- ☉ Peter Green guitar (for one night ☉)
- ☉ Ric Grech bass, violin (previously with *FAMILY, BLIND FAITH* and *AIR FORCE* ☉ to *TRAFFIC, CRICKETS, KGB*, the *BEE GEES* and *RON WOOD*. Died on March 17, 1990)
- ☉ Rod Mayall org (Mayall's half brother, previously played with *IVAN'S MEADS* and *LOS BUENOS* ☉ to *FLAMING YOUTH*, then *NEVADA*)
- ☉ Aynsley Dunbar drums (back for one night ☉)

RECORDINGS: No recordings with this "one-night stand" line-up.
CONCERTS: 1970: One show at the Bath Festival of Blues and Progressive Music, UK, June 27–28, on the same bill with Canned Heat, Flock, Zappa's Mothers, Jefferson Airplane, the Keef Hartley Band, Johnny Winter, Led Zeppelin, Colosseum, Pink Floyd, Steppenwolf, Dr. John and many more.

THE FIRST US BANDS
(1970–1971)

JOHN MAYALL BAND # 16. July 1970 to June 1971
- John Mayall vocals, harmonica, guitar ☉
- ☉ Harvey Mandel guitar (previously with *BARRY GOLDBERG, BUDDY GUY, CHARLIE MUSSELWHITE*, the *BUSTERS* and *CANNED HEAT* ☉ left to form *PURE FOOD AND DRUG ACT* with Sugarcane Harris and Paul Lagos, did a lot of recording work with *RON CARTER, LOVE*, the *ROLLING STONES*, rejoined *CANNED HEAT* in the 90s, then the *CHICAGO BLUES REUNION* plus his own *SNAKECREW*)

- • ☉ **Larry Taylor** bass ☉ (previously with the *MONKEES, TEDDY RANDAZZO, TOMMY BOYCE & BOBBY HART, JERRY LEE LEWIS* and *CANNED HEAT*, the latter with Harvey Mandel)
- • ☉ **Don Sugarcane Harris** violin (violin wizard Harris began his career 1957 with the *SQUIRES*, continued with his duo *DON & DEWEY*, then played with the *LITTLE RICHARD REVUE*, the *JOHNNY OTIS SHOW* and *FRANK ZAPPA & THE MOTHERS OF INVENTION* ☉ left to form *PURE FOOD AND DRUG ACT* with Harvey Mandel and Paul Lagos, then went solo and returned to John Mayall in 1975) Sugarcane couldn't make the tour of Japan in December 1970.
- • ☉ **Paul Lagos** drums, from January 1971 on (previously with *KALAIDOSCOPE*, the *JOHNNY OTIS SHOW* and *SHUGGIE OTIS* ☉ left to form *PURE FOOD AND DRUG ACT* with Harvey Mandel and Sugarcane Harris. Died October 19, 2009)

RECORDINGS: USA UNION recorded July 27 & 28, 1970 in Los Angeles (4-piece without Lagos) plus the double *BACK TO THE ROOTS* recorded November 15–25, 1970 in Los Angeles and London, with additional musicians and former members Eric Clapton guitar, Mick Taylor guitar, Johnny Almond tenor and alto sax, flute, Keef Hartley drums, Steve Thompson bass, plus Jerry McGee guitar and Paul Lagos drums. Live recordings on *ROCK THE BLUES TONIGHT* recorded in Canada, September 26, 1970 (five tracks without Lagos) and April 2, 1971 (six tracks with Lagos). Two more live tracks from German TV recorded February 1971 with Lagos on drums, released on DVD *THE LOST BROADCASTS* in 2012, plus two further live tracks recorded April 1971 in Germany, on *HISTORIC LIVE SHOWS VOL. 1*
CONCERTS:
- • *1970:* Fillmore San Francisco Aug. 27–29, then a tour of USA and Canada from Sept. 11 to Oct 18 including Fillmore East NYC Oct 9 & 10. 2 UK dates in November. A 1st tour of Japan starting Dec 12 (7 dates), Sugarcane Harris was denied a work permit for Japan and didn't play.

- *1971:* a two weeks tour of Europe in Feb. and March with a show for German TV (Beat Club) and dates in Montreux (CH) on Feb. 20, Milan, Amsterdam, Stockholm, Munich, Hamburg, Düsseldorf, Paris, plus dates in the UK. Sugarcane recorded his album *FIDDLER ON THE ROCK* in Germany with the above band, but without Mayall. Another two-week UK tour in early March plus dates in USA and Canada in April, including Fillmore San Francisco April 9 & 10 and Fillmore East NYC April 16–17.
Dates in Germany in June

JOHN MAYALL BAND # 17. July and August, 1971
- John Mayall vocals, harmonica, keyboards, guitar ☙
- ☙ Jerry McGee guitars, sitar (came from the *CANDY STORE PROPHETS* [*BOBBY HART'S* backing band], the *VENTURES, DELANEY & BONNIE, NANCY SINATRA* ☙ played with *RITA COOLIDGE, KRIS KRISTOFFERSON, BILLY SWAN, BARBARA STREISAND* and many others after that)
- Larry Taylor bass ☙

RECORDINGS: The album *MEMORIES* recorded July 7–9, 1971 in Los Angeles
CONCERTS: 1971: only on the West Coast

JOHN MAYALL BAND # 18. September 12 to October 5, 1971
- John Mayall vocals, harmonica, guitar ☙
- ☙ Jimmy McCulloch guitar (previously with *ONE IN A MILLION* and *THUNDERCLAP NEWMAN* ☙ went on to play with *BRENT FRAME, STONE THE CROWS, BLUE, JOHN ENTWISTLE, WINGS, SMALL FACES* and *DUKES.* Died of an overdose on September 27, 1979)
- Larry Taylor bass ☙
- ☙ Keef Hartley drums (had just disbanded the *KEEF HARTLEY BAND* ☙ joined *VINEGAR JOE* after this tour and returned to Mayall in 1972)

- ⟲ **Chris Mercer** tenor sax (joined on at least one date in Britain on Sept. 26 in Croydon ⟲)

RECORDINGS: 1 live track recorded Sept. 15, 1971 in Frankfurt, Germany, available on *HISTORIC LIVE SHOWS VOL. 1*
CONCERTS: 1971: A tour of Europe from Sept 12–22 (Germany and Switzerland, 10 dates) and a British tour from Sept. 23–Oct. 5 (11 dates), plus Scandinavia

THE JAZZ-BLUES BANDS
(1971–1973)

In late August and early September 1971, Mayall recorded and produced two albums with US bluesmen: *THE LOST SESSION* with *ALBERT KING*, with Blue Mitchell on trumpet, Clifford Solomon, tenor and alto sax, and Ron Selico, drums, and *THE DEVIL'S HARMONICA* with *SHAKY JAKE HARRIS* featuring Freddy Robinson on guitar and Ron Selico, drums. These four became new members of Mayall's Jazz-blues band later in 1971.

JOHN MAYALL BAND # 19. October 1971 to December 1973
- **John Mayall** vocals, harmonica, keyboards, guitar ⟲
- ⟲ **Freddy Robinson** guitar, vocals (previously with *LITTLE WALTER, JIMMY ROGERS, HOWLIN' WOLF, WILLIE DIXON, EARL GAINES, JERRY BUTLER,* the *CRUSADERS, MONK HIGGINS, BLUE MITCHELL, QUINCY JONES, STANLEY TURRENTINE* and *RAY CHARLES* ⟲ continued with a new name *ABU TALIB* after 1973 and recorded with blues artists like *LOUIS MYERS, BIG LEON BROOKS, BOBBY BLUE BLAND, VERNON GARRETT* and *JIMMY WITHERSPOON.* Died October 8, 2009)

- **Larry Taylor** bass (↻ stopped touring for health reasons in February 1972 and spent some time studying string bass before returning in 1974) then

  ↻ **Putter Smith** bass (a friend of Larry Taylor's who replaced him for the Australian tour in March 1972. Previously with *MOSE ALLISON* and *MASON WILLIAMS* ↻ recorded with *LEE KONITZ, CHARLIE HADEN* and other jazzmen afterwards) then

  ↻ **Victor Gaskin** bass, joined March 1972 (previously with the *DUKE ELLINGTON ORCHESTRA, LES McCANN, CANNONBALL ADDERLEY, MOSE ALLISON, THELONIOUS MONK, DEXTER GORDON* and *CHICO HAMILTON* ↻ continued with the *CRUSADERS, NAT ADDERLEY, DEXTER GORDON* and the *BILLY TAYLOR TRIO* after 1973. Died July 14, 2012)

- ↻ **Ron Selico** drums, from November 1971 (no drummer at the start of this line-up) until December 1971 (previously with *JAMES BROWN*, the *SHUGGIE OTIS BAND* and *FRANK ZAPPA'S MOTHERS OF INVENTION* ↻ joined soul man *ERIC MERCURY*) then

  ↻ **Keef Hartley** drums, rejoined January 1972 (left *VINEGAR JOE* ↻ returned to the *KEEF HARTLEY BAND*, formed *DOG SOLDIER*, then to *MICHAEL CHAPMAN* and *MAINSQUEEZE*. Died 26 November 2011, after a long illness)

- ↻ **Richard Blue Mitchell** trumpet, flugelhorn (a jazz giant; previously with *EARL BOSTIC, JIMMY SMITH, BOBBY TIMMONS, JACKIE McLEAN, LES McCANN, ELVIN JONES, PHILLY JOE JONES, SONNY STITT, STANLEY TURRENTINE, RICHARD HOLMES, YUSEF LATEEF, JIMMY McGRIFF, GRANT GREEN, CHICK COREA*, the *HORACE SILVER QUINTET*, his own groups and *RAY CHARLES* ↻ continued after 1973 with the *LOUIE BELLSON SEPTET, HANK MOBLEY* and many more. Died May 21, 1979)

- ↻ **Clifford Solomon** tenor and alto sax (well-known for his work with *RAY CHARLES*, the *JOHNNY OTIS SHOW*,

CLIFFORD BROWN, QUINCY JONES, LIONEL HAMPTON, IKE AND TINA TURNER and *ART FARMER* ☉ left in summer 1972 to work with *JOHNNY OTIS, BIG JOE TURNER, VERNON GARRETT* and *CHARLES BROWN*. Died June 21, 2004) then

☉ **Fred Clark** tenor sax, joined Sept. 1972 (previously played with *SONNY THOMPSON* in the fifties ☉ left end 1972, to *PEE WEE CRAYTON, JOHNNY OTIS, LOUIS JORDAN, ROD PIAZZA*) then

☉ **James W. Red Holloway** tenor and alto sax, flute, vocals ☉ (joined early 1973, previously with *CHARLIE PARKER, JOHN COLTRANE, JACK McDUFF, GENE AMMONS, BILLIE HOLLIDAY, DUKE ELLINGTON, SONNY ROLLINS, BEN WEBSTER, SONNY STITT, LESTER YOUNG, ELLA FITZGERALD, MILES DAVIS, LIONEL HAMPTON, NAT KING COLE, BILL DOGGETT, B.B. KING, OTIS RUSH, ARETHA FRANKLIN, JIMMY REED, MUDDY WATERS, ROOSEVELT SYKES, JIMMY WITHERSPOON, WILLIE DIXON, MEMPHIS SLIM, CHUCK BERRY*)

RECORDINGS: The live albums *JAZZ BLUES FUSION* recorded November 18, 1971 in Boston and December 3 & 4 in New York, and *MOVING ON* recorded July 10, 1972 in Los Angeles with guest musicians Ernie Watts tenor sax, Fred Jackson baritone and tenor sax, Charles Owens tenor and soprano sax, flute, and Larry Taylor bass. The double album *TEN YEARS ARE GONE* (studio album recorded March to May 1973 in Los Angeles with Sugarcane Harris on violin; live album end 1972 with Fred Clark in New York), plus three live tracks on the album *ROCK THE BLUES TONIGHT* in late 1972 with Fred Clark, recorded in Canada. Eight more live tracks on the album *ROLLING WITH THE BLUES* recorded in Frankfurt in May 1972 (3 tracks with Clifford Solomon) and May 1973 (five tracks with Red Holloway)

CONCERTS:
- *1971:* US tour in late October, November and December
- *1972:* Australian tour in March (7 dates), then a tour of Europe in April & May, US dates in summer and a US and Canada tour from September to December
- *1973:* May 8–19 Germany (7 dates) plus Switzerland, Paris, Vienna & London as part of an eight-week tour of Europe including GB (3 dates), Australia & New Zealand. Then another European tour. US dates in summer, including the Newport Jazz Festival on July 1 (session with Roy Buchanan), & Philharmonic Hall in NYC

MORE BANDS
(1974–1976)

JOHN MAYALL BAND # 20. 1974
- **John Mayall** vocals, harmonica, keyboards, guitar ☮
- ☮ **Hi Tide Harris** guitar, vocals (Bluesman from San Francisco, previously played and recorded with *JOHNNY TAYLOR, LOWELL FULSON, JIMMY McCRACKLIN*, the *ROGER COLLINS BAND, BIG MAMA THORNTON*, the *BOB GEDDINS Jr. BAND, SHAKY JAKE HARRIS* and *CHARLIE MUSSELWHITE* ☮ solo from 1975 on)
- ☮ **Randy Resnick** guitar (came from *PURE FOOD AND DRUG ACT* where he played with former Mayall musicians Sugarcane Harris, Harvey Mandel and Paul Lagos. Also played on *SUGARCANE's* solo albums ☮ to *JOHN KLEMMER, JOHN LEE HOOKER* and *FREDDIE KING*, before going to Paris to live and work after 1975)
- **Red Holloway** tenor and alto sax, flute, vocals (☮ had a solo career as a jazz player, returned for a short stint in 1976 (see

217

band # 22), played with *HORACE SILVER, ETTA JAMES* and *EDDIE CLEANHEAD VINSON* before forming the *RED HOLLOWAY-CLARK TERRY SEXTET*)

- ʘ ***LARRY TAYLOR*** bass ʘ (returned to the fold; had worked with *RICHARD GREENE* and *HARVEY MANDEL* in the meantime)
- ʘ ***SOKO RICHARDSON*** drums ʘ (previously played with the *IKE AND TINA TURNER SHOW, TERRY REID, EARL HOOKER* and *BOBBY WOMACK*)

RECORDINGS: THE LATEST EDITION plus the singles ***BRAND NEW BAND/LET ME GIVE/PASSING THROUGH*** and probably ***AL GOLDSTEIN BLUES*** recorded March and April 1974
CONCERTS: 1974: A tour of GB in late April and Europe in May and June including dates in Germany, Italy, Spain and Switzerland (4 dates) as well as tours of Japan, China, Australia & New Zealand in October. On July 19, 1974, Mayall jammed with *ERIC CLAPTON'S BAND* at Long Beach, CA.

JOHN MAYALL BAND # 21. COUNTRY BLUES. January 1975 to autumn 1976

- **John Mayall** vocals, harmonica, guitar ʘ
- ʘ **Dee McKinnie** vocals (from Memphis, she sang in a band led by Jay Spell ʘ returned to Memphis in 1976 to gig locally)
- ʘ **Rick Vito** guitar, vocals (previously with *MATRIX*, the *WRIGHT BROTHERS, TROY NEWMAN, SPANKY & OUR GANG*, the *VITO-VALENTI BLUES BAND, DELANEY & BONNIE, DOBIE GRAY, LITTLE RICHARD, JOHN PRINE, TODD RUNDGREN & UTOPIA* and *BOBBY WHITLOCK* ʘ played and recorded with *ROGER Mc GUINN'S THUNDERBYRD, BONNIE RAITT, ANGEL CITY RHYTHM BAND, JACKSON BROWNE, BOB SEGER, RITA COOLIDGE, DOLLY PARTON, ROY ORBISON, MARIA MULDAUR, GLENN FREY* and *DELBERT Mc CLINTON* before joining *FLEETWOOD MAC* in 1987, toured with *STEVIE NICKS* and

later solo with his own band the *LUCKY DEVILS*, toured with *JOHN FOGERTY*, then with the *MICK FLEETWOOD BLUES BAND*)

○ **Mick Radford** guitar, replaced Rick Vito for some shows

- ○ **Don Sugarcane Harris** violin, vocals (returned here ○ left around end of 1975 to reunite with *DEWEY TERRY*, then recorded with *TUPELO CHAIN SEX*. Returned to record one tune with Mayall in 1984. Died November 30, 1999)
- ○ **Jay Spell** keyboards ○ (the blind keyboardist previously with *TOWER OF POWER*, *DON NIX*, *EDDIE FLOYD* and *ERIC MERCURY*) replaced for 1975 autumn European tour by ○ **Ronnie Barron** keyboards, vocals (an excellent singer and keyboardist from New Orleans, previously played with *DR. JOHN*, *SMILEY LEWIS*, *SUGARBOY CRAWFORD* and *PAUL BUTTERFIELD'S BETTER DAYS* ○ then recorded with *B.B. KING*, *DR. JOHN*, *TOM WAITS*, *RY COODER*, *ERIC BURDON* plus several albums under own name before joining *CANNED HEAT* for a tour in 1985. Died March 20, 1997)
- **Larry Taylor** bass ○
- **Soko Richardson** drums (until spring 1976 ○ returned in 1977) then ○ **Roy McCurdy** drums (from *CANNONBALL ADDERLEY QUINTET*, the *JAZZTET*, *BOBBY TIMMONS*, *ART FARMER* and *SONNY ROLLINS* ○ recorded with *BLOOD, SWEET AND TEARS*, *CLARK TERRY* and *MILT JACKSON* after 1976)

RECORDINGS: *NEW YEAR, NEW BAND, NEW COMPANY* recorded January 1975, ***NOTICE TO APPEAR*** with Allen Toussaint in late summer 1975 in New Orleans, the two live TV tracks ***SO MUCH TO DO*** and ***TAXMAN BLUES*** for The Old Grey Whistle Test in GB in October 1975 (on ***LIVE AT THE BBC***), plus ***A BANQUET IN BLUES*** in May 1976 with 17 guest musicians, including former band members John McVie, Blue Mitchell, Red Holloway, Jon Mark, Johnny Almond, Alex Dmochowski, Sugarcane Harris and Ronnie Barron.

CONCERTS: 1975: US dates plus a tour of Europe in autumn including London's Royal Albert Hall on Sept. 26 and TV recordings for The Old Grey Whistle Test, plus 3 dates in Switzerland in October.

STILL MORE BANDS
(1976–1978)

JOHN MAYALL BAND # 22. Autumn 1976 to end 1976
- John Mayall vocals, harmonica, keyboards, guitar ◑
- ◑ **Pepper Watkins** vocals (previously with *TOWER OF POWER* doing backing vocals in 1976 ◑ afterwards sang with *GENE CLARK, MARIA MULDAUER* and many others)
- ◑ **Patty Smith** vocals (previously sang backing vocals with *BARRY GOLDBERG* and *BLUE OYSTER CULT* ◑)
- ◑ **Gary Rowles** guitar (previously played with *LOVE, COTTON-WOOD, FLO & EDDIE, RICHARD TORRANCE* and *LEON RUSSELL* ◑)
- **Jay Spell** keyboards (◑ left to play with *CAROL GRIMES, RICHARD TORRANCE, JIMMY BUFFET,* the *SAM LAY BLUES BAND, CANNED HEAT, ROSCOE SHELTON, CLIFFORD CURRY, EDDIE FLOYD, DON NIX, EMMYLOU HARRIS* and *EARL GAINES.* Died of cancer December 30, 2010)
- ◑ **Red Holloway** tenor sax (◑ see band # 20. Died February 25, 2012)
- ◑ **Ann Patterson** tenor and alto sax, oboe (leader of *MAIDEN VOYAGE,* an all-female jazz orchestra from Los Angeles ◑ to *DON ELLIS ORCHESTRA*)
- **Larry Taylor** bass (◑ previously recorded with *HOLLYWOOD FATS, RONNIE BARRON, TOM WAITS, LITTLE MILTON, JOHN LEE HOOKER, RY COODER, J.J. CALE, JOHN*

HAMMOND, CANDYE KANE, TRACY CHAPMAN and *ROD PIAZZA*, before rejoining *CANNED HEAT* in 1988)
- ◑ **Frank Wilson** drums (◑ joined *JIMMY SMITH*)
- ◑ **Warren Bryant** percussion (◑)

RECORDINGS: *LOTS OF PEOPLE* recorded November 24, 1976 at the Roxy in Los Angeles, with "big band" horn section featuring: Nolan Smith, trumpet, Jimmy Roberts, tenor sax, David Li, baritone sax and Bill Lamb, trumpet and trombone.
CONCERTS: 1976: US tour in autumn.

JOHN MAYALL BAND # 23. February 1977 to end 1978
- **John Mayall** vocals, harmonica, keyboards, guitar ◑
- ◑ **James Quill Smith** guitar, vocals ◑ (previously with *POLLUTION* and *SYLVESTER & THE HOT BAND, DOBIE GRAY, DR. JOHN* and *THREE DOG NIGHT*)
- ◑ **Steve Thompson** bass (rejoined ◑) replaced end 1977 by ◑ **Ed Lee** bass, only until end 1977 (recorded with CMU in 1971 ◑)
  ◑ **Steve Thompson** bass, back for 1978 (◑ returned 1982)
- ◑ **Soko Richardson** drums (rejoined ◑ returned 1982)
- ◑ **Jody Linscott** percussion, only from February to spring 1977 (◑ previous studio work with *DANA GILLESPIE, ROBERT PALMER, DAN FOGELBERG, KOKOMO, DAVID SANBORN, ELTON JOHN*, the *WHO*, the *PET SHOP BOYS, SNOWY WHITE, SANTANA, PAUL McCARTNEY AND WINGS*)

RECORDINGS: *A HARD CORE PACKAGE* studio album recorded March 1977, with Ann Patterson on flute, six extra horns plus five female singers including Pepper Watkins.
The live album ***THE LAST OF THE BRITISH BLUES*** recorded during spring 1978 in Baltimore, Cincinnati and New York, with seven additional female vocalists, including Pepper Watkins.

CONCERTS:
- ***1977:*** A three month/twelve country European tour in April, May and June including dates in Germany (7), France, Britain, Scandinavia and Switzerland. US dates in summer.
- ***1978:*** US dates in spring.

YET MORE BANDS
(1979–1981)

JOHN MAYALL BAND # 24. Jan. 1979 to Sept. 1979
- **John Mayall** vocals, harmonica, guitar ☺
- ☺ **Maggie Parker** vocals ☺ (previously sang with *HARVEY MANDEL'S BAND*, later became John Mayall's 2ⁿᵈ wife)
- ☺ **Kathrin Fields** vocals (☺fired in May 1979 for "non-professional attitude" during a European tour) replaced by ☺ **Becky Burns** vocals, from June 1979 on (☺ to *MARIA MULDAUR, LOUDON WAINWRIGHT III, JOHN JUKE LOGAN*)
- **James Quill Smith** guitar, vocals ☺
- ☺ **Chris Cameron** keyboards (☺ recorded with *PETER MADCAT RUTH, KITARO, BIG TWIST & THE MELLOW FELLOWS, GEORGE MICHAEL, TERENCE TRENT D'ARBY, RAMSEY LEWIS,* the *COMMODORES, SONIA DADA, ELTON JOHN, TAD ROBINSON,* the *PET SHOP BOYS, CHRIS DE BURGH, RANDY CRAWFORD, PATRICIA KAAS* and *CLIFF RICHARD* later on)
- ☺ **Christiaan Mostert** sax, flute (previously with *POLLUTION* and *SYLVESTER & THE HOT BAND* before, together with James Quill Smith, and with *GOOSE CREEK SYMPHONY* ☺ to *GLENN FREY, BRUCE COCKBURN.* Released the instrumental album *Midnight Breeze* under his own name in 2001)

- ○ **Angus Thomas** bass (from *HARVEY MANDEL* ○ to *BRAD GOODE, HANS THEESSINK, JIMMY MACK, MILES DAVIS, ALBERT KING, PETER WOLF, STANLEY CLARKE, RAHSAAN ROLAND KIRK, EDDIE HARRIS, JOHNNY WINTER, PHILIPP FANKHAUSER*)
- ○ **Ruben Alvarez** drums (○ to *BIG TWIST & THE MELLOW FELLOWS*, the *COMMODORES, JUNIOR WELLS, RAMSEY LEWIS* and *MISSISSIPPI HEAT*)

RECORDINGS: NO MORE INTERVIEWS recorded July 16–31, 1979 in Los Angeles with the above-mentioned band plus Rick Vito guitar, Ronnie Barron vocals, and three horns. *BOTTOM LINE* was recorded in January 1979 with 41 studio musicians (no recent band members)
CONCERTS: 1979: among others a tour of Europe in May, including dates in Germany (with an appearance on German TV), the Netherlands and France. On September 16, 1979, Mayall's Laurel Canyon house in Los Angeles was incinerated in a forest fire. It destroyed all his earthly belongings, including his scrupulously kept diaries, master recording tapes, extensive book and magazine collection, artwork and much more.

JOHN MAYALL BAND # 25. Winter 1979 to spring 1981
- John Mayall vocals, harmonica, keyboards, guitar ○
- James Quill Smith guitar, vocals (○previously with *BILLY JOEL*, Maggie Mayall-Parker in her band *MAGGIE & THE BLUE KATS*, the *RANDY FULLER FOUR, ROGER McGUINN* and *FISHING WITH DYNAMITE*, before he formed his own *JAMES QUILL SMITH BAND*)
- ○ **Kevin McCormick** bass (previously with *BROOKLYN DREAMS* ○ returned in 1982)
  ○ **Larry Taylor** bass (back only for the Australian tour in May & June 1980 ○ see band # 22)
- ○ **Soko Richardson** drums (rejoins for the last time ○ then teamed up with *ALBERT COLLINS*. Died January 4, 2004)
- Maggie Parker vocals, until summer 1980 (also occasionally performed as guest vocalist with Mayall's band in 1982

and 1987) ○ built her own career singing in all female groups such as *MAGGIE MAYALL & THE CADILLACS* with Debbie Davies, or the *LOS ANGELES HOUSEWIVES*, then formed *MAGGIE & THE BLUE KATS* with James Quill Smith, and later the *JAZZ PROPHETS*)

RECORDINGS: ROAD SHOW BLUES recorded July 1980, studio and live at the Golden Bear Club at Huntington Beach, CA, featuring Christiaan Mostert on sax & flute. Four tracks on *ROLLING WITH THE BLUES* recorded May 1980 (same venue as above), with Red Holloway on sax & flute.
CONCERTS:
- *1980:* Mexico City; Huntington Beach CA in May, as above. Australian tour: May 20–June 8. In July, Huntington Beach CA, as above. Autumn European tour, with dates in Poland and London (29 & 30 November).
- *1981:* A tour of Australia in early 1981 with 42 shows in 49 days.

THE RETURN OF THE BLUESBREAKERS
(1981-1982)

MEMPHIS BLUESBREAKERS # 26. May 1981 to August 4, 1981
- John Mayall vocals, harmonica, keyboards, guitar ○
- ○ Don McMinn lead-guitar (from *MEMPHIS SLIM* and *DON NIX BAND* ○ formed *DON McMINN AND THE MEMPHIS BLUES REVUE* afterwards)
- ○ Bobby Manuel rhythm-guitar (former Stax/Vault session guitarist, previously with *WILLIAM BELL*, the *MGs*, *LITTLE MILTON*, *THE EMOTIONS*, *ALBERT KING*, *RUFUS THOMAS*, the *BAR KEYS*, *DON NIX* and *LEON RUSSELL* ○

224

left July 31 and missed the last four shows of the Italian tour, joined *SHIRLEY BROWN*, *MAVIS STAPLES* and *JOHNNY TAYLOR*)
- ◑ **Larry Raspberry** piano (from the *GENTRYS*, *LARRY RASPBERRY AND THE HIGHSTEPPERS*, *ALAMO* and *DON NIX BAND* ◑)
- ◑ **Jeff Davis** bass (from the *AMAZING RHYTHM ACES* and *DON NIX' BAND* ◑ to *DON McMINN AND THE MEMPHIS BLUES REVUE*)
- ◑ **Mike Gardner** drums (from the *GENTRYS*, *JIMMY BUFFET'S CORAL REEFER BAND* and *DON NIX BAND* ◑ to *DON McMINN AND THE MEMPHIS BLUES REVUE*, returned to the *BLUESBREAKERS* in 1984)

Note: the *MEMPHIS BLUESBREAKERS* were in fact Don Nix's house band!

RECORDINGS: An album of ten tracks was recorded in May 1981 in Memphis that has never been released. Eight of these songs surfaced in 1994 on **CROSS COUNTRY BLUES**, five tracks appeared in 1985 on **RETURN OF THE BLUESBREAKERS**
CONCERTS: 1981: Among others, a tour of Europe from July 2 to August 4, with 25 dates in Italy, plus an appearance at the Nyon Festival in Switzerland. In November, Mayall played a session with *MUDDY WATERS* at the Roxy in Los Angeles. On December 31, Mayall played a New Year's Eve party at his eldest son's club Gossips in London, backed by Diz Watson's 7-piece *DIZ & THE DOORMEN*, with *ALEXIS KORNER* as special guest.

BLUESBREAKERS # 27. January 14, 1982 to June 20, 1982
- **John Mayall** vocals, harmonica, keyboards, guitar ◑
- ◑ **Mick Taylor** guitar ◑ (back after 13 years)
- ◑ **John McVie** bass (back after 15 years ◑ returned to *FLEETWOOD MAC*) until June 18, 1982, then
  ◑ **Kevin McCormick** bass (back after only about one year)

until September 1982, but probably for 2 shows only on
June 19 & 20 (◐ joined *MARTIN BALIN*, *STEVE PERRY*, then
MELISSA ETHERIDGE and *JACKSON BROWNE*)
- ◐ **Colin Allen** drums (◐ (back after 13 years)

RECORDINGS: THE 1982 REUNION CONCERT recorded at the
Wax Museum in Washington DC, June 17, 1982, with ten eleven
tracks, released 1994. Five of these were issued in 1985 on the
Australian release *RETURN OF THE BLUESBREAKERS*. Four
more live tracks are available on the album *ROLLING WITH THE
BLUES* recorded June 3, 1982, at Minneapolis and June 5, 1982,
in Chicago. Also the live VHS/DVD/2CD *BLUES ALIVE/JAMMIN'
WITH THE BLUES GREATS/IN THE SHADOW OF LEGENDS*
recorded at the Capitol Theatre in Passaic, NJ, June 18, 1982, with
guest appearances by Albert King, Buddy Guy, Junior Wells, Etta
James and Sippie Wallace.
CONCERTS: 1982: 7 in California from January 15 to 22, a tour of
Hong Kong, Australia (17d), New Zealand (1d) and Hawaii (2d) from
late January to February 21. 3 in California from May 20 to 22, a US
East Coast Tour from June 2 to 20 (20d)

BANDS
(1982–1984)

BLUESBREAKERS # 28. November 1982 to June 1983
- **John Mayall** vocals, harmonica, keyboards, guitar ◐
- **Mick Taylor** guitar (◐ returns in January 1984 already,
  see band # 30)
- ◐ **Steve Thompson** bass (back to complete the Laurel
  Canyon line-up (see band # 13) ◐returned to England and
  joined *TREAT*. Died December 2007)

- **Colin Allen** drums (☽married and moved to Stockholm, then toured with *BOB DYLAN* together with Mick Taylor in 1984, and later joined *MICK TAYLOR'S NEW ELECTRIC BAND* in 1986 and then *THE BRITISH BLUES QUINTET* with Zoot Money, Miller Anderson and Maggie Bell)
- ☽ **Maggie Mayall-Parker** vocals (guested on some concerts of the Italian tour in late 1982)

RECORDINGS: Just two live tracks on *ROLLING WITH THE BLUES* recorded December 7, 1982 at Rome, Italy, and December 10, 1982 at Lugo, Italy, plus one more live track (*French Toast*), recorded May or June 1983 in Concerneau, France, issued on *EXCLUSIVE LIVE RARITIES*.

CONCERTS:
- *1982:* Italian tour from November 25 to December 10 (9 dates).
- *1983:* European tour from May 20 to June 14 with dates in Austria, France, Spain, Switzerland (3 dates from June 12 to 14) and London.

BAND # 29, CANNED HEAT. October to November 1983
- **John Mayall** vocals, harmonica ☽
- ☽ **Walter Trout** guitar (☽ joined the Bluesbreakers in 1985)
- ☽ **Mike Halby** guitar
- ☽ **Ernie Rodriguez** bass
- ☽ **Fito de la Parra** drums

John Mayall was guest artist on this tour, playing a set of about five songs with Canned Heat.

CONCERTS: 1983: US tour with 28 concert dates. October 12 at the Lone Star Café in New York City saw a session with Johnny Winter. Probably also dates in Canada.

BLUESBREAKERS # 30. January 19 to April 28, 1984
- **John Mayall** vocals, harmonica, keyboards, guitar ☽
- ☽ **Mick Taylor** guitar (returned ☽ joined *BOB DYLAN* on tour, moved to NYC and formed own groups *NEW ELECTRIC*

227

BAND, HOT WATER BAND, PROFESSORS OF PLEASURE, TUMBLING DICE, HOLLYWOOD BLUES KINGS and *MICK TAYLOR & THE DOGS* etc. as well as with *CORKY LAING'S ALL STARS, CARLA OLSON*, the *JAMES HARMAN BAND, TERRY REID, BILL WYMAN'S RHYTHM KINGS, TODD SHARPEVILLE, PETER KARP & THE ROAD SHOW BAND*, the *WENTUS BLUES BAND*, the *ALL STAR BAND WITH BUDDY GUY*, the *STEPHAN PETIT BAND* plus many more. Rejoined the Bluesbreakers as a guest on UK tour in late 2004)

- ⟲ **Tim Drummond** bass (known to Mayall as one of the studio musicians to record *Bottom Line* back in 1979, previously with the *BEACH BOYS, LONNIE MACK, CHARLIE DANIELS, J.J. CALE, GRAHAM BELL, STRAY GATOR, RONNIE HAWKINS, PAUL BUTTERFIELD, FENTON ROBINSON, CROSBY, STILLS, NASH and YOUNG, RY COODER, BOB DYLAN, DAVE DAVIES* and *JAMES BROWN* ⟲ toured and recorded with *LONNIE MACK, BOB DYLAN, NEIL YOUNG, ERIC CLAPTON, ROY BUCHANAN, JOHN HAMMOND* and *BOBBY BYRD*)
- ⟲ **Mike Gardner** drums (back from the Memphis Bluesbreakers (see band # 26) ⟲ returned to Memphis to front his own group and recorded with *RUFUS THOMAS* and *BILLY SWAN*. Died May 18, 1991).

RECORDINGS: Two live tracks on the album *BLACKTOP BLUES-A-RAMA, LIVE FROM TIPITINA'S, NEW ORLEANS, 1977–1989* recorded April 17, 1984 at New Orleans.
CONCERTS: 1984: Californian dates from January 19 to 21 (6 shows), US tour with 16 concerts from April 5 to 28 (April 5, 7 & 8: Californian dates with Walter Trout)

BANDS
(1984-1989)

BLUESBREAKERS # 31. June 14, 1984 to May 16, 1985
- **John Mayall** vocals, harmonica, keyboards, guitar ↺
- ↺ **Coco Montoya** guitar, vocals ↺ (played drums with *FREDDIE KING* and *ALBERT COLLINS*, then switched to guitar and had his own band in LA)
- ↺ **Kal David** guitar, vocals (previously played with the *EXCEPTIONS, ILLINOIS SPEED PRESS, NEIL MERRYWHEATHER*, the *FABULOUS RHINESTONES, ROBBIE DUPREE* and *BONNIE RAITT*. Mayall met Kal during an all-star jam with Bonnie Raitt ↺ Preferred session work with *WOODSTOCK* and local work in LA to being on the road, formed his own group, then joined *JOHNNY RIVERS*)
- ↺ **Bobby Haynes** bass ↺ (previously played with the *CRUSADERS, T-BONE WALKER, BIG JOE TURNER, PAUL BUTTERFIELD, PERCY MAYFIELD, DEXTER GORDON*, the *CHICO HAMILTON QUINTET* among many others. Red Holloway recommended Bobby Haynes to Mayall)
- ↺ **Willie McNeil** drums (a friend of Mayall's son Jason ↺ left spring '85 to join *TUPELO CHAIN SEX, JUMP WITH JOY*, the *UNTOUCHABLES* and *MAGGIE MAYALL'S* band)
  ↺ **Keith John** drums, vocals (from spring '85 on, US gigs only, played with *ALL OF THE ABOVE, LESLIE WEST, BILLY IDOL, DANNY GATTON*, the *BACK DOORS* before ↺ to play with the *VENTURES, NEIL YOUNG* and *QUAVER*)

RECORDINGS: A studio album at Sunswept Studio in LA in July 1984 that has never been released as such. All nine tracks were issued ten years later on ***CROSS COUNTRY BLUES***. One live track (Parchman Farm) appears on the 4 CD set ***CELEBRATING 20 YEARS OF THE FESTIVAL INTERNATIONAL DE JAZZ DE MONTREAL 1980-2000*** recorded July 4, 1984.

CONCERTS:
- *1984:* Italian tour June 14 to July 3, Montreal Jazz festival on July 4, US dates until end 1984.
- *1985:* A tour of Scandinavia and Germany in Jan, then a US-tour in Feb & 4 dates in Canada in April.

BLUESBREAKERS # 32. May 28, 1985 to July 1988 and February to May 6, 1989
- **John Mayall** vocals, harmonica, keyboards, guitar ☉
- **Coco Montoya** guitar, vocals ☉
- ☉ **Walter Trout** guitar, vocals (previously with *JOHN LEE HOOKER, BIG MAMA THORNTON, JOE TEX, PERCY MAYFIELD, PEE WEE CRAYTON,* the *RIGHTEOUS BROTHERS, HANK BALLARD* and *CANNED HEAT* ☉ formed the *WALTER TROUT BAND,* later *WALTER TROUT AND THE FREE RADICALS*)
- **Bobby Haynes** bass ☉
- ☉ **Joe Yuele** drums ☉ (previously with the *VEE JAYS, DOBIE "DRIFT-A-WAY" GRAY* and the *JUKE RHYTHM BAND,* where he backed artists like *ALBERT COLLINS, LOWELL FULSON, BIG JOE TURNER, GEORGE HARMONICA SMITH* and *BIG MAMA THORNTON,* then with *SIMON STOKES & THE NIGHTHAWKS* and the *COCO MONTOYA BLUES BAND,* before becoming Mayall's longest-ever band member)
  ☉ **Paul Hines** drums (came from *TEENA MARIE,* replaced Yuele from Oct 30 to Nov 2, 1985 for four gigs to try it out, says Mayall ☉ to *ROY MERIWETHER, CREFLO A. DOLLAR JR.*)

RECORDINGS: BEHIND THE IRON CURTAIN (Szeged, Hungary, June 6, 1985) and *THE POWER OF THE BLUES* (Frankfurt, Bonn & Münster, Germany, April 19–21, 1987) as well as *CHICAGO LINE* (a studio effort, Tutzing, Germany, April 5–10, 1988). One more live track (Racehorse Man) recorded July 8, 1986, at Montreux, Switzerland, appeared on *EXCLUSIVE LIVE RARITIES.* Also a

DVD *LIVE AT THE IOWA STATE UNIVERSITY* (Ames, Iowa, Oct 31, 1985) with Paul Hines on drums, plus CD & DVD *LIVE IN GERMANY 1988* (TV, March 16, 1988)
CONCERTS:

- *1985:* Tour of Eastern Europe & Germany from May to June, then US dates June to July, Germany again in August, California in Sept, Buenos Aires on Oct 12, plus dates in USA & Canada until Dec (Oct 24 & 25, an all-star jam with *BO DIDDLEY* and Chuck Berry, Ron Wood, Mick Fleetwood, Mitch Mitchell, Carl Wilson and 17 more musicians in LA with Mayall on harmonica and keyboards. No Bluesbreakers. Concert filmed as *BO DIDDLEY AND FRIENDS, ROCK 'N' ROLL ALL STAR JAM*)
- *1986:* Tour of Europe in February (DK, S, N, D, CH, F, 30 concerts in 29 days), US and CDN dates in June, European summer festivals in July including Montreux July 8 (radio & TV broadcast, a session with Luther Allison), USA and CDN: 19 dates in Aug & Sept, Australian tour with 26 dates Oct 15–Nov 9.
- *1987:* Feb 4 to 14 US south 10d AR, CA, AL, FL. European tour in March & April (58 shows in Scandinavia, D, A, CH, H, YU, DDR, London), New Orleans Jazz and Heritage Festival plus US east coast (New York & Boston) end of May, Italian tour in December
- *1988:* Canada, USA, European tour in March & April (D, A, plus German TV broadcast on March 16, two dates in Switzerland April 22 & 25). US east coast dates in July.
- *1989:* A tour of Scandinavia in January during which Mayall fell ill and Trout took over. A tour of Europe from Feb to May (D, A, CH in April)

BANDS
(1988–1993)

BAND # 33, PETER MAFFAY'S GROUP. July 25 to October 9, 1988
- John Mayall vocals, harmonica, guitar ☉
  ☉ Pascal Kravetz organ
- Peter Maffay vocals, guitar ☉ Bobby Stern alto & electric sax
- Chris Thompson vocals, percussion ☉ Eddie Taylor
  tenor sax
- Carl Carlton guitar ☉ Thomas Zoller baritone sax
- Frank Diez guitar ☉ Steffi Stefan bass
- Jean-Jacques Kravetz piano, keyboards ☉ Bertram Engel
  drums

Mayall was the guest artist on German star Peter Maffay's *Lange Schatten tour '88*. He played harmonica & guitar on some songs and performed *Room to Move* and others.
RECORDINGS: A live album and video **LANGE SCHATTEN TOUR '88** recorded Sept. 17, at Dortmund, Germany.
Prior to this, Mayall added harp on one studio track with Maffay in Dec. 1987 for the album **LANGE SCHATTEN**.
CONCERTS: 1988: LANGE SCHATTEN TOUR from August 17 to October 9 (34 dates in Germany and one in Zurich, Switzerland).

BLUESBREAKERS # 34. May 1989 to November 7, 1993
- John Mayall vocals, harmonica, keyboards, guitar ☉
- Coco Montoya guitar, vocals (☉solo)
- ☉ (Don Sugarcane Harris) violin, vocals (back. Rehearsed but didn't show up when they went on tour ☉)
- Bobby Haynes bass, until December 1989 (☉ formed his own *BOBBY HAYNES BLUES BAND*), then
  ☉ Rick Cortes bass (from New Orleans, previously with *IRMA THOMAS, LEE DORSEY, JOHN MOONEY, JOSEPH "ZIGABOO" MODELISTE, LEO NOCENTELLI, ANDY FOREST, IVAN NEVILLE, RAZIN' CAIN* and *LITTLE*

QUEENIE & THE PERCULATORS ◔) from December 1989 to January 1990, then
  ◔ **Freebo (Dan Friedberg)** bass (previously with the *EDISON ELECTRIC BAND, BONNIE RAITT* and the *BLUES BUSTERS* ◔ left end 1990 to join *DOUG LEGACY & THE ZYDECO PARTY BAND*, recorded with own name from 1999), then
  ◔ **Rick Cortes** bass ◔ (back) from January 1991
- **Joe Yuele** drums ◔

RECORDINGS: A SENSE OF PLACE (December 1989 in Los Angeles) with Bobby Haynes and Freebo on bass, plus six guest musicians including Sonny Landreth on slide guitar. *WAKE UP CALL* (autumn 1992 in Burbank) with Rick Cortes on bass, plus eleven guest musicians including Buddy Guy, Albert Collins, Mick Taylor and Mavis Staples. The DVD *LIVE FROM THE BOTTOM LINE NEW YORK* (June 2, 1990 in NYC) with Freebo. Radio recordings for BBC, July 10, 1990 with Freebo (four tracks), plus one live track on *EXCLUSIVE LIVE RARITIES* recorded May 1990 in Tokyo with Freebo. Three more live tracks recorded in Japan May 1990 plus one in Germany from Oct 1990 (with Lee Mayall adding sax) on *HISTORIC LIVE SHOWS VOL. 1*, all with Freebo. On *HISTORIC LIVE SHOWS VOL. 2* one track from Sept 1990 in Austin, TX with Freebo, all others with Rick Cortes on bass: Two from March 1992 in Germany, three from June 6, 1992 in Ben Lomond, CA, and thrtee more from Fort Worth, TX in Sept 1993. *LIVE FROM AUSTIN, TX* (recorded Sept 13, 1993) with Rick Cortes on bass.
CONCERTS:
- *1989:* US dates including the Great Wood Blues festival in Boston on June 25 with Stevie Ray Vaughan, Johnny Winter and Ronnie Earl on the same bill
- *1990:* US dates, Tour of Japan (6 dates in May), USA & CDN tour from May to August with 2 European dates in July (Helsinki & London), US west in July & Aug (10d), Tour of Europe in fall with Germany (22 dates from Sept. 18 to Oct. 20) plus CH, A, B, NL and Luxemburg. A 30 cities tour of

Australia (prob. in Aug) and a two weeks US tour with ZZ Top mostly in Texas prob. in early Sept

- **1991:** US dates in March (west coast), May 3 Jazz Heritage Festival New Orleans. Australian tour in spring, Europe in June & July (GR, DK, NL, D, F, S, CH, E, B, N, SF) plus US dates (east coast festivals August 16. & 17, New York in October e. g.)
- **1992:** 10 US dates in Jan./Feb. On Feb. 20, Mayall performed at Gossips in London, backed by his son's Gaz's band the Blues Rockers. Tour of Europe March 6 to 27 (D, A, CH, Lux, 22d), 5 US dates in April, Scandinavia & France May 1 to 27 (23 dates: 7 DK, 5 S, 2 SF, 1 N, 7 F, 1 B), 3 US dates June 5. & 6. Tour of Europe June 24 to July 5 (12 dates: 3 E, 2 F, 2 GB, 1 B, 4 NL), USA 17 dates in July & Sept
- **1993:** US dates in March (as a package with Buddy Guy), a European tour from May 12 to June 2: 18 dates in Germany & 1 in CH. Among the German dates 4 shows from May 12 to 16: Blues in the summer with Buddy Guy, Pete York's Superblues & Mose Allison on the same bill. London in June. Montreal Jazz Festival CDN on July 3, Paleo Festival in Nyon CH on July 24. Cambridge Folk Festival GB on Aug. US dates in Sept. & Nov. Also a tour of Asia including Hong Kong and Singapore (Oct. 5 & 6)

BANDS WITH BUDDY WHITTINGTON
(1993–2000)

BLUESBREAKERS # 35. November 1993 to end 2000
- John Mayall vocals, harmonica, keyboards, guitar �
- � Buddy Whittington guitar, vocals � (previously with *SHORT CHANGE, POINT BLANK* and his own Texan group

THE SIDEMEN, before joining Mayall for the longest stint for a guitar player

- **Rick Cortes** bass (until October 1995 ↺ started working as a web producer and kept playing, occasionally with *CHUCK BERRY, MITCH RYDER, SPENCER DAVIS* and *CHET McCRACKEN* among others) then

  ↺ **John Paulus** bass (from November 1995 on. Played with *BOBBY CALDWELL* before ↺ left end September 1999 to join *CANNED HEAT* on guitar) then

  ↺ **Greg Rzab** bass (from Oct. 1, 1999 on. Previously with *BUDDY GUY* (for twelve years), *OTIS CLAY, OTIS RUSH, EDDIE CLEARWATER, JAMES COTTON, ALBERT COLLINS, LUTHER ALLISON, WILLIE DIXON, JOHN LEE HOOKER, JUNIOR WELLS, ROBERT JR. LOCKWOOD, TAB BENOIT, CARLOS SANTANA, ERIC CLAPTON, JEFF BECK* and *BERNARD ALLISON* before ↺ walked out during the British tour on May 22, 2000 because he had an offer from the *BLACK CROWES*, but joined *JIMMY PAGE* instead, later to *GOV'T MULE* and *MELVIN TAYLOR*, to rejoin in 2009) then

  ↺ **Neil Simpson** bass (from the *CLIMAX BLUES BAND*, substituted for Greg Rzab from May 23 to June 2, 2000 for 11 UK gigs to finish the tour ↺ back to *CLIMAX BLUES BAND* and *ROY WOOD*) then

  ↺ **Greg Boaz** bass (from June 2000 on, played in *MICK TAYLOR's* band in 1993, recorded with *JOHN 'JUKE' LOGAN* and *DAVE ALVIN* before, until the end of August 2000 ↺ to *GEORGE FRIEND*, then to *GROOVE DIVINITIES*, and *IMPERIAL CROWNS*) then

  ↺ **Hank van Sickle** bass ↺ (from Sept 1, 2000 on, previously with *GUITAR SHORTY, SMOKEY WILSON, CANDYE KANE, DENNY FREEMAN, ROSIE FLORES, SKIP HELLER, JAMES INTVELD, WANDA JACKSON, YMA SUMAC, JUDY TENUTA* and the *DRIFTERS*)

- **Joe Yuele** drums ↺

RECORDINGS: SPINNING COIN (May & Aug 1994 in Burbank and Hollywood) with Rick Cortes on bass, plus two live tracks recorded summer 1994 in Madrid on *EXCLUSIVE LIVE RARITIES* and four more live tracks recorded in Jan 1995 in Salt Lake City, UT on *HISTORIC LIVE SHOWS VOL. 2*. One live track on the Various Artists album *FM 101,9, LIVE FROM THE MUSIC HALL VOL. 2* recorded March 14, 1995 in LA. *BLUES FOR THE LOST DAYS* (Oct 1996 in Calabasas) with John Paulus on bass, plus nine guest musicians including Red Holloway, Clifford Solomon and Tommy Eyre. Four live tracks recorded Nov 1997 in Houston, TX, plus six more from the North Sea Festival in Den Haag, Holland in July 1998 on *HISTORIC LIVE SHOWS VOL. 3. PADLOCK ON THE BLUES* (Oct 1998 in Calabasas and San Francisco) with John Paulus on bass, plus eight guest musicians, including John Lee Hooker, Ernie Watts, Coco Montoya and Tommy Eyre. *UK TOUR 2K* (May 2000 live in Great Britain), with Greg Rzab or Neil Simpson on bass. *ALONG FOR THE RIDE* (Oct to Dec 2000 in Calabasas, London, Nashville and Chicago) with mostly *DAVID SMITH* from Memphis on bass (studio only, he also recorded with Luther Allison, Coco Montoya, Debbie Davies, Melvin Taylor, Carl Wheatersby, Ana Popovic and Mighty Sam McClain) plus 26 famous guest musicians.
CONCERTS:

- *1994:* Singapore, Israel (Tel Aviv), Scandinavia & Italy plus dates in South America (Buenos Aires on March 2). Germany: 7 dates on June 16 and 24–27, plus July 1 & 12. July 17 Gurtenfestival Berne in CH. Spanish dates in summer. A two-week US-mid-west tour with ZZ Top.
- *1995:* US tour (5 weeks) in March & April. Tour of Europe 42 dates in April & May: D (11 dates, 4 with the Eric Burdon Band on the same bill), CH (2), F (11), GB (5), IRL (2) plus NL, B, TR & Rumania. US dates in June
- *1996:* US dates in spring. Blues Cruise France & Italy from May 25 to June 1. July: 7 dates in Germany, 1 in London.
- *1997:* Germany March 18–20, US dates in July. Sept. 24 in Athens, Greece with an all-star Band featuring Mayall

(vocals, harmonica), Mick Taylor (guitar), Max Middleton (piano), Kuma Harada (bass), Jeff Allen (drums), Snowy White (guitar), Rick Wakeman (keyboards), Alvin Lee (guitar), Hillary Briggs (organ), Michael Bailey (bass). European tour Oct 9–Nov 14 with concerts in Germany (17), Austria (5) and Switzerland (3). British dates in late November.

- **1998:** Piazza Blues Festival in Bellinzona June 27 and Monteux July 11 (both CH), as part of a 18 country/53 day European tour in June and July, with concerts in Spain, Greece, Turkey, Hungary, Poland, Germany and Britain (June 18, 20, 21 with the Mick Taylor Band on the same bill). Sept 6 Long Beach CA with Mick Taylor, Peter Green, Kim Simmonds, Ronnie Earl, Keith Emerson, Chris Dreja, Jim McCarty. Nov 14 Clarksdale, with Buddy Guy and Koko Taylor (a festival to benefit the Delta Blues Museum).
- **1999:** US west coast in February and festivals in July. Europe in October with CH (3d).
- **2000:** UK tour together with Peter Green's Splinter Group May 1–June 2 (31d). US tour together with Peter Green's Splinter Group in Sept.

BANDS WITH BUDDY WHITTINGTON II (2001–2008)

BLUESBREAKERS # 36. 2001 to September 20, 2003
- **John Mayall** vocals, harmonica, keyboards, guitar ↻
- **Buddy Whittington** guitar, vocals ↻
- ↻ **Tom Canning** keyboards, joined 2001 (previously with *T-BONE BURNETT, DELBERT McCLINTON, FREDDIE KING, JOHNNY SHINES, AL JARREAU, WAYNE SHORTER, BONNIE RAITT, ROBBIE ROBERTSON, GLENN FREY, JOE*

*WALSH, ELVIS COSTELLO, ALBERT LEE, JOHN 'JUKE'
LOGAN* and *JOHNNY HALLYDAY*) ☊ left Sept. 21, 2003 to
continue working with French "Elvis" *JOHNNY HALLYDAY*,
rejoined in 2009
- **Hank van Sickle** bass ☊
- **Joe Yuele** drums ☊

Musicians taking part in the 70th birthday concert, July 19, 2003,
in Liverpool:
- ☊ **Eric Clapton** guitar, vocals, back with the Bluesbreakers
  after 37 years! ☊
- ☊ **Mick Taylor** guitar, ☊
- ☊ **Chris Barber** trombone☊
- ☊ **Henry Lowther** cornet, back with the Bluesbreakers
  after 35 years! ☊
- ☊ **Dave Lewis** tenor sax ☊
- ☊ **Julian Argüelles** baritone sax ☊

RECORDINGS: STORIES (Feb & March 2002 in Calabasas).
NO DAYS OFF (recorded live Nov 2002 at Reading UK). The DVD
COOKIN' DOWN UNDER (Feb 12, 2003 in Sydney AUS). *70TH
BIRTHDAY CONCERT* (July 19, 2003 at Liverpool UK) with six
guest musicians including Eric Clapton, Mick Taylor, Chris Barber
and Henry Lowther (also on DVD).
CONCERTS:
- *2001:* Tour of Europe & UK June 14–July 22 (GB, LUX, NL,
  B, H, CZ, D, N, F, CH, IT, DK, SF, S, IRL). US dates from Sept
  to Dec.
- *2002:* US tour Sept 7–Oct 12 (15d), UK tour with Peter Green's
  Splinter Group Oct 27–Dec 4 (39d)
- *2003:* Hawaii in Jan, Australian tour in Feb,
  Germany (8d) & Britain (1d) in March. Liverpool July 19.
  US dates in Aug & Sept.

BLUESBREAKERS # 37. September 21, 2003 to Nov 2007,
and April 12 to October 24, 2008

- **John Mayall** vocals, harmonica, keyboards, guitar ☺
- **Buddy Whittington** guitar, vocals ☺ stayed 15 years before going solo
- **Hank van Sickle** bass ☺ after 8 years
- **Joe Yuele** drums ☺ after 23½ years ☺ **Danny Cochran** drums, Buddy Whittington's pal, subbed during the tour of Canada in spring and summer 2005 for Yuele, whose passport did not make the visa deadline ☺

Guests on tour:
- ☺ **Eric Steckel** guitar, vocals, (aged 13) for the Scandinavian tour in July 2004 ☺
- ☺ **Mick Taylor** guitar, back for the UK tour in late 2004 ☺
- ☺ **Robben Ford** vocals, guitar, on the US tour 2005, Sept 21 to Nov 20 ☺

RECORDINGS: ROAD DOGS (January & February 2005 at Calabasas) and ***IN THE PALACE OF THE KING*** (July 2006 at LAFX, North Hollywood), plus one live track recorded July 28, 2007 in Murcia, Spain on DVD ***SWEET LITTLE ANGEL***.
CONCERTS:
- ***2003:*** Beirut, Lebanon in Sept. D & E in Nov, Mexico in autumn.
- ***2004:*** Scandinavia in July with Eric Steckel as guest. UK tour Oct 12–Nov 16 (35d), with Mick Taylor as guest.
- ***2005:*** European tour in Feb and March; F, D (13d), CH (1d). US and Canadian dates in spring and summer like June 9: Chicago Blues Festival with Mick Taylor as a guest. US tour Sept 21–Nov 20: The Rockin' Blues Revue with Robben Ford and Eric Bipp (32d).
- ***2006:*** 4 dates in Hawaii Feb 1–4. Tour of Europe March 2–Apr 3: D (6d), B (2d), LUX (1d), CH (1d), F (22d), London (1d). June–Sept 14 US dates.

UK tour Oct 17–Nov 24 (37d) with Stan Webb's Chicken Shack. (2006: 88 shows).

- **2007:** 3 dates in California Feb 22–24. 8 dates US east coast Apr 13–21. Tour of Europe July 5–Aug 5 (30d): E (7d), It (5d), B (3d), NL (3d), F (3d), CH (2d), PL (2d), Malta, A, H, CZ, GB (1d each). St. Louis Sept 2 & Seattle Sept 6–9. Two US tours: East coast & mid west Oct 5–21 (14d), west coast Nov 9–17 (7d). (2007: 67 shows)
- **2008:** Apr 12–19: 4 US dates CA & NV. Tour of South America May 15–23 (Brazil 6d, Argentina 1d). Tour of Europe June 27–July 31 (30d): N, SF, F, NL, CH, IT, A, H, CZ, PL, LT, DK, S, E, GB, incl. the Montreux Festival, CH, July 7. US Blues Festivals CA Aug 30–31, Springfield MO, Sept 6. Tour of Europe Sept 24–Oct 24 (31d): NL (10d), F (18d), CH (1d), B (1d), Monaco (1d). (2008: 75 shows).

BANDS
(2008–2010)

BAND # 38, MARK HUMMEL'S HARMONICA BLOW OUT
January 24 to February 1, 2008
- **John Mayall** vocals, harmonica, keyboards, guitar �
- **Mark Hummel** vocals, harmonica �
- **Kenny Neal** vocals, harmonica
- **Lazy Lester** vocals, harmonica
- **Greg Fingers Taylor** vocals, harmonica
- **Rusty Zinn** guitar �
- **Bob Welsh** piano, guitar
- **Richard W Grigsby** bass �
- **Marty Dodson** drums

Hummel invited Mayall to guest at his annual harmonica blow out. These events go back to 1991 and have included great blues harp players such as Billy Branch, James Harman, Kim Wilson and Carey Bell.

CONCERTS: 2008: Tour of California January 24–February 1 (8 dates)

BAND # 39, MARK HUMMEL'S HARMONICA BLOW OUT # 2
February 4 to 15, 2009
- **John Mayall** vocals, harmonica, keyboards, guitar ☉
- **Mark Hummel** vocals, harmonica
- **Charlie Musselwhite** vocals, harmonica (for the first 4 dates)
- **Lee Oskar** vocals, harmonica (for the first 4 dates)
- **Curtis Salgado** vocals, harmonica (for the first 4 dates)
- **Rick Estrin** vocals, harmonica (for the last 2 dates)
- **James Harman** vocals, harmonica (for the last 2 dates)
- **Rusty Zinn** guitar
- **Chris Burns** keyboards
- **Richard W Grigsby** bass
- **Willie Panker** drums

Hummel invited Mayall to guest at his annual harmonica blow out with another series of concerts in California and Nevada.
CONCERTS: 2009: Tour of California February 4–15 (6 dates)

BAND # 40. March 20, 2009 to Oct. 18, 2010
- John Mayall vocals, harmonica, keyboards, guitar ☉
- ☉ **Rocky Athas** guitar ☉ (previously with *LIGHTNING, BLACK OAK ARKANSAS, BUDDY MILES & the BLUES BERRIES* and his own *ROCKY ATHAS GROUP* before)
- ☉ **Tom Canning** keyboards (back after 5 years ☉ left Oct. 19, 2010 during European tour)
- ☉ **Greg Rzab** bass ☉ (back after 9 years)
- ☉ **Jay Davenport** drums ☉ (previously with the *DELLS, SUGAR BLUE, JUNIOR WELLS, VALERIE WELLINGTON,*

PINETOP PERKINS, DION PATON and *MELVIN TAYLOR* together with Rzab)

RECORDINGS: *TOUGH* (March 2009 at LAFX studio, North Hollywood) with Maggie Mayall.
CONCERTS:

- ***2009:*** US 4 dates March 20–May 3. 1st tour of Europe May 8–31 (24 dates): DK 1, D 14, A 3, CH 1, NL 4, B 1. 2nd tour of Europe June 24–July 25 (27 dates) UK 16 dates (including June 24–28 four with B.B. King), E 7, B 1, IRL 3. Seattle Nov 8, and a tour of Canada, Nov 10–22 (12 dates). (2009: 74 shows)
- ***2010:*** US 12 East Coast dates Feb 9–21. Tour of Australia (13 d) and New Zealand (9d) March 26–April 24. California, April 28–May 1 (4d). Tour of Europe May 21–June 21 (30d): E 9, LUX 1, A 1, CZ 4, ISR 1, H 1, D 7, NL 1, PL 3, SK 1, GB 1. USA 2 Blues festivals WA, OR July 1 & 2, 5 East Coast dates Aug 11–15. Another tour of Europe Oct 1–18 (16d F, 1d CH)

BANDS
(2010–2015)

JOHN MAYALL BAND # 41. Oct 20, 2010 to present
- **John Mayall** vocals, harmonica, keyboards, guitar
- **Rocky Athas** guitar
  ↻ **Oli Brown** guitar, replaced Rocky Athas for one show in Jakarta, Dec 17, 2011 ↻
- **Greg Rzab** bass
- **Jay Davenport** drums

RECORDINGS: The DVD & 2CD ***LIVE IN LONDON*** (Nov 1, 2010 at Leicester Square Theatre), plus four more live tracks recorded

and filmed at one or two unknown places in 2010, plus Hideaway recorded and filmed July 9, 2011 in Odense, Denmark, all on DVD
SWEET LITTLE ANGEL. A SPECIAL LIFE (November 2013 at Entourage Studios, North Hollywood) with C.J. Chenier as guest
CONCERTS:

- ***2010:*** Tour of Europe (cont.): Oct 20–Nov 1: F 5, D 2, NL 2, B 2, GB 1. US west coast (CA, AR, NV) Nov 11–16 (5d), Hawaii Nov 18–21 (4d). (2010: 113 shows)
- ***2011:*** USA 8 East coast dates March 27 to April 4. GA & FL 4 dates April 28 to May 1. 5 more US-east cost dates from May 18–22. European tour June 10–July 13 (29d) NL 3, E 8, CH 2, It 3, D 4, SF 1, N 1, S 4, DK 1, PL 1, CZ 1. Canada & USA Aug 3–20 (8 CDN, 8 US). Tour of Britain Oct 25–Nov 18 (25d). 8 more Canadian dates Nov 27 to Dec 3. Jakarta, Indonesia Dec 17. (2011: 95 shows)
- ***2012:*** US dates: 10 East coast dates (CT, NY, PA, MD, VA, VT, NH, MA) Feb 15–25. March 24 NC. 2 shows in Ontario, CDN June 21 & 22. 11 more East coast dates (PA, CT, NH, DE, NY, VA, RI, MA, ME) July 5–16. 6 West coast dates (CA, OR, WA) July 17–22. Aug 11 Snowshoe WV, 3 Texan dates Aug 16–18. Harvest Jazz & Blues Festival in Fredericton, NB, CDN Sept 14 & 15. 6 shows in mid-west USA Sept 17–22. 8 dates in Arizona & California Oct 19–27. An extended tour of Europe from Nov 6 to Dec 17 with 39 shows in N 1, S 2, DK 1, RO 1, CZ 1, D 13, A 1, CH 3, F 8, It 2, NL 4, B 1 and London 1. (2012: 89 shows 2 with Mark Hummel)
- ***2013:*** US dates: 8 East coast dates (MA, CT, NH, NY, NJ, PA, MD, VA) Jan 31–Feb 11. 4 Hawaiian dates May 16–19. 5 Californian dates May 22–26. Greenly Colorado Blues Jam June 8. Sao Paolo, Brazil on June 12–13 (Best of Blues Festival with Buddy Guy, Taj Mahal & Shemekia Copeland), 6d Oregon & Seattle July 9–14. San José CA, Fountain Blues Festival July 20. Tour of Europe Aug. 2–15 with 11 shows in PL 1, N 2, S 2, DK 3, NL 1, CZ 1 and B 1. US dates again: 3 shows in Texas Aug 30–Sep 1. 15 East coast & Midwest dates (NY,

NJ, DC, DE, MD, PA, CT, NH, OH, MI, IL) Oct 3–19, plus the 80th birthday show in Sarasota FL on Nov 29. El Paso TX (private party) Dec 7 (2013: 58 shows)

- **2014:** 80th Anniversary tour of Europe Feb 16–Apr 19 with 55 shows in CZ 1, PL 2, A 4, IT 3, E 6, CH 4, F 10, B 1, NL 3, D 18, SF 1, LUX 1 & GB 1. North American dates: 1 NC May 3, 3 CA May 23–25, 5 CDN July 8–12, 3 Seattle July 17.20, 2 CA July 25–26, SD Aug 4, 3 TX Aug. 14–16, 16 East Coast Sept 9–25. Moscow & St. Petersburg Oct 13 & 14, Extended UK-tour Oct 16–Nov 26 (36d), including Barcelona in between on Nov. 18. (2014: 128 shows 13 with Mark Hummel)
- **2015:** Australian dates in April, Florida in May, US West Coast in July, another extended European tour in Sept & Oct with shows in SF, S, N, DK, D, NL, B, F, It, CH, A, H, PL, CZ.

BANDS
(2012–2014)

BAND # 42, MARK HUMMEL'S HARMONICA BLOW OUT # 3.
January 22 to 23, 2012
- **John Mayall** vocals, harmonica, keyboards, guitar �
- **Mark Hummel** vocals, harmonica
- **Billy Boy Arnold** vocals, harmonica
- **Curtis Salgado** vocals, harmonica
- **Sugar Ray Norcia** vocals, harmonica
- **Little Charlie Baty** guitar
- **Billy Flynn** guitar
- **Richard W Grigsby** bass
- **June Core** drums

Hummel invited Mayall to guest at his annual harmonica blow out, this time to replace Charlie Musselwhite for two Californian concerts.
CONCERTS: 2012: California Jan 22 San Juan Capistrano and Jan 23 Solana Beach

BAND # 43, MARK HUMMEL'S HARMONICA BLOW OUT # 4.
January 3 to 19, 2014

- **John Mayall** vocals, harmonica, keyboards, guitar
- **Mark Hummel** vocals, harmonica
- **Rick Estrin** vocals, harmonica
- **Curtis Salgado** vocals, harmonica
- **James Harman** vocals, harmonica
- **Little Charlie Baty** guitar
- **Bob Welsh** piano, guitar
- **Richard W Grigsby** bass
- **June Core** drums

Hummel invited Mayall to guest at his annual harmonica blow out; this was the Sonny Boy Tribute.
CONCERTS: 2014: 13 dates from Jan 3–19 in CA, WA, OR including San Francisco Jazz Festival.

CHAPTER 15

Discography

JOHN MAYALL ALBUMS
(not including compilations)

		tracks studio or live	formats	recording date	first released	record companies
A1	TIME CAPSULE (*Powerhouse Four, Blues Syndicate*)	16 L	CD	57–62	3.00	Private Stash
A2	JOHN MAYALL PLAYS JOHN MAYALL/LIVE	12 L	LP CD	12.64	3.65	Decca/ London
A3	BLUESBREAKERS WITH ERIC CLAPTON	12 S	LP CD	3.66	7.66	Decca/ London
A4	RAW BLUES (6 tracks without John Mayall)	8 S	LP CD	65 & 66	1.67	Decca/ London
A5	A HARD ROAD	14 S	LP CD	10. & 11.66	2.67	Decca/ London
A6	BLUESBREAKERS WITH PAUL BUTTERFIELD	4 S	EP CD	11.66	1.67	Decca/ London
A7	THE BLUES ALONE/ BROKEN WINGS	12–14 S	LP CD	5.67	11.67	Decca/ London
A8	CRUSADE	12 S	LP CD	7.67	9.67	Decca/ London
A9	THE DIARY OF A BAND VOL. 1	6 L	LP CD	10. & 11.67	2.68	Decca/ London
A10	THE DIARY OF A BAND VOL. 2/LIVE IN EUROPE	7 L	LP CD	10. & 11.67	2.68	Decca/ London
A11	BARE WIRES	13 S	LP CD	4.68	6.68	Decca/ London

		tracks studio or live	formats	recording date	first released	record companies
A12	*BLUES FROM LAUREL CANYON*	12 S	LP CD	8.68	11.68	Decca/ London
A13	*LOOKING BACK (UK/ US) [single sampler]*	1 L/10 S	LP CD	64–67	8.69	Decca/ London
A14	*THRU THE YEARS [single sampler]*	14 S	LP CD	64–68	10.71	Decca/ London
A15	*PRIMAL SOLOS*	8 L	LP CD	66–68	77	Decca/ London
A16	*LIVE AT THE BBC*	14 L	CD	65–75	1.07	Decca
A17	*THE MASTERS*	18 L	2CD	5. & 6.69	4.99	Eagle
A18	*LIVE AT THE MARQUEE 1969*	7 L	CD	6.69	4.99	Eagle
A17/ 18+	*THE TURNING POINT SOUNDTRACK/ LIVE: 1969*	17 L	2CD	5. & 6.69	6.04	Eagle
A19	*THE TURNING POINT*	7–10 L	LP CD	7.69	9.69	Polydor
A20	*EMPTY ROOMS*	12 S	LP CD	8–12.69	3.70	Polydor
A21	*USA UNION*	10 S	LP CD	7.70	10.70	Polydor
A22	*BACK TO THE ROOTS*	18–26 S	2LP 2CD	11.70	4.71	Polydor
A23	*MEMORIES*	10 S	LP CD	7.71	11.71	Polydor
A24	*JAZZ BLUES FUSION*	7 L	LP CD	11. & 12.71	4.72	Polydor
A25	*ROCK THE BLUES TONIGHT/JOHN MAYALL-LIVE*	9–14 L	2CD CD	70 & 71	2.99	Indigo/ Rialto
A26	*MOVING ON*	9 L	LP CD	7.72	12.72	Polydor/ Lemon

		tracks studio or live	formats	recording date	first released	record companies
A27	*TEN YEARS ARE GONE*	4 L/9 S	2LP 2CD	5.73	10.73	Polydor/ Lemon
A28	*THE LATEST EDITION*	10 S	LP CD	3. & 4.74	9.74	Polydor/ Lemon
A29	*ARCHIVES TO EIGHTIES (revised version of A22)*	8–13 S	LP CD	11.70 & 1.88	4.88	Polydor
A30	*NEW YEAR, NEW BAND, NEW COMPANY*	10 S	LP CD	1.75	3.75	ABC/MCA ONE WAY
A31	*NOTICE TO APPEAR*	10 S	LP CD	9.75	11.75	ABC/MCA ONE WAY
A32	*A BANQUET IN BLUES*	8 S	LP CD	5.76	8.76	ABC/MCA ONE WAY
A33	*LOTS OF PEOPLE*	8 L	LP CD	11.76	4.77	ABC/MCA ONE WAY
A34	*A HARD CORE PACKAGE*	10 S	LP CD	3.77	8.77	ABC/MCA ONE WAY
A35	*THE LAST OF THE BRITISH BLUES*	10 L	LP CD	78	78	ABC/MCA ONE WAY
A36	*BOTTOM LINE*	8 S	LP	1.79	5.79	DJM
A37	*NO MORE INTERVIEWS*	9 S	LP	7.79	11.79	DJM
A38	*ROAD SHOW BLUES/ WHY WORRY/ LOST & GONE*	2 L/7 S	LP CD	7.80	4.81	DJM/ Success/ Yeaah!
A39	*RETURN OF THE BLUESBREAKERS*	5–8 S/5 L	LP CD	5.81 & 6.82	85	AIM
A40	*THE 1982 REUNION CONCERT*	10–11 L	LP CD	6.82	4.94	ONE WAY/ Repertoire
A41	*IN THE SHADOW OF LEGENDS*	12 L	2CD DVD	6.82	9.11	Blues Boulevard
A42	*CROSS COUNTRY BLUES*	17 S	CD	5.81 & 7.84	4.94	ONE WAY

		tracks studio or live	formats	recording date	first released	record companies
A43	ROLLING WITH THE BLUES; LIVE/PRIVATE COLLECTION	18 L	2CD	72–82	11.03	Shake-down/ Secret
A44	BEHIND THE IRON CURTAIN/LIVE IN CONCERT	7 L	LP CD	6.85	3.86	GNP Crescendo/ PRT
A45	THE POWER OF THE BLUES	6–8 L	LP CD	4.87	8.87	Entente/ Charly
A46	LIVE IN GERMANY 1988	8 L	CD DVD	3.88	4.11	Immortal
A47	CHICAGO LINE	10 S	LP CD	4.88	7.88	Entente/ Charly/ Island
A48	A SENSE OF PLACE	11 S	LP CD	12.89	5.90	Island
A49	WAKE UP CALL	12 S	LP CD	10. & 11.92	4.93	Silvertone
A50	LIVE FROM AUSTIN TX	9 L	CD DVD	9.93	10.07	New West
A51	SPINNING COIN	11 S	LP CD	5. & 8. 94	2.95	Silvertone
A52	BLUES FOR THE LOST DAYS	12 S	LP CD	10. & 11.96	3.97	Silvertone
A53	PADLOCK ON THE BLUES	13 S	CD	10.98	4.99	Eagle/ Cleopatra
A54	UK TOUR 2K Live recordings from Britain 2000	8 L	CD	5.00	2.01	Private Stash
A55	BOOGIE WOOGIE MAN Live solo concerts	11 L	CD	5.00	2.01	Private Stash
A56	ALONG FOR THE RIDE John Mayall & friends	13 S	CD	10. & 12.00	4.01	Eagle/ Red Ink
A57	STORIES	14 S	CD	2. & 3.02	8.02	Eagle/ Red Ink
A58	NO DAYS OFF A live recording from the 2002 British tour	10 L	CD	11.02	4.03	Private Stash

		tracks studio or live	formats	recording date	first released	record companies
A59	70TH BIRTHDAY CONCERT John Mayall & friends	19 L	2CD DVD	7.03	11.03	Eagle/ Red Ink
A60	ROAD DOGS	15 S	CD	1. & 2.05	6.05	Eagle
A61	EXCLUSIVE LIVE RARITIES from Essentially 5 CD set	11 L	CD	66–94	11.06	Eagle
A62	IN THE PALACE OF THE KING	14 S	CD	7.06	4.07	Eagle
A63	TOUGH	11 S	2LP CD	3.09	9.09	Eagle
A64	LIVE IN LONDON	13 L	2CD DVD	11.10	10.11	Private Stash
A65	HISTORIC LIVE SHOWS, VOL. 1	10 L	CD	1.70–10.90	11.12	Private Stash
A66	HISTORIC LIVE SHOWS, VOL. 2	12 L	CD	9.90–1.95	11.12	Private Stash
A67	HISTORIC LIVE SHOWS, VOL. 3	10 L	CD	11.97–7.98	11.12	Private Stash
A68	A SPECIAL LIFE	11 S	2LP CD	11.13	5.14	Forty Below
A69	BLUES ALIVE NYC 1976	12 L	CD	10.76	3.15	Rockbeat
A70	LIVE IN 1967 Never re- leased live performances	13 L	CD	4–.5.67	4.15	Forty Below
VA1	CELEBRATING 20 YEARS OF THE FESTIVAL INTERNATIONAL DE JAZZ DE MONTREAL 1980–2000	1 L	4CD	7.84	01	Spectra
VA2	FM 101,9 LIVE FROM MUSIC HALL VOL. 2	1 L	CD	3.95	96	KSCA
VA3	BLACKTOP BLUES- A-RAMA Live from Tipitina's 1977–1989	2 L	2CD	4.84	10.14	Rockbeat

JOHN MAYALL 7" SINGLES AND EPS

S: original single tracks:
    recorded, produced and released as single or EP
A: tracks taken from albums

		s/A	formats	recording dates	first released	record companies
S1	CRAWLING UP A HILL/MR. JAMES	s (A13/A14)	7"	3. & 4.64	5.64	Decca
S2	CROCODILE WALK/BLUES CITY SHAKEDOWN	s (A13/A14)	7"	2.65	4.65	Decca
S3	I'M YOUR WITCHDOCTOR/ TELEPHONE BLUES	s (A3 bis)	7"	6.65	10.65	Immediate
S4	LONELY YEARS/ BERNARD JENKINS	s (A4)	7"	2.66	8.66	Purdah
S5	PARCHMAN FARM/ KEY TO LOVE	A3	7"	4.66	9.66	Decca/ London
S6	ALL YOUR LOVE/ HIDEAWAY	A3	7"	4.66	3.67	London
S7	LOOKING BACK/ SO MANY ROADS	s (A13)	7"	9.66	10.67	Decca
S8	SITTING IN THE RAIN/OUT OF REACH	s (A13/A14)	7"	10.66	1.67	Decca
S9	CURLY/RUBBER DUCK (The Bluesbreakers only)	s (A14/A5*)	7"	2.67	3.67	Decca/ London
S10	DOUBLE TROUBLE/ IT HURTS ME TOO	s (A13)	7"	4.67	6.67	Decca
S11	SUSPICIONS PARTS 1 & 2	s (A13/A14)	7"	9.67	10.67	Decca
S12	SUSPICIONS PART 1/ OH, PRETTY WOMAN	s/A8	7"	7. & 9.67	11.67	London
S13	OH, PRETTY WOMAN/ THE SUPER NATURAL	A8/A5	7"	10.66/7.67	68	London J
S14	JENNY/PICTURE ON THE WALL	s (A13)	7"	12.67	2.68	Decca/ London

		s/A	formats	recording dates	first released	record companies
S15	NO REPLY/SHE'S TOO YOUNG	A11	7"	4.68	6.68	Decca
S16	BROKEN WINGS/ SONNY BOY BLOW	A7	7"	5.67	6.68	London
S17	THE BEAR/2401	A12	7"	8.68	11.68	Decca
S18	WALKING ON SUNSET/LIVING ALONE	A12/A5	7"	8.68/66	11.68	London
S19	CROCODILE WALK/ WHEN I'M GONE	A2	7"	12.64	6.69	Decca D
S20	I NEED YOUR LOVE/ SNOWY WOOD	A2/A8	7"	12.64/7.67	69	London J
S21	DON'T WASTE MY TIME/DON'T PICK A FLOWER	s (A20)	7"	6.69	10.69	Polydor
S22	ROOM TO MOVE/SAW MILL GULCH ROAD	A19	7"	7.69	1.70	Polydor D
S23	THINKING OF MY WOMAN/PLAN YOUR REVOLUTION	A20	7"	ca. 10.69	7.70	Polydor
S24	TOOK THE CAR/ MY PRETTY GIRL	A21	7"	7.70	70	Polydor D
S25	DREAM WITH ME/ MR. CENSOR MAN	A22	7"	11.70	71	Polydor D
S26	PRISONS ON THE ROAD/MARRIAGE MADNESS	A22	7"	11.70	71	Polydor D
S27	PRISONS ON THE ROAD/BLUE FOX	A22	7"	11.70	71?	Polydor J
S28	MOVING ON/KEEP OUR COUNTRY GREEN	A26	7"	7.72	72	Polydor US
S29	NATURE'S DISAPPEARING/ MOVING ON	A21/A26	7"	7.70 & 7.72	73	Polydor US
S30	GASOLINE BLUES/ BRAND NEW BAND	A28/s	7"	3. & 4.74	74	Polydor D

		s/A	formats	recording dates	first released	record companies
S31	LET ME GIVE/ PASSING THROUGH	s	7"	3. & 4.74	74	Polydor US
S32	STEP IN THE SUN/ AL GOLDSTEIN BLUES	A30/s	7"	1.75	75	ABC/ Blue Thumb
S33	A HARD DAY'S NIGHT/ THE BOY MOST LIKELY TO SUCCEED	A31	7"	ca. 10.75	76	ABC E
S34	YOU CAN'T PUT ME DOWN/TABLE TOP GIRL	A32	7"	5.76	76	ABC E
S35	CROCODILE WALK/ SITTING IN THE RAIN	s1/s8	7"	2.65 & 10.66	10.78	Decca
S36	BOTTOM LINE/ DREAMBOAT	A36	7"	1.79	7.79	DJM
S37	BOTTOM LINE/ COME WITH ME	A36	7"	1.79	79	DJM E
S38	HARD GOING UP/ SWEET HONEY BEE	A37	7"	7.79	79/80	DJM PL
S39	FALLING/GIPSY LADY	A37	7"	7.79	80	DJM E
S40	BURN OUT YOUR BLIND EYES/ – (flexi disc)	A4	7"	11.66	?	B & H PL
S41	SENSITIVE KIND/ JACKSBORO HIGHWAY	A48	7"	12.89	8.90	Island US
S42	SENSITIVE KIND/ SUGARCANE	A48	7"	12.89	90	Island GB
S43	SENSITIVE KIND/ SUGARCANE/ CONGO SQUARE	A48	CD single	12.89	90	Island GB
S44	CONGO SQUARE/ SUGARCANE	A48	CD single	12.89	90	Island D
S45	BLACK CAT MOAN/ I WANT TO GO	A48	7"		90	Island D
S46	MAIL ORDER MYSTICS/ WAKE UP CALL/ I COULD CRY	A49	CD single	10. & 11.92	93	Silvertone US

		s/A	formats	recording dates	first released	record companies
S47	*MAIL ORDER MYSTICS/ I COULD CRY/ NOT AT HOME*	A49	CD single	10. & 11.92	93	Silvertone GB
S48	*AIN'T NO BRAKEMAN/ SPINNING COIN/ WHEN THE DEVIL STARTS CRYING*	A51	CD single	5. & 8. 94	95	Silvertone D
S49	*PRIDE AND FAITH*	A57	CD single	2. & 3.02	02	Eagle US?
EP1	*JOHN MAYALL'S BLUESBREAKERS WITH PAUL BUTTERFIELD*	A6	EP, CD	11.66	1.67	Decca/ Deram
EP2	*JOHN MAYALL'S BLUESBREAKERS*	s7/A3	EP, CD	4. & 9.66	11.66	Decca F/ Eva
EP3	*JOHN MAYALL & THE BLUESBREAKERS VOL. 1*	A3/A5/A8	EP	4.66–7.67	69	London J
EP4	*JOHN MAYALL & THE BLUESBREAKERS VOL. 2*	A5/A8	EP	10.66–7.67	69	London J
EP5	*JOHN LEE BOOGIE/ WHY WORRY/ MAMA TALK TO YOUR DAUGHTER*	A38	EP	7.80	6.81	DJM GB

JOHN MAYALL VIDEOS & DVDS

		tracks studio or live	formats	recording date	first released	record companies
V1	THE TURNING POINT 26 mins	film	VHS	5–6.69	4.99	Eagle Rock Entertainment
V2	BEAT CLUB The best of '70 Vol. 1 50 mins	1/13 L	DVD	1.70	00	ARD Radio TV
V3	JOHN MAYALL & JOY FLEMMING Live in Germany 44 mins	3 L	DVD-R	1–2.70	02	
V4	THE LOST BROADCASTS 23 mins	4 L	DVD	1.70 + 2.71	2.12	Gonzo Multimedia
V5	BLUES ALIVE 52–90 mins	10–13 L	VHS LD	6.82	10.84	RCA, Castle, PNE
V5	JAMMIN' WITH THE BLUES GREATS 90 mins	13 L	DVD	6.82	5.02	Eagle Rock Entertainment
V5	IN THE SHADOW OF LEGENDS 90 mins	13 L	DVD 2CD	6.82	9.11	Blues Boulevard Records
V6	LIVE AT IOWA STATE UNIVERSITY 85 mins	9 L	DVD	10.85	3.04	Quantum Leap
V7	LIVE IN GERMANY 1988 Ohne Filter SWF 56 mins	8 L	DVD CD	3.88	4.11	Immortal
V8	LIVE FROM THE BOTTOM LINE, NEW YORK 90 mins	12 L	DVD	6.90	10.04	Masterplan
V9	LIVE FROM AUSTIN TX 56 mins	9 L	DVD CD	9.93	10.07	New West
V10	ROLLING WITH THE BLUES Interview 38 mins	interv.	DVD	11.02	11.03	Shakedown Records
V11	COOKIN' DOWN UNDER (Live in Sydney) 79 mins	9 L	DVD	2.03	6.04	Private Stash Records
V12	70TH BIRTHDAY CONCERT 137 mins	16 L	DVD 2CD	7.03	12.03	Eagle Rock Entertainment

		tracks studio or live	formats	recording date	first released	record companies
V13	THE GODFATHER OF BRITISH BLUES/ THE TURNING POINT 83 mins	film	DVD	69–03	6.04	Eagle Rock Entertainment
V14	ROLLIN' WITH THE BLUES 71 mins	9 L/7 S	DVD	85–03	2.05	Planet Song
V15	BITS AND PIECES ABOUT… JOHN MAYALL 37 mins	film	DVD	69–06	9.06	Delta Entertainment
V16	LIVE IN LONDON 97 mins	13 L	DVD 2CD	11.10	6.11	Private Stash Records
V17	SWEET LITTLE ANGEL 62 mins	11 L	DVD	6.70–7.11	11.12	IMV Blueline/XXL Media

JOHN MAYALL BOOTLEGS

		tracks studio or live	formats	recording date	first released	record companies
B1	BLUESBREAKING (9 BBC Recordings)	6 L/14 S	CD-R	65, 66	99	3BR US
B2	CROCODILE WALK (11 BBC Recordings)	3 L/11 S	CD	65, 67, 69	91	Lost Rose – Wild Bird It
B2	BULLDOGS FOR SALE (11 BBC Recordings)	3 L/11 S	CD	65, 67, 69	9?	Teddy Bear Records It
B3	BEANO'S BOYS (9 BBC Recordings)	5 L/9 S	CD	65, 68, 69	9?	Tendolar J
B4	THE FIRST FIVE YEARS (18 BBC Recordings)	2 L/23 S	CD	65–69	?	Pontiac
B5	SIMPLY OUTSTANDING	5 L	CD-R	2.68	?	Vintage Masters
B6	LIVE IN SWITZERLAND	5 or more L	LP	1.69	69	Python
B7	FALKONER TEATRET COPENHAGEN 7/10/1971	? L	CD	10.71	?	
B8	HORNY BLUES/ HORNY TOAD	9 L	CD	4.72	00	
B9	MINNEAPOLIS 1971	5 L	CD	9–12.72	?	
B10	MICK TAYLOR – TOAD'S PLACE – JOHN MAYALL	11 L	CD	6.82	?	
B11	BLUES ALIVE (limited to 100)	8 L	LP	6.82	85	Wilbour
B12	LIVE IN MILAN – DAL VIVO A MILANO	10 L	CD	11.82	3.94	FU It
B13	THE DARK SIDE OF MIDNIGHT (limited to 100)	11 L	2LP	5.83	83?	"???"
B14	"THE FLAMINGO ALBUM"	8 L	LP	11.65 + 5.83	88?	MCB

		tracks studio or live	formats	recording date	first released	record companies
B15	*MAYALLAPOLIS BLUES*	10 L	CD	3.93	1.94	Blues Tune
B16	*BACK IN TOWN AGAIN, LIVE IN LUCERN 1997*	10 L	CD	10.97	97	Blue Nose CH
B17	*ROCKIN BLUES REVUE 2005*	10 L	CD	9-11.05	?	
BV1	*JOHN MAYALL & FRIENDS/POP2/ LYON FRANCE JUNE 1970/BEAT CLUB*	11L	DVD	1.70-3.71	?	
BV2	*BERLIN 1987*	13L	DVD	4.87	?	

JOHN MAYALL AS GUEST MUSICIAN

		tracks with Mayall/ total tracks on album	formats	recording date	first released	record companies
G1	*CHAMPION JACK DUPREE FROM NEW ORLEANS TO CHICAGO*	2/14	LP CD	11.65	4.66	Decca/ London
G2	*EDDIE BOYD AND HIS BLUES BAND FEATURING PETER GREEN*	4/16	LP CD	3.67	9.67	Decca/ London/ Deram
G3	*McGOUGH AND McGEAR SAME*	?/13	LP CD	67/68	4.68	EMI Parlophone
G4	*CANNED HEAT LIVING WITH THE BLUES*	2/8	2LP CD	7. & 8.68	10.68	Liberty/See For Miles
G5	*SHAKEY JAKE AND THE ALL STARS FURTHER ON UP THE ROAD*	4/11	LP CD	10.68	2.69	Liberty/ Sequel
G6	*ALBERT KING THE LOST SESSION*	6/10	LP CD	8.71	86	Stax
G7	*SHAKY JAKE HARRIS THE DEVIL'S HARMONICA*	7/10	LP	9.71	72	Polydor-Crusade
G8	*BLUE MITCHELL BLUES' BLUES*	3/5	LP CD	71/72	72	Mainstream
G9	*SONNY TERRY & BROWNIE MCGHEE SONNY & BROWNIE*	4/12	LP CD	73	73	A&M
G10	*KEITH CARRADINE I'M EASY*	1/10	LP CD	76	76	Asylum
G11	*ROD STEWART FOOT LOOSE & FANCY FREE*	1/8	LP CD	76/77	10.77	Warner Brothers/ WEA
G12	*TED GARDESTAD BLUE VIRGIN ISLES*	1/10	LP CD	77/78	78	Polar/Epic
G13	*THE BOYS TO HELL WITH THE BOYS*	2/11	LP CD	79	79	Safari
G14	*PETER MAFFAY LANGE SCHATTEN*	1/21	2LP 2CD	12.87	88	Teldec
G15	*PETER MAFFAY LANGE SCHATTEN TOUR 88*	3–5/10	LP CD	9.88	88	Teldec

		tracks with Mayall/ total tracks on album	formats	recording date	first released	record companies
G15	PETER MAFFAY LANGE SCHATTEN TOUR 88	5/15	VID	9.88	88	BMG-Ariola
G16	BO DIDDLEY AND FRIENDS ROCK 'N' ROLL JAM	6/6	VID	10.85	89	Castle Hendring
G16	CHUCK BERRY & BO DIDDLEY ROCK 'N' ROLL ALL STAR JAM	10/10	CD	10.85	4.09	Angel Air
G17	LAQUAN NOTES OF A NATIVE SON	1/14	LP CD	90	90	4TH&BWAY (Island)
G18	BUDDY GUY FEELS LIKE RAIN	1/11	LP CD	10./11.92	3.93	Silvertone
G19	COCO MONTOYA GOTTA MIND TO TRAVEL	1/10	LP CD	93?	94	Silvertone/ Blind Pig
G20	HOUSEWIVES GET THE DIRT!	1/13	CD	89	4.95	Beachwood
G21	DICK HECKSTALL- SMITH BLUES AND BEYOND	1/12	CD	12.00	6.01	Blue Storm
G22	DON NIX & FRIENDS GOING DOWN	2/13	CD	12.00	10.02	Evidence
G23	ROBBEN FORD KEEP ON RUNNING	2/12	CD	5./6.03	10.03	Concord Jazz
G24	RUDY ROTTA & FRIENDS SOME OF MY FAVORITE SONGS FOR...	2/14	CD	9.04	2.05	Zyx Music
G25	MAGGIE MAYALL DIG THIS	3/14	CD	89/91	6.06	Private Stash
G26	WALTER TROUT FULL CIRCLE	2/13	CD	1.–3.06	6.06	Ruf
G27	RZAB AND DAVENPORT R & B DEPT.	1/8	CD	11		(promo)
G28	ROCKY ATHAS LET THE GUITAR DO THE TALKING... WITH MY FRIENDS	1/10	CD	11	2.14	RockyAthas. com

		tracks with Mayall/ total tracks on album	formats	recording date	first released	record companies
G*1	KEEF HARTLEY BAND HALFBREED	narrative only	LP CD	10.68	3.69	Deram
G*2	AYNSLEY DUNBAR RETALIATION TO MUM FROM AYNSLEY AND THE BOYS	production	LP CD	69	10.69	Liberty/ Blue Thumb/ MCA
G*3	THE FLOCK FLOCK	liner notes	LP	69	69	CBS
G*4	J.B. LENOIR CRUSADE	narrative only	LP	66/70	71	Polydor-Crusade
G*5	DEBBIE DAVIES KEY TO LOVE	liner notes	CD	02	1.03	Shanachie
G*6	BOOGIE WOOGIE PIONEERS PICKING THE BLUES	liner notes & compilation	CD	28–60	7.06	Document

JOHN MAYALL COMPILATIONS/SAMPLERS

		tracks	formats	first released	record companies	countries
C1	SO MANY ROADS	12	LP	67	Decca	NL/D
C2	LOOKING BACK (different from A12)	21	2LP	69	Decca	D
C3	THE BEST OF JOHN MAYALL	14	LP	70	Decca	D
C4	THE WORLD OF JOHN MAYALL VOL. 1	14	LP	70	Decca	GB/D/ NL/AUS
C5	BLUES GIANT	24	2LP	70	Decca	NL/D
C6	JOHN MAYALL	14	LP	70	Decca	D
C7	DOUBLE DELUXE	22	2LP	70	London	J
C8	THE WORLD OF JOHN MAYALL VOL. 2/ John Mayall	12	LP	71	Decca/ Superstar	GB/It/NL
C9	JOHN MAYALL (freundin)	12	LP	71	Decca	D/F
C10	BEYOND THE TURNING POINT	9	LP	71	Polydor	GB/D
C11	SOMETHING NEW/ ROOM TO MOVE/ BEST OF Vol.1	10	LP	71	Karussell	D/NL/ GB/ISR
C12	DOWN THE LINE	22	2LP	72	London	US
C13	POP GIANTS VOL. 13	9	LP	ca. 72	Brunswick	D
C14	DIE JOHN MAYALL STORY	9	LP	ca. 72	Polydor	D
C15	POP HISTORY VOL. XIV/GREATEST HITS/IL BLUES	17	2LP	73	Polydor	D/It

		tracks	formats	first released	record companies	countries
C16	THE BEGINNING VOL. 13	10	LP	73	Decca	D
C17	STARPORTRAIT/ HIGHLIGHTS	18	2LP	73	Polydor	D/GB
C18	THE BEST OF JOHN MAYALL	16	2LP	73	Polydor	US/D
C19	THE STORY OF JOHN MAYALL	19	2LP	74	Polydor	D
C20	JOHN MAYALL	10	LP	76	Polydor	GB
C21	BLUES ROOTS/ THE VERY BEST OF/HISTORIA	11	LP	78	Decca	GB/NL/E
C22	PROFILE	12	LP	79	Decca	D
C23	THE LEGENDS OF ROCK	24	2LP	80	Decca	D
C24	RARE TRACKS VOL. 1	13	LP	81	Decca	D
C25	RARE TRACKS VOL. 2	11	LP	81	Decca	D
C26	DIE WEISSE SERIE: JOHN MAYALL	12	LP	82	Decca	D
C27	HISTORY OF ROCK	8	LP	82	Orbis	GB
C28	THE JOHN MAYALL STORY VOL. 1	16	LP	83	Decca	GB/NL
C29	THE JOHN MAYALL STORY VOL. 2	13	LP	83	Decca	GB/NL
C30	STORMY MONDAY	25	MC	84	Decca	GB
C31	SOME OF MY BEST FRIENDS ARE BLUES	11	LP	86	Charly Decal	GB

		tracks	formats	first released	record companies	countries
C32	*THE COLLECTION*	22	2LP	86	Castle	GB
C33	*THE COLLECTION*	17	CD	86	Castle	GB
C34	*LO MEJOR DE JOHN MAYALL*	9	LP	86	Polydor	E
C35	*JOHN MAYALL 1966-1972*	34	2CD	89	Polygram/ London	D/US
C36	*THE BEST OF YESTERYEARS*	15	CD	90	Dark Blue	D
C37	*WAITING FOR THE RIGHT TIME*	19	CD	91	Elite	GB
C38	*LIFE IN THE JUNGLE/RIDIN' ON THE L&N*	8	CD	92	Charly R&B	GB
C39	*LONDON BLUES 1964-69*	40	2CD	92	Deram Chronicles	USA
C40	*ROOM TO MOVE 1969-74*	30	2CD	92	Polydor Chronicles	USA
C41	*JOHN MAYALL'S BLUESBREAKERS*	11	CD	92	Castle	D
C42	*STORMY MONDAY*	14	CD	94	Spectrum Karussell	D
C43	*AS IT ALL BEGAN 64-69 THE BEST OF JOHN MAYALL*	20	CD	97	Deram	GB
C44	*MASTER SERIES*	18	CD	97	Decca	
C45	*DRIVING ON, THE ABC YEARS 1975 TO 82*	32	2CD	98	MCA	USA
C46	*SILVER TONES - THE BEST OF JOHN MAYALL*	14	CD	98	Silvertone	EU
C47	*BLUE FOR YOU*	10	CD	00	Dressed To Kill	GB

		tracks	formats	first released	record companies	countries
C48	**STEPPIN' OUT** *An Introduction To John Mayall*	17	CD	01	Decca	GB
C49	**BEST OF, 20TH CENTURY MASTERS**	11	CD	04	Universal	CDN
C50	**BITS AND PIECES ABOUT... JOHN MAYALL**	16	CD	06	Delta Entertainment	D
C51	**THE STATESMAN OF BRITISH BLUES**	16	CD	07	Music Session	GB
C52	**SO MANY ROADS** *An Anthology 1964–1974*	74	4CD	10	Universal	GB

CHAPTER 16
Bibliography

- **Aeppli, Felix:** *HEART OF STONE*, The Definitive Rolling Stones Discography 1962–1983; Pierian Press, Ann Arbor 1985
- **Aeppli, Felix:** *THE ROLLING STONES*, 1962–1995, The Ultimate Guide, Record Information Services, Bromley 1996
- **Brown, Tony:** *JIMI HENDRIX*, V.I.P. music, Paul Zsolay Verlag, Wien 1994
- **Brunning, Bob:** *BLUES – THE BRITISH CONNECTION*, Blandford Press, Poole 1986
- **Brunning, Bob:** *BLUES IN BRITAIN*, Blandford, London 1995
- **Carter, Phil:** *JOHN MAYALL*, Record Collector, London 1985
- **Celmins, Martin:** *PETER GREEN*, the Biography, Castle Communications, Chessington 1995
- **Chesher, Debby:** *STAR ART*, Johnny Mitchell, John Mayall, Cat Stevens, Klaus Voormann, Ron Wood, Commander Cody. Starart Prod. DeWinton, Alberta, Canada 1979
- **Clapton, Eric:** *CLAPTON, THE AUTOBIOGRAPHY*, Broadway Books, New York 2007
- **Clarke, Steve:** *FLEETWOOD MAC*, Proteus, London, 1984
- **Clifford, Mick:** *THE HARMONY ILLUSTRATED ENCYCLOPEDIA OF ROCK* 6th edition, Harmony Books, New York 1988
- **Coleman, Ray:** *CLAPTON*, the Authorised Biography, Pan Books, London 1994
- **De la Parra, Fito:** *LIVING THE BLUES*, Canned Heat's Story, Little Big Beat Musikverlag, Lindewerra 2001
- **Douse, Cliff:** Guitarist presents *BLUES GUITAR HEROES*, Future Publishing Ltd, Bath 2010

- Fancourt, Leslie: *BRITISH BLUES ON RECORD* (1957–1970), revised edition, Faversham 1992
- Fleetwood, Mick & Davis, Stephen: *MEIN LEBEN MIT FLEETWOOD MAC*, Moewig, Rastatt 1991
- Frame, Pete: *ROCK FAMILY TREES* (Vol. 1 & 2), Omnibus Press, London 1980
- Harris, Sheldon: *BLUES WHO'S WHO*, Da Capo Press, New York 1989
- Hartley, Keef: *HALFBREED*, A rock and roll journey that happened against all the odds, self edition 2007
- Heckstall-Smith, Dick: *THE SAFEST PLACE IN THE WORLD*, Quartet Books, London 1989
- Heckstall-Smith, Dick & Grant, Pete: *BLOWING THE BLUES*, Clear Books, Bath 2004
- Hjort, Christopher: *STRANGE BREW:* Eric Clapton and the British Blues Boom 1965–1970, Jawbone, London 2007
- Hounsome, Terry: *NEW ROCK RECORD 3rd Ed.* Blanford Press, Poole 1987
- Hounsome, Terry: *ROCK RECORD 7*, Record Researcher Publ. Llandysul 1997
- Hunt, Marsha: *REAL LIFE*, The story of a survivor, Headline Books, London 1986
- Hüttenrauch, Oliver: *ERIC CLAPTON & CO*, Moewig, Rastatt 1990
- James, Etta & Ritz David: *RAGE TO SURVIVE, THE ETTA JAMES STORY*, Da Capo Press, New York 1995
- Kubernik, Harvey: *CANYON OF DREAMS*, The Magic and the music of Laurel Canyon, Sterling, New York 2009
- Larkin, Colin: *THE GUINESS WHO'S WHO OF BLUES*, Guiness Publishing, London 1993
- Larkin, Colin: *THE GUINESS WHO'S WHO OF SOUL MUSIC*, Guiness Publishing, London 1993
- Laufenberg, Frank: *ROCK & POP ALMANACH*, Bastei Lübbe, Bergisch Gladbach 1987
- Logoz, Dinu: *JOHN MAYALL: HIS RECORDS, HIS BANDS, HIS SIDEMEN*, self edition, Otelfingen 1992

- Mayall, Gaz: *GAZ'S ROCKIN' BLUES, THE FIRST 30 YEARS*, Trolley Ltd, Great Britain 2010
- Mayall, John: *THE LYRICS OF JOHN MAYALL*, a history of a bluesman through his songs, Magnolia Blue, Tarzana CA, 2001
- McStravick, Summer & Roos, John: *BLUES-ROCK-EXPLOSION*, Old Goat, Mission Viejo, CA 2001
- Miller, Jim: *THE ROLLING STONE ILLUSTRATED HISTORY OF ROCK & ROLL*, Rolling Stone Press, New York 1976
- Mumenthaler, Samuel: *BEAT, POP, PROTEST*, Der Sound der Schweizer Sixties, Edition Plus, Lausanne 2001
- Newman, Richard: *JOHN MAYALL, BLUES BREAKER*, Castle Communications, Chessington 1995
- Pidgeon, John: *ERIC CLAPTON*, the biography of the world's greatest rock guitarist, Panther Books, Frogmore, St Albans 1976
- Reichold, Martin: *JOHN MAYALL OLDIE-MARKT DISCOGRAPHIE*, Oldie Markt Stuttgart, 8. & 9. 1986
- Roberty, Marc & Welch, Chris: *ERIC CLAPTON, THE ILLUSTRATED DISCO/BIOGRAPHY*, Omnibus Press, London 1984
- Roberty, Marc: *ERIC CLAPTON, A VISUAL DOCUMENTARY*, Omnibus Press, London 1986
- Roberty, Marc: *ERIC CLAPTON*, in his own words, Omnibus Press, London 1993
- Roberty, Marc: *ERIC CLAPTON, THE COMPLETE CHRONICAL*, Pyramid Books, London 1991
- Roberty, Marc: *ERIC CLAPTON*, The complete recording sessions 1963–1992, Blanford, London 1993
- Roberty, Marc: *ERIC CLAPTON, DAY BY DAY*, the early years, 1963–1982, Backbeat Books, Milwaukee 2013
- Sanford, Christopher: *ERIC CLAPTON*, vgs Verlagsgesellschaft, Köln 1996
- Schober, Ingeborg: *ROCK DREAMS/ROCK LEXIKON*, Schünemann Verlag, München 1973
- Schwager, Edi: *MICK TAYLOR AND THE STONES* in *IDOLE 9*, Ullstein Verlag, Frankfurt 1986

- Shapiro, Harry: *ALEXIS KORNER*, the Biography, Bloomsbury, London 1996
- Shapiro, Harry: *ERIC CLAPTON, SLOWHAND*, Ein Leben für den Blues, Hannibal Verlag, St. Andrä-Wördern 1993
- Stuckey, Fred: *BLUES GUITARISTS*, Guitar Player Prod., Saratoga 1975 (1970)
- Talevski, Nick: TOMBSTONE BLUES, The encyclopedia of rock obituaries, Omnibus Press, London 1999
- Tracy, John: *TWENTY YEARS ON...*, all the liner notes in the Deram and London Mayall CDs, London 1987–1994
- Wyman, Bill: *BLUES*, Christian Verlag, München 2002
- Wyman, Bill: *ROLLING STONES STORY*, Dorling Kindersley Verlag, Starnberg-München 2002
- Zentgraf, Nico: *MICK TAYLOR, TAYLOR-MADE WORKS* 1964–2004 (3rd update), Stoneware Publ. Hamburg 2004

WEBSITES:

www.allmusic.com
www.johnmayall.com
www.chromoxid.com
www.johnmayall.net (now defunct)
www.freebomusic.com
www.johntherelevator.nl
www.imbd.com

THANKS!

A huge *THANK YOU* for their generous help, support, contributions, live tapes, CDs, press clippings, "know how" and patience goes to: Marcel Aeby (CH), Felix Aeppli (CH), Nicholas Aleshin aka Delta Nick (US), Heike Angerer (A), Rocky Athas (US), Richard Brown (GB), Kansas J. Canzus (US), Giampiero Colombo (CH), Jack R. Conrad (CH), Rick Cortes (US), Robert Egloff (CH), Leslie Fancourt (GB), Freebo (US), Klaus Griesbeck (D), Keef Hartley (GB), Diane Hatz (US), Christopher Hjört (N), Terry Hounsome (GB), Mark Hummel (US), Keith John (US), Joachim Kirstein (D), Sonny Landreth (US), Rolf LL Lüthi (CH), Lee Mayall (D), Chris Mercer (US), Chris Mitchell (CH), Christoph Müller (CH), Norbert Muller (CH), Samuel Mumenthaler (CH), Kim Neat (AUS), Bernd Olschewsky (D), Randy Resnick (F), Bryan S. Reid (US), Rudy Rotta (It), Markus Rudin (CH), Greg Rzab (US), Gary B. Shaw (US), Walter Schäppi (CH), Edi Schwager (CH), Neil Simpson (GB), Roland Sommer (CH), Keith Tillman (GB), Markus Tschudi (CH), Hank van Sickle (US), Dieter Schöni (CH), Buddy Whittington (US), Joe Yuele (US), Nico Zentgraf (D), and most of all John B. Mayall (US) himself.

A special thank you must go to leading Mayall expert Richard Brown for amending and correcting the original text, and to Eugene Edwards for shortening and transforming it for publication as popular biography.